COMPETING WESTERN STRATEGIES AGAINST THE PROLIFERATION OF WEAPONS OF MASS DESTRUCTION

Comparing the United States to a Close Ally

David A. Cooper

Westport, Connecticut
London

Library of Congress Cataloging-in-Publication Data

Cooper, David A., 1965–
    Competing Western strategies against the proliferation of weapons of mass destruction :
comparing the United States to a close ally / David A. Cooper.
        p.   cm.
    Includes bibliographical references and index.
    ISBN 0–275–97477–4 (alk. paper)
    1. Weapons of mass destruction.   2. United States—Military policy.   3.
Australia—Military policy.   4. World politics—1989–
    U793.C66   2002
    327.1'745—dc21   2001041188

British Library Cataloguing in Publication Data is available.

Library of Congress Catalog Card Number: 2001041188
ISBN: 0–275–97477–4

First published in 2002

Praeger Publishers, 88 Post Road West, Westport, CT 06881
An imprint of Greenwood Publishing Group, Inc.
www.praeger.com

Printed in the United States of America

The paper used in this book complies with the
Permanent Paper Standard issued by the National
Information Standards Organization (Z39.48–1984).

10 9 8 7 6 5 4 3 2 1

The views expressed in this study are those of the author and do not reflect the official
policy or position of the Department of Defense or the U.S. government.

Contents

Author's Note

This book was just going to press on September 11, 2001, when terrorists attacked the soul of the United States and the very concept of national security. It is impossible to know how the repercussions of this calamity will alter fundamental policies of the United States, its allies, and the entire international community.

WMD terrorism traditionally has been seen as a law enforcement rather than a proliferation issue. However, such distinctions are unlikely to survive. Defense Secretary Donald Rumsfeld and other senior U.S. officials have already stressed that, because most state sponsors of terrorism are also active proliferators, there is a direct link between proliferation and the likelihood that future terrorist attacks will involve mass destruction weapons. The clear implication is that curbing proliferation is likely to be a vital long-term element of the unfolding coalition campaign against global terrorism. This lends fresh urgency to the need to improve Western cooperation against proliferation.

October 6, 2001

Acknowledgments

I am indebted to Andrew Mack for his perspicacious advice throughout the preparation of this study. I would also like to acknowledge the substantial input that I received from James L. Richardson, W. Seth Carus, Trevor Findlay, and Graeme Cheeseman, as well as various feedback at different stages from Greg Austin, Desmond Ball, Gail Craswell, Greg Fry, Brian Job, Greg Noble, Richard Speier, and Ramesh Thakur. Thanks also to Mike Fitzgibbon, Ted Greenwood, and Henry Sokolski for helping to come up with the initial idea for this study. I am also grateful to those who worked so hard on the mammoth freedom of information requests that I generated, especially Anne Moores and John Scott at DFAT and William Harris at the Bush Presidential Library. Finally, I would like to thank the many past and present officials who spared their valuable time for the often lengthy interviews that made the case studies possible.

This book is dedicated to my wife Cynthia Skelton, and to my parents, Samuel James and Doris Jean Cooper.

Abbreviations

ACDA	Arms Control and Disarmament Agency (U.S.)
ACME	Arms Control Middle East initiative (also known as P-5 Process)
ADF	Australian Defence Force
AG	Australia Group
AHG	BWC Ad Hoc Group (compliance protocol negotiations)
ARF	ASEAN Regional Forum
BDA	Bilateral Destruction Agreement (U.S.–USSR/Russia)
BMD	ballistic missile defense
BMDO	Ballistic Missile Defense Organization, DOD (U.S.)
BW	biological/bacteriological and toxin weapons
BWC	Biological Weapons Convention
CBM	confidence building measure
CB/M	chemical and biological weapons and missiles
CBW	chemical and biological/bacteriological and toxin weapons
CD	Conference on Disarmament, Geneva
CEP	circular error of probability
CFE	Conventional Forces Europe treaty (NATO–Warsaw Pact)
CMA	Chemical Manufacturers Association (U.S.)
COCOM	Coordinating Committee on Multilateral Export Controls

CPI	Counterproliferation Initiative, DOD (U.S.)
CTBT	Comprehensive Test Ban Treaty (nuclear)
CTR	Cooperative Threat Reduction program, DOD (U.S.)
CW	chemical weapons
CWC	Chemical Weapons Convention
CWRI	Chemical Weapons Regional Initiative (AUS)
DIA	Defense Intelligence Agency (U.S.)
DOD	Department of Defence (AUS); Department of Defense (U.S.)
DOE	Department of Energy (U.S.)
DFA	Department of Foreign Affairs (AUS) (became DFAT)
DFAT	Department of Foreign Affairs and Trade (AUS)
DGP	Defense Group on Proliferation (NATO)
DSTO	Defence Science and Technical Organisation (AUS)
DTRA	Defense Threat Reduction Agency (U.S.)
EC	European Community (became EU)
EPCI	Enhanced Proliferation Control Initiative (U.S.)
EU	European Union
FOI	Freedom of Information
FPA	foreign policy analysis (academic literature)
FSU	former Soviet Union (USSR successor states)
G-7	group of seven industrialized countries
GPALS	global protection against limited strikes
GPS	Global Positioning System
IAEA	International Atomic Energy Agency
IC	Intelligence Community (U.S.) (includes all intelligence agencies)
ICBM	intercontinental ballistic missile (over 5500km)
INF	Intermediate Nuclear Forces treaty (U.S.–USSR/FSU)
IRBM	intermediate/medium range ballistic missile (500–5500km)
JCS	Joint Chiefs of Staff (U.S.)
MOU	memorandum of understanding
MRMB	Medium Range Missile Ban (proposal)
MTAG	Missile Technology Analysis Group (U.S. interdiction group)
MTCR	Missile Technology Control Regime
MTEC	Missile Technology Export Committee (U.S. export licensing group)
MTOPS	millions of theoretical operations per second (computer capability)
NAM	nonaligned movement
NIS	Newly Independent States (non-Russian USSR successor states)

NMD	national missile defense (element of U.S. BMD program)
NPT	Nuclear Nonproliferation Treaty
NSAM	National Security Action Memorandum (U.S.)
NSC	National Security Council (U.S.)
NSDD	National Security Decision Directive (U.S.)
NSG	Nuclear Suppliers Group
ONA	Office of National Assessments (AUS) (intelligence agency)
OPCW	Organization for the Prevention of Chemical Weapons, The Hague
OSCE	Organization for Security and Cooperation in Europe, Vienna
OSD	Office of the Secretary of Defense (U.S.)
OSIA	On-site Inspection Agency, DOD (U.S.)
P-5	UNSC Permanent-5 (China, France, Russia, U.K., U.S.)
PDD	Presidential Decision Directive (U.S.)
PhRMA	Pharmaceutical Research and Manufacturers of America
PrepCom	Preparatory Commission (OPCW), The Hague
RCA	riot control agent
RevCon	Review Conference, BWC
SDI	Strategic Defense Initiative (U.S.)
SDIO	Strategic Defense Initiative Organization, DOD (U.S.) (became BMDO)
SLBM	sea-launched ballistic missile (strategic)
SLV	space launch vehicle
SNF	short-range nuclear forces negotiations (U.S.–USSR)
SRBM	short-range ballistic missile (less than 500km)
START	Strategic Arms Reduction Treaty I & II (U.S.–USSR/FSU)
TMD	theatre missile defense (element of U.S. BMD program)
UAV	unmanned air vehicle
UNGA	U.N. General Assembly
UNSC	U.N. Security Council
UNSCOM	U.N. Special Commission on Iraq
VEREX	BWC ad hoc group of verification experts
WEOG	Western Group (Geneva negotiations caucus)
WHO	World Health Organization
WMD	weapons of mass destruction

Introduction

In a hasty bid to retaliate for the American bombing of Tripoli in 1986, Libya launched a missile strike against a remote U.S. Coast Guard station on the Italian island of Lampedusa. This attack remains the first and only case of outside aggression against the military forces of a NATO country on NATO territory. Fortunately, because Libya only had obsolete, early-generation SCUDs (limited in range, inaccurate, and armed solely with conventional munitions), the missiles fell harmlessly into the sea, leaving the incident as a largely forgotten footnote to the last chapter of the Cold War epoch. Almost farcical in itself, Libya's hapless attack nonetheless was a harbinger of what would soon emerge as a dominant Western security concern: the proliferation of weapons of mass destruction (WMD) and their means of delivery.

Today the catastrophic potential for such attacks is becoming increasingly grave. A burgeoning number of hostile states are currently striving to acquire the capacity to deliver mass destruction. The botched Libyan retaliation occurred in a world that was preoccupied by East–West tensions. In this context relatively little attention at the time was given to proliferation threats. The marginal energies expended on the problem tended to focus narrowly on nuclear weapons, with scant thought directed toward chemical and biological weapons (CBW) and missiles. By contrast, over the past decade or so the international community, and particularly Western governments, have come to see all aspects of proliferation as, in the words of former U.S. Secretary of State Madeleine Albright, "The overriding security interest of our time" (*Washington Post*, 02/22/98).

Despite intensifying official alarm about proliferation and parallel academic interest in both its underlying causes and the various international structures created to control it, scholarly examination of national responses to proliferation has been surprisingly limited. Even the proliferation response policies of the United States—leader of the Western antiproliferation coalition—have been subject to curiously little systematic examination.[1] Following from this, there necessarily has been virtually no meaningful attempt at comparing the national antiproliferation strategies of different Western states. This gap in scholarly knowledge has too often fostered misleading assumptions about the cohesiveness, and by extension the efficacy, of Western responses to proliferation.

The present study offers the first published comparison of antiproliferation efforts over time and across different proliferation areas. Chapters 1 and 2 expound a broad conceptual and normative framework for understanding national proliferation response on an abstract level. Chapters 3 and 4 then apply this analytical framework in a series of comprehensive empirical case studies, comprising two sets of national case studies. These case studies constitute the heart of the study. Each can stand on its own as a separate, complete account. However, the study's main analytical focus is on structured comparison, which is taken up in Chapter 5. This establishes that the United States and one of its close allies, in this case Australia, although belonging to a common security community and sharing the same broad antiproliferation goals, nonetheless frequently disagree on the specific policy means by which to achieve them. These differences in specific policy preferences amount to systematically divergent patterns of national proliferation response, patterns that have been more or less consistent over time and across the various proliferation areas. The chapter seeks to explain why two close strategic allies and dedicated antiproliferation partners might lean toward different antiproliferation strategies. The study concludes by warning that fissures in the Western antiproliferation coalition inevitably undermine international efforts to deal effectively with proliferation.

SCOPE

The study embraces a relatively broad conception of national proliferation response. It encompasses the full spectrum of instruments—

diplomatic, military, and economic; unilateral, bilateral, and multilateral—directly intended to respond to the spread of chemical weapons (CW), biological weapons (BW) and Missile Technology Control Regime (MTCR)-class delivery systems.[2]

It is important to note that nuclear proliferation is specifically not examined. Although somewhat arbitrary, there are several good reasons for this admittedly significant omission. First, in contrast to other proliferation areas, there is already a mature literature on nuclear proliferation (Ogilvie-White, 1996). This alone would seem to justify focusing in greater detail than would otherwise be possible on the other, relatively neglected areas. A second consideration is that nuclear proliferation response instruments are conceptually anomalous. For example, the nuclear nonproliferation regime, based on the Nuclear Nonproliferation Treaty (NPT), was created in the 1960s and reflects the priorities, alignments, and dynamics of the early Cold War era. It is difficult to compare this regime to the comparatively recent policies and instruments in the other areas. Finally, the atypical "have–have not" division of Western states codified in the NPT poses a particular problem for the most-similar case comparison at the heart of the present study, given that the United States and its ally Australia, the comparative subject, remain on opposite sides of the nuclear divide.

Conventional weapons issues are excluded because the United States and most other Western states typically define their antiproliferation policies as applying only to WMD and associated missile means of delivery. The United States in particular has been careful to differentiate between its nonproliferation and its conventional arms transfer policies.[3] For similar reasons the study does not directly address the topic of WMD-related terrorism, which traditionally Washington has viewed as a law enforcement issue rather than a proliferation problem (Oehler testimony [tst.], 1996). Therefore, while antiterrorism clearly overlaps with antiproliferation in important respects, it is also by definition beyond the scope of the present study because the countries being studied do not define it as an element of their proliferation response policies.

Finally, the study omits direct examination of policies put in place against Iraq following the 1990–1991 Gulf War. The rationale for not covering these country-specific antiproliferation policies is that collectively they represent an utterly unique case. The post–Gulf War responses to Iraqi proliferation were imposed on Iraq as the result of its military defeat in a conflict fought over an entirely unrelated cause. As such, they are not representative of proliferation response generally, and more important, could not realistically be replicated elsewhere. These issues therefore are examined only to the extent that they have influenced broader proliferation response policy.

The approximate chronological starting point for the study is the mid-1980s. The primary research cutoff date is January 1999, although major developments through July 2001 are referenced.

METHODOLOGY

Case Study Selection

A broad multiactor comparison of several or more Western countries is infeasible due to the lack of existing empirical data on national antiproliferation efforts (Cooper, 1999). The current study therefore approaches the subject of Western proliferation response through a two-actor most-similar case comparison. It is hoped that the resulting data can be further enriched, and that the generalized conclusions based on this data can be further validated, by complementary future studies examining other Western states.

The United States has been chosen as the main research focus because of its singular role as the leader of international antiproliferation efforts, commensurate with its current status as lone superpower. Australia has been selected as a most-similar case comparative subject based on a hierarchy of three interconnected criteria: (1) leadership role and active participation in all facets of the international nonproliferation system, (2) commonality in commitment to shared antiproliferation goals, and (3) commonality in other pertinent respects.

Bertsch and Cuppit (1993, 59) suggest that states' roles in the international nonproliferation system can be divided into five general categories: (1) *coordinating* states that play roles in all components, (2) *collaborating* states that play roles in some components, (3) *sensitive* states that may have relevant industries or technological capacities but do not play a significant role and are not hostile (i.e., do not import, export, or produce targeted weapons systems), (4) *threatening* states that oppose the system (i.e., attempt to acquire, produce, or export applicable weapons or associated technology), and (5) *peripheral* states that do not play a role and are irrelevant to the proliferation issue. The first of these categories includes about twenty states, fewer than half of which can be said to be activists across the nonproliferation spectrum. It is this latter subgroup of less than ten key actors that demarcates the pool of comparative subjects based on the first of the criteria.

Australia has been winnowed from this pool based on a high cumulative ranking for all criteria. It represents what Cooper, Higgot, and Nossal (1993) term a first-follower to U.S. leadership in this sphere. Australia scores high in the categories of international leadership and participation. It is fair to say that Australia is universally recognized as among the most active players in the nonproliferation realm.

Through a series of high-profile initiatives over many years—like creating the Australia Group in the early 1980s, hosting an unprecedented proliferation-related conference of governments and representatives of national chemical industries in the late 1980s, brokering the final resolution of the CWC negotiations in the early 1990s, and most recently assembling most of the world's foreign ministers in 1998 to bolster efforts to strengthen the BWC—Australia is widely acknowledged to be among the one or two most influential players after the United States (Dorling interview [int.], 1998; Evans, 1997; McNamara int., 1998).

Australia also has a strong sense of common purpose with, and in the eyes of, the United States. Former U.S. Assistant Secretary of State Thomas McNamara (int., 1998) states, "They're probably our strongest partner in nonproliferation overall. We cooperate better with the Aussies on average than we do with almost anyone else." Such perceptions are reciprocal and widespread. In research interviews, over 90 percent of present and past officials from both countries affirm that the two share the same antiproliferation objectives.

There are a few other Western states that to a greater or lesser extent are also leaders in the international nonproliferation system and also strongly share U.S. antiproliferation objectives. However, Australia offers several additional advantages as a comparative subject. For instance, citing their sociocultural commonalties, Lijphart (1971) asserts that the Anglo-American countries generally represent one of the more advantageous categories of nonregionally contiguous states for purposes of like-case comparative foreign policy case studies. In addition, whereas the United States and Australia are profoundly dissimilar structurally in terms of national attributes (i.e., regional middle power versus lone global superpower), geopolitics, and so on, they share an unusual degree of commonality in the politico-military arena. This is reflected in uncommonly close intelligence sharing, including on proliferation and related strategic issues.[4] It would be difficult to overstate the importance of the U.S.–Australian intelligence nexus for purposes of the present study. Many scholars of foreign policy decision making see the availability and processing of information as central to understanding foreign policy behavior (Ripley, 1993). Officials often stress the critical role that access to reliable intelligence plays in making policy decisions on nonproliferation (Freedenberg tst., 1989; Oehler tst., 1995; Woolsey tst., 1993b). Indeed, in interviews a number of senior Australian officials cited the intelligence relationship as a key factor in explaining the high degree of commonality between Australian and U.S. antiproliferation objectives relative to other Western countries, in that most other Western countries simply do not share the same understanding of the gravity of the proliferation threat. In addition to intelligence cooperation, the two countries have an unusually close strategic alliance relationship underpinned by regular bilateral consultation and cooperation, including specifically on proliferation issues.

Although there are other countries that roughly match Australia in offering all of these various advantages, most notably Britain and Canada, a number of appurtenant factors nonetheless make Australia a preferable subject for comparison. Britain, for example, would seem an intuitive choice as a most-similar case because it is widely perceived as Washington's most faithful ally. However, notwithstanding the vaunted specialness of the Anglo-American relationship, the increasingly significant role that the European Union (EU) plays in this and other foreign and security policy areas makes British policy as such increasingly hard to isolate and define. This factor would hopelessly complicate any comparative analysis. Canada is therefore left as the most promising alternative to Australia. Yet its contiguous geographic proximity and extreme cultural resemblance to the United States lends an incestuous quality to a Canadian comparison that seems undesirable. In addition, Ottawa's policies are thought to be shaped to an unusual degree by the desire to demonstrate independence from its powerful neighbor, leading it to espouse opposing positions "as a matter of principle rather than interest" far more than other U.S. allies (Handel, 1981, 145). For purposes of a similar-case comparison, being different for difference's sake represents an unhelpful dynamic. And so we are left with Australia.

Case Study Design

The study employs the comparative case studies method. The specific case study design is adapted from the "multiple case studies design" suggested by Robert Yin (1984), and specifically the "embedded multiple case" version of this design involving both multiple units of analysis and multiple cases for each unit of analysis. "What distinguishes this type of analysis," Yin explains, "is that the unit of analysis is clearly embedded within a larger case, and the larger case is the *major* interest of the study. . . . The results should be interpreted at the single-case level. . . . The patterns . . . for each single case may then be compared across cases, following the replication mode for multiple cases. Finally, the conclusions drawn for multiple cases can become the conclusions for the overall study" (p. 115).

For the present study, each of the two countries represents a unit of analysis, with differentiated cases for each of the three issue areas. Thus, the study employs a two-by-three structure, with three cases each for two units of analysis, equaling six differentiated cases. This structure permits three levels of comparative analysis: (1) for each ac-

tor comparing policies within each issue area over time (i.e., tracing
the evolution of policies), (2) for each actor comparing policies among
the three issue areas, and (3) comparing patterns between actors.

Empirical data for each case study is derived from official material,
interviews, legislative testimony and statements by government officials, newspapers and specialized news services, and relevant secondary sources. Official material (including primarily hitherto classified
documents) is derived from sources including U.S. and Australian freedom of information procedures. Interview data are derived from nearly
sixty interviews with present and past officials, ranging in rank from
desk officers to cabinet ministers.

NOTES

1. The terms "antiproliferation" and "proliferation response" denote the
full spectrum of diplomatic, military, or economic instruments intended to
stem, reverse, or mitigate the consequences of horizontal proliferation. "Nonproliferation" refers specifically to a subset of mostly diplomatic and economic
tools intended to stem or reverse proliferation. "Counterproliferation" refers
specifically to a subset of mostly military tools designed to mitigate the consequences of proliferation.

2. The MTCR Annex defines "Category 1" as any system (e.g., rocket, ballistic missile, cruise missile) inherently capable of delivering a 500-kilogram
payload to a range of 300 kilometers.

3. Confusingly, there have been occasional official references by the U.S.
and other Western governments to "conventional proliferation," but these have
usually been stated in a context that carefully distinguishes the issue as a separate policy area from "nonproliferation."

4. See Ball (1985) for a description of the unrivalled intelligence cooperation among Australia, Canada, New Zealand, the United Kingdom, and the
United States. New Zealand has more recently been largely excluded from
this privileged club.

Chapter 1

Conceptual Framework for Analysis: A Typology of National Antiproliferation Strategies

This chapter constructs a comprehensive typology of national proliferation response. It is tailored to serve as a framework for comparable national case studies spanning multiple proliferation areas. Such a novel typology is necessitated by the paucity of existing conceptual models offering a fully satisfactory basis for this type of national-level comparative analysis (Cooper, 1999).

The chapter begins by establishing the outer boundaries of proliferation response by distinguishing it from closely related concepts. It then posits three basic antiproliferation strategies: (1) *capability-denial*, (2) *nonpossession norm-building*, and (3) *consequence-management*. Finally, it describes various policy instruments that support each of these strategies. Examination of the strengths, weaknesses, and compatibility of these strategies is taken up in Chapter 2.

WHAT IS NOT ANTIPROLIFERATION: SETTING CONCEPTUAL PARAMETERS

It is important to set the conceptual parameters of proliferation response by demarcating cognate concepts. Antiproliferation as a distinctive class of activities evolved from various Cold War antecedents like traditional arms control, strategic trade controls, and strategic deterrence and WMD warfighting. Overlap still exists with many of these concepts. For example, export control–based elements of non-proliferation bear a pronounced resemblance to the concept of strategic trade controls, and treaty-based nonproliferation is closely related to traditional arms control and disarmament. At the same time, proliferation response is conceptually distinguishable in significant ways from these concepts rooted in bipolar superpower confrontation.

Strategic Trade Controls

Nonproliferation is sometimes portrayed as a North–South reorientation of earlier West–East tools. Thus, relatively recent nonproliferation export controls are associated with earlier strategic trade controls. Nevertheless there are important conceptual and structural differences. These are based both on what is controlled, and to where.

Nonproliferation export controls focus only on exports associated with a narrow class of weaponry (i.e., WMD and associated missiles) that is deemed so abhorrent that exports to anywhere that contribute to it are to be prevented. By contrast, strategic trade controls focus on a broad spectrum of militarily relevant trade, but only to a narrow class of destination (i.e., enemies) in order to stymie organic military-industrial capabilities. Put another way, whereas nonproliferation export controls target only specific classes of armaments but do so for all countries, strategic trade controls target only specific classes of recipient countries but do so for all militarily relevant items.

These conceptual distinctions between strategic trade controls and nonproliferation export controls are reflected in pronounced structural differences. International cooperation on the former, as embodied by the now defunct Coordinating Committee on Multilateral Export Controls (COCOM), requires a strong consensus on just who, precisely, are the common adversaries.[1] This type of consensus then allows for an extremely draconian approach. Because COCOM targeted an enemy alliance that posed a clear and present danger to its members, it could function on the basis of economic warfare; in essence, a sharp stick used to punch holes in militarily relevant industrial bases (Bryen tst., 1989, [State] int.). COCOM hence was able to exercise a virtual veto over all East–West transfers of militarily relevant equipment and technology.

In striking polarity, nonproliferation does not assume any political consensus whatsoever about the nature of the countries targeted. This allows nonproliferation export controls to be practiced by, and theoretically coordinated among, a much more heterogeneous group of countries. But it also means that these countries will have to apply such controls to recipients that they do not necessarily regard as hostile. Indeed, Western countries often apply nonproliferation export controls to suspected proliferators who also happen to be friendly countries (e.g., Israel, South Korea), and even to countries that are not suspected proliferators, including other Western states. It goes without saying that no country wants to use too sharp a stick against its friends and allies, nor to get poked with such a stick itself. Multilateral nonproliferation export controls consequently bear only the most superficial resemblance to the COCOM model. They do not target the industrial base of any country, but instead employ narrower, more flexible, and inevitably weaker methods. It is left to individual countries to make decisions that take into account their own assessments of the proliferation risk posed by both the specific commodity and the specific end user on a case-by-case basis. A dramatic illustration of this is the effective loosening seen in Western dual-use exports to China once the basis for controls on such items shifted in the mid-1990s from strategic trade to nonproliferation (Clarke & Johnston, 1999).

The bottom line is that unilateral strategic trade controls may be an effective way for an individual state to augment nonproliferation efforts against unambiguous national adversaries. However, other than in highly unusual cases (e.g., Iraq), it is difficult in practice to multilaterize such efforts with strict, COCOM–style arrangements under the banner of nonproliferation.

Traditional Arms Control and Disarmament

Treaty-based nonproliferation is closely linked to traditional Cold War–style arms control and disarmament. At times the two occur in tandem. As with strategic trade controls, this aspect of nonproliferation is often thought of merely as traditional arms control reoriented from West–East to North–South. Here too, though, there are important conceptual and structural distinctions. That said, although distinguishing between disarmament and nonproliferation is useful and in fact quite common, the lines are both indistinct and inconsistently drawn. Moreover, the distinction is likely to become even blurrier over time, as hybrid policies increasingly emerge that intermingle arms control and nonproliferation goals and methods (Davis, 1999).

One of the most widespread forms of differentiation, both within the proliferation literature and in some official usage, equates the term "disarmament" expansively with any and all legal treaty instruments, and the term "nonproliferation" narrowly with export-control instruments. There is a strong undertone of political expediency to parsing the concepts in this way, since many Third World countries have visceral objections to nonproliferation, and so prefer not to have the term associated with global treaty instruments to which they are parties (Herby, 1991). But this politically motivated division is not especially helpful for conceptualizing national proliferation response. Instead, a more useful distinction is between traditional arms control and disarmament (e.g., START, INF, CFE) on the one hand, and treaty-based nonproliferation on the other.

In many ways this conceptual distinction is analogous to the distinctions that once were drawn between the concepts of "arms control" and "disarmament." Seminal theorists, such as Schelling and Halperin (1961) and Bull (1965), carefully distinguished between these concepts. As J. L. Richardson (1986) explains,

The goals of arms control were generally taken . . . to be to reduce the risk of war, especially nuclear war; to reduce its destructiveness, if it should occur; and to reduce the cost of preparedness (the burden of the arms race), in that order of priority. An important implication of this ranking of the goals was that disarmament, the reduction of arms, was not *necessarily* desirable unless it could be shown as likely to promote the primary goal, reducing the risk of war. The arms control school did not assume, as the disarmers had tended to, that agreed measures of disarmament would *ipso facto* achieve this. In the same way, arms control agreements were not desirable for their own sake, but for their consequences. (p. 5)

Today the concepts of arms control and disarmament have come to be used almost interchangeably. If they are differentiated at all, it is merely by a rather narrow technical distinction along the lines of, "Arms control refers to agreements designed to regulate arms levels either by limiting their growth or by restricting how they may be used . . . [whereas] disarmament . . . seeks to reduce or eliminate weapons" (Kegley & Wittkopf, 1991, p. 461). This receding of the differentiation between these once battling concepts resulted from the supremacy achieved by the arms control school as the dominant paradigm for Cold War arms control and disarmament as a whole, wherein the value of constraints, reductions, or elimination is not seen as inherent, but instead as contingent on whether the consequences enhance security or promote other beneficial objectives (Dougherty & Pfaltzgraff, 1990, p. 413; Fergusson, 1991).

It is this fundamentally contingent premise of traditional Cold War arms control and disarmament that brings us to its basal conceptual distinction from treaty-based nonproliferation, whose objectives are fixed and absolute. As with nonproliferation export controls, nonproliferation treaties do not encompass all types of armaments, but only those weapons deemed to be so intrinsically abhorrent (i.e., WMD and associated missiles) as to warrant an unconditional goal to prevent or reverse their spread in any and all circumstances. To illustrate, whereas

arms control dictates that attitudes about a given country's possession of a hundred or a thousand tanks could be positive or negative depending on any number of factors (e.g., political relationships, regional
military balance), nonproliferation dictates that attitudes about any
proliferator's possession of even a single offensive biological weapon is
unconditionally negative.[2] This difference in goals—based on the difference between the contingent versus inherent judgement of the *legitimacy*
of the targeted weapons—separates all aspects of nonproliferation from
all aspects of traditional arms control and disarmament. The conceptual foundation of nonproliferation is that preventing new proliferation and eliminating proliferated weapons is always beneficial.

The focus on "proliferators" as the target raises another basic conceptual distinction between traditional arms control and disarmament
and nonproliferation. That is that the latter is implicitly embedded in
the notion of a preexisting status quo demarcating "haves" and "have
nots." Accordingly, "By definition, any legal instrument giving expres-
sion to the goal of non-proliferation implicitly defines the freezing of
the . . . status quo as the minimum floor of success" (Leaver, 1997b, p.
167). This minimum floor can then be raised to include reversing instances where prevention has failed in order to restore the status quo.
However, going beyond this to impact the status quo "haves" is, at
least from their perspective, crossing the conceptual line that separates nonproliferation from traditional arms control and disarmament.
Although conceptually important, this distinction can get rather murky.
For example, traditional disarmament among "haves" can occur in
parallel, or even in conjunction with, nonproliferation targeting "have
nots." For example, under the aegis of the CWC negotiations the United
States and the Soviet Union (as the two acknowledged CW–possessor
states) engaged in traditional bilateral disarmament between themselves, while they and all of the other participants at the same time
were negotiating nonproliferation for everyone else. Indeed, many
"have not" countries insist that disarmament among "haves" is a necessary parallel activity, or even a prerequisite, for their cooperative
participation in nonproliferation treaties.

The definitional emphasis on a proliferation status quo begs the
question: Where and by whom is this benchmark set? This question
poses no difficulty in the nuclear milieu, where the concept of nonproliferation originally was invented. In the context of the NPT, the benchmark of "haves" and "have nots" was formally established at a fixed
point in time and has been carried forward. The division of labor between nuclear arms control and disarmament and nuclear nonproliferation is thus clearly drawn. India and Pakistan may now be overt
nuclear powers, but the rest of the world still declines to treat them as
status quo "haves." But determining comparable benchmarks is more

difficult for the other proliferation areas, since the status of "haves" and "have nots" is ad hoc and variegated.[3] At least one analyst defines the status quo simply as any proliferation beyond the U.N. Security Council's (UNSC) five permanent (P-5) members (Müller, 1997).[4] Others merely assume that the status quo is defined by the situation that existed at some representative point in the Cold War, typically the late 1960s or early 1970s. The salient point in any case is that there is no broad consensus on where to draw the line.

The concept of a proliferation status quo is only germane when there are acknowledged "haves." Once the number of acknowledged "haves" reaches zero—for example, in the BW area after the United States and Soviet Union signed the BWC in the early 1970s—the conceptual line of demarcation is eliminated and the endeavor becomes the same as the inherent nonproliferation goal: to prevent the existence of a proscribed type of weapon everywhere. The concept of a status quo therefore is very important in cases where there are no global bans, or while such bans are being negotiated, but is largely irrelevant thereafter.

The example of India and Pakistan helps to illustrate some of these complex conceptual distinctions. Neither state is acknowledged as a status quo "have." But each having acquired nuclear weapons and nuclear-capable missile delivery systems (i.e., the preventative element of nonproliferation having failed), they and others see value in measures to manage the risks posed by this situation (e.g., capping weapons levels, restricting deployments, establishing hot-line procedures) (Kamal, 1999; Talbott, 1999; Yasmeen, 1999). Such contingent measures, however, constitute traditional arms control rather than nonproliferation. In fact, to the extent that other states endorse such arrangements, nonproliferation goals could actually be undermined by legitimizing non–status quo possession. Even deep reductions—probably highly desirable to achieve traditional arms control and disarmament goals—would not constitute nonproliferation if residual inventories were left permanently intact. It is even imaginable for reductions short of total elimination to be harmful from a nonproliferation perspective. For instance, imagine if India and Pakistan agreed to cut their inventories of relatively primitive missiles, but that in return they demanded that others not impede upgrading the quality of the residual inventory. This hypothetical outcome still may or may not be a positive outcome from a contingent arms control and disarmament perspective, but it assuredly would be a nonproliferation catastrophe, because it would facilitate *qualitative proliferation.* So while qualitative and quantitative enhancements to the capabilities of non–status quo "haves" always constitutes proliferation, the opposite (i.e., reductions of their capabilities) counterintuitively does not automatically constitute nonproliferation.

The various distinguishing conceptual features of nonproliferation—inherent objectives based on a fixed status quo—lead to a number of structural differences between the scope and content of nonproliferation versus traditional arms control and disarmament treaties. For example, because the latter are designed to achieve goals such as minimizing the risk or cost of conflict, they are only worthwhile to the extent that they involve potential enemies, since such goals are irrelevant among countries that would not fight or prepare for war in any case (Gray, 1993). Consequently, traditional arms control and disarmament in practice tends to occur in bilaterally oriented instruments between potential enemies (e.g., START) or between groupings of potential enemies (e.g., CFE). In contrast, treaty-based nonproliferation—encompassing friend and foe alike—occurs in broad multilateral instruments among heterogeneous groups of states.

Finally, whereas traditional arms control and disarmament concentrates largely on existing weapons, nonproliferation treaties tend to focus on preventing future acquisition of weapons. They therefore in fact involve little or no actual disarming (Fergusson, 1995). Consequently, whereas traditional arms control and disarmament deals primarily with armaments and secondarily with associated production capabilities, treaty-based nonproliferation deals primarily with production and even preproduction capabilities. This means that functionally the scope of nonproliferation treaties tends to cover a much wider range of dual-use facilities and activities.

DISTINGUISHING ANTIPROLIFERATION STRATEGIES: CAPABILITY-DENIAL, NONPOSSESSION NORM-BUILDING, CONSEQUENCE-MANAGEMENT

Having considered at length some of what proliferation response is not, we are now ready to categorize what it is. There are a variety of ways in which to parse this class of activity conceptually. For example, nonproliferation instruments may be grouped by focus (e.g., nuclear regimes [NPT, NSG] versus CW regimes [CWC, AG]), by structure (e.g., legal bans [BWC, CWC, NPT] versus export control arrangements [MTCR, AG, NSG]), or by characteristic (e.g., coercive versus cooperative, limited membership versus universal, unilateral versus multilateral). For the study of national proliferation response, however, it is most useful to group instruments by the purpose for which countries use them.

Whereas multilateral regimes represent the basic unit of analysis for studies of the international nonproliferation system, national policies represent the basic unit of analysis for studies of an individual actor's responses to proliferation. Consider that individual instruments, and particularly multilateral regimes, can serve multiple purposes as instruments of national policy. For example, Washington essentially regards the CWC as two separate tools in one, serving two purposes: a mechanism for U.S.–Russian bilateral disarmament, and a global nonproliferation vehicle (ACDA & State Department tst., 1990, p. 281; Christopher tst., 1996; Deutch tst., 1994; Perry tst., 1996). In fact various countries look to the CWC for a wide variety of sometimes contradictory purposes, including not only as a ban on CW possession, but also, for example, as a source for export controls, or technology sharing and economic development. Ergo, the fact that country X and country Y each support the CWC—a statement that at one level is equally valid for the United States and Iran—does not tell us for what purposes they do so. This observation is true of many instruments that simultaneously support different nonproliferation and other purposes.

The premise that instruments can most usefully be grouped according to the purposes that they serve suggests three broad proliferation response categories: (1) capability-denial, (2) nonpossession norm-building, and (3) consequence-management.

Capability-Denial: Supply-Side Nonproliferation

One of the two basic approaches to preventative nonproliferation is for supplier countries—be they "haves" or "have nots"—to deny the capability of "have not" countries to acquire proscribed weapons. This is accomplished not only by impeding access to actual weapons, but also access to equipment, technology, services, and knowledge that could contribute to indigenous development of such weapons. The approach focuses primarily on inherent capability, with a recipient's intentions only a secondary factor. Virtually every "have not" country is a potential target for supply-side nonproliferation.

The primary characteristic of this approach is that it is the exclusive domain of supplier and transshipment countries. It is most effective when there is cooperation among all or most suppliers so that they do not undercut one another with inconsistent rules or implementation. But while this type of supplier cooperation may or may not exist, by definition it does not extend to recipients. In other words, "The target country is not a participant in the establishment and execution of the rules" (Zanders, 1997, p. 19). This means that the approach does not require the consent of, or participation by, recipients in order to function. Rather, its effectiveness depends largely on the extent to which a given proliferator relies on outside sources to acquire a given capability.

The overall goal of this category of activity at any point in time is to prevent further quantitative or qualitative proliferation from occurring. It is therefore explicitly prophylactic in character. Moreover, the goal of preventing proliferation often in reality translates to the more modest objective of merely impeding or slowing it down. Supply-side measures are only able to reverse proliferation indirectly, by thwarting programs of proliferation concern for long enough, or to such an extent, that the proliferators themselves give up the game.

The broad formula for supply-side strategies is well established. Because capability-denial focuses on preventing the spread of inherent capability, it seeks to do so at the earliest feasible stage. The approach is therefore innately concerned as much, or more, with production capabilities as it is with weapons per se. At the same time, it only seeks to target capabilities that directly contribute to proscribed weapons. Decisions about whether to deny a particular country's access to a particular item are therefore based on subjective judgements regarding (1) the inherent proliferation risk posed by a given item, defined as precisely how directly it could contribute to a proscribed capability, and (2) the proliferation threat posed by a given country, defined as whether and to what extent it is suspected of trying to attain proscribed weapons in defiance of the nonproliferation status quo. The approach is thus grounded in an ongoing series of case-by-case evaluations by suppliers regarding primarily inherent capability and secondarily intentions. In cases where an item is judged to have an extremely high inherent capability to contribute to proscribed weapons, this consideration generally takes precedence over considerations of possible intent. In cases where the item poses a moderate inherent proliferation risk, and particularly if it has other nonproscribed uses (i.e., dual-use items), then intention is taken heavily into account. In cases where the item poses a low inherent risk, then intention is the lone consideration.

Nonpossession Norm–Building: Cooperative Nonproliferation

A second basic preventative nonproliferation strategy is to get governments to consent to abide by legally constructed norms against possession of proscribed weapons. In other words, this approach seeks to secure and enforce pledges that whether a state has the latent capability to proliferate it does not intend to do so.

Under this approach, countries agree to forswear acquiring a specified class of weapons, and to eliminate any that have been acquired already in contravention to the nonproliferation status quo. This approach is accomplished by working to build, broaden, strengthen, and maintain agreements that ban possession. Because this approach requires the consent of its targets, it can be thought of as cooperative or consensual nonproliferation. The ultimate objective of the approach is to eliminate demand for proscribed weapons by codifying and demonstrating that, regardless of whether participating countries have the inherent capability to possess them, they have no intention to do so.

Although the main characteristic of the norm-building approach is that it is consensual, a variety of means may be used to secure a government's consent, including coercion. To take an extreme example, UNSCOM was strictly speaking a consensual arrangement, even though the means used to obtain and maintain Iraq's consent were highly coercive. Once Iraq withdrew consent, the tool collapsed utterly. The CWC offers a more typical example of coercively induced cooperation, building in automatic economic penalties against non-members as a means to encourage wide participation.

It is important to note that the conception of norm-building used here reflects a specialized understanding of what constitutes a norm. This term is generally used in international relations theory to describe a common consensus that has evolved around a particular issue (e.g., it is bad for states to kill one another's diplomats). In this sense, a norm exists to the extent that it has already come to be widely recognized and adhered to internationally. However, in the nonproliferation context, the term "norm" generally refers to a formal agreement of one sort or another that bans possession of specified weaponry.[5] According to this specialized understanding, norms can be legislated through diplomatic processes. Unlike traditional customary norms, which are binding upon all states, this type of legislated or constructed norm is only binding on the contracting parties (Thomas & Thomas, 1970). The effectiveness of the norm-building approach therefore depends largely on the proportion of states that agree to participate, as well as the quality of their compliance in choosing or being compelled to follow the rules.

There is considerable variation in the nature of these normative rules and the means by which they are implemented. But as with supply-side measures, the basic demand-side formula is well established. The operative prohibition almost by definition focuses on the weapon per se. As a rule, a nonpossession norm cannot prohibit capabilities that merely *could* facilitate the production of proscribed weapons, but only those that are demonstrably intended to do so (Robinson, 1987). Mutimer (1998) elaborates, "The focus of [nonproliferation] disarmament practices is not on the technology which 'inevitably' gives rise to military capability, but on that capability itself. Disarmament practices seek to reduce or eliminate the weapons which pose military threats, not to constrain the movement of technologies underlying those capabilities" (p. 115).

In practice, this means that restrictions on inherent capabilities tend to be narrowly limited to those very few that have no other conceivable purpose but to produce prohibited weapons. Dual-use research, development, and production capabilities, as well as defensive military programs, may or may not be monitored, but they are almost never disallowed, and in fact usually are explicitly authorized in order to provide a positive incentive for participation.

Consequence-Management: Beyond Nonproliferation

A third approach to proliferation response seeks to ameliorate the consequences of actualized proliferation by using primarily military countermeasures to deny the proliferator effective use of, or the capacity to coerce by the threat of use of, proliferated weapons. This is accomplished by preemptively eliminating an enemy's WMD capabilities before they can be used—for instance, Coalition SCUD-hunting efforts during the Persian Gulf War—or deterring, defending against, or coping with such use. The operative characteristic of this approach is its postproliferation focus. Instead of targeting development and possession, it concentrates on denying proliferators the capacity effectively to use or threaten to use proliferated capabilities. In a sense this strategy can be thought of as capability denial after the fact.

Consequence-management is premised on the basic assumption that "a country determined to obtain NBC [nuclear, biological, and chemical] weapons and their means of delivery . . . can in all likelihood succeed despite the strongest prevention efforts" (Miller tst., 1997). Only actualized proliferators (i.e., countries that have successfully circumvented capability denial and/or cheated, withdrawn from, or opted out of nonpossession norms) with perceived hostile intentions are targets. Consequently, international cooperation on this strategy requires a shared perception that at least some proliferators are potentially hostile and represent a common danger. Because this strategy mainly involves latent military preparedness, it does not require the cooperation of its targets.

POLICY INSTRUMENTS SUPPORTING THESE STRATEGIES

Capability-Denial Instruments

National Export Controls

National export controls are often perceived as nothing more than the implementing mechanism by which Western countries carry out commitments under multilateral supplier regimes, and so tend to be disregarded as an independent policy tool. However, national export control regulations, procedures, and individual licensing decisions can represent important independent tools of national policy. In a sense, the rules of the supplier regimes are negotiated as least common denominators, representing minimum acceptable standards of conduct for participants. Thus, individual countries may choose to cleave to the letter of these multilateral rules or even to abuse their national discretion by bending them. But they are equally free to go beyond them by applying stricter approval standards, by insisting on stringent extra precautions (e.g., government-to-government assurances, technical safeguards), or by controlling additional items. Such augmented measures can be applied across the board, or particular countries or regions may be singled out for exceptional vigilance, again based entirely upon national discretion.

Limited-Membership Global Export-Control Regimes

The most visible capability-denial instruments are multilateral export-control arrangements such as the MTCR and the AG. The key purpose of these regimes is to develop common export-control rules for specified items and to coordinate national implementation by participating supplier countries. The effectiveness of these regimes is affected by a combination of factors, including the extent to which all major suppliers participate, the extent to which the rules and lists unambiguously apply to all relevant transfers, and the extent to which members conscientiously follow the rules in their national implementation. Beyond this core mission, supplier regimes also serve to focus the attention of members on specific proliferation problems, facilitate the sharing of intelligence and technical information among members, and help members identify and respond quickly to emerging proliferation threats (Van Ham, 1993).

Although supplier regimes are global in scope, their membership is restricted, and they are not recognized as part of the U.N. system (Lyons, 1995). Because they operate as consensus organizations, there is a strong imperative to limit membership in order to facilitate cohesion and avoid cumbersome decision-making processes. Determining who is allowed to join the club is therefore usually a key (and potentially thorny) issue. Specific considerations boil down to a candidate's degree of commitment to nonproliferation and role or potential role as a supplier of relevant equipment and technology.

Supplier regimes seek to regulate activities like commercial transactions that are intrinsically difficult to monitor for compliance (Boutin, 1994; Wright, 1993). They therefore of necessity must rely on members to implement their commitments in good faith, with few or no formal enforcement mechanisms. In practice, this means the effectiveness of supplier regimes depends on the "like mindedness" of their members, both in their desire not to contribute to proliferation by others and in not having proliferation ambitions themselves.[6]

Wider Export-Control Norms

The inherent membership limitations of export-control regimes exclude a number of countries that otherwise might contribute to the overall capability-denial enterprise. These include those with an imperfect commitment to nonproliferation (e.g., nonmembers of nonpossession norms), proliferants and other countries that could act as second-tier suppliers, and nonsupplier transshipment countries. Supply-side nonproliferation can therefore be greatly enhanced if such countries are persuaded to adopt responsible export control standards. This can be achieved in a number of ways. The most common is to promote unilateral adherence to the rules of a limited-membership supplier regime by countries outside the regime. For example, both the AG and the MTCR have invited nonmember countries to apply the rules of the regime unilaterally, in effect suggesting that these rules become a quasi-universal export-control norm.

Supplier regime rules also can be extended on a more formal basis through bilateral agreements, essentially bilateralizing unilateral adherence. For example, the United States has obtained binding political commitments to apply the MTCR Guidelines and Annex from a number of missile technology suppliers that, for one reason or another, are unwilling, or have not been permitted, to join the MTCR.

Alternatively, export-control obligations can be incorporated into global treaty instruments (e.g., CWC Article I(d), BWC Article III). Because such instruments are negotiated among an extremely diverse set of countries, such obligations are rarely thoroughgoing. Instead, they usually consist of vague prohibitions against assisting proscribed weapons, with no concrete rules or coordinated implementation (Müller, 1994, pp. 255–256). What this device lacks in rigor it compensates for by getting a wide spectrum of states to acknowledge implicitly that sensitive exports should somehow be regulated.

Targeted (Reinforced) Export-Control Regimes

In cases where a significant number of supplier countries shares a common perception that a certain country, group of countries, or region poses either an unusually high proliferation risk or a clear and present danger to collective strategic interests it may be possible to apply the tenets of strategic trade control to the nonproliferation mission. This tool works on the premise that "the proliferation problem is not global and generic, but regional and specific" (Müller, 1997, p. 65). For example, since the defeat of Iraq following its invasion of Kuwait, and the ongoing failure to disarm Iraq's WMD and missile programs, the United States has worked within the U.N. system to maintain severe restrictions on dual-use transfers to Iraq. Likewise, after the Gulf War the P-5 countries considered augmenting their own constraints on dual-use transfers to the entire Middle East region, under the auspices of the Bush administration's Arms Control Middle East (ACME) initiative. Along less formal lines, the United States has for years tried to rally its Western allies to join it in taking a similar approach vis-à-vis a group of countries that it has termed "rogue states." However, the abject failure of the ACME initiative, and the difficulties that the United States has experienced in maintaining support for Iraq sanctions, and also in selling the rogue state approach even to its closest allies (Bertsch, Cupitt, & Yamamoto, 1997), illustrate the difficulty in achieving the high level of political consensus on shared threats that is needed in order to apply stringent targeted controls.

Compliance Mechanisms

Compliance and enforcement mechanisms are among the most conspicuous arrows in the quiver of both supply- and demand-side approaches to nonproliferation. For the former, enforcement tools run the gamut of interdiction actions, diplomatic pressure, punitive sanctions, positive incentives, indirect linkages (i.e., tying outcomes on unrelated issues to proliferation behavior), and verification mechanisms. These instruments are primarily intended to encourage suppliers to exercise appropriate restraint in transferring proliferation-relevant capabilities. A secondary purpose is to encourage recipients to account for how they use the capabilities that they do receive. These tools are often directly or indirectly linked to multilateral export-control norms.

Interdicting specific transfers is the lynchpin of supply-side enforcement activity. Despite the colorful images that this conjures, interdiction in the nonproliferation context involves mostly mundane activities. The term applies broadly to any national action undertaken to block a specific transfer of proliferation concern. The interdiction workhorse is the humble diplomatic démarche, a formal request to a foreign government to take some specified action. When a government becomes aware of a pending transfer of concern, it may have its embassy deliver a démarche to the government of the sending country asking it to intervene to block the transfer. Alternatively, if the government of the originating country is hostile or uncooperative, or if the item has already left its jurisdiction, a démarche may be sent to an intermediate transshipment country requesting confiscation. Failing these steps, the government trying to stop the transfer might even publicize the transaction, attempting to shame the governments or companies involved into taking action. Finally, as a last resort, and only in very rare circumstances, a state may opt to take military action to seize or turn back a shipment.

In addition to interdiction, various positive and negative incentives can be used as "carrots and sticks" to encourage appropriate behavior. These include economic or political sanctions punishing problematic transfers, or similar kinds of rewards explicitly linked to refraining from unacceptable behavior (Bertsch, Cuppit, & Yamamoto, 1997; Dunn, 1998). Even cooperative verification, usually associated with treaty-based nonproliferation, can to a limited degree be used as an adjunct to capability-denial. For example, a supplier country can institute a program to verify the end-use assurances that it obtains as a condition for approving export licenses (Mussington, 1995).

It would be difficult to overstate the importance of compliance mechanisms. Indeed, the extent of a state's commitment to one or another nonproliferation approach may, in large measure, be judged by the extent to which it takes national actions to help enforce it. For example, one analyst, noting that "the use of sanctions—and the threat to use them—has been a valuable tool in enhancing international adherence to international export-control norms," concludes that countries that have failed to use this tool are "not acting . . . aggressively . . . to police international export control norms" (Spector, 1996, p. 173). In other words, failure to use enforcement tools aggressively to promote supply-side compliance is seen as indicative of a lack of commitment to the capability-denial approach.

Sabotage–Destruction

The most direct and controversial means of capability-denial is to attack weapons-related research or production facilities in order to prevent a country from achieving capabilities. One of the best known examples of this most muscular form of capability-denial was the 1980s Israeli attack on an Iraqi nuclear facility. A more recent example was the U.S. attack on an alleged CW–related production facility in Sudan. Because such actions require compelling evidence about the details of a program of proliferation concern, as well as a profound conviction that the country in question poses a clear and present danger, they are extremely rare.

Indirect Capability-Denial

Some things that impede proliferation nevertheless should not properly be seen as elements of national proliferation response. Anything that detracts from the resources that a would-be proliferator can direct toward its proliferation programs indirectly bolsters supply-side nonproliferation. For example, a former U.S. intelligence chief has noted that economic sanctions that were imposed on Libya for involvement in terrorism have had a spin-off impact on Tripoli's proliferation programs (Woolsey tst., 1993a). By extension, global economic downturn might also deny proliferators resources and force them to slow or halt their WMD programs in order to divert resources to more urgent national priorities. Global recession surely should not be counted as an instrument of national nonproliferation policy, however, because it is not a result of government action intended to reduce proliferation risks. Only policies directly intended to address proliferation—versus those that merely have inadvertant benefits—can be counted as proliferation-response instruments, at least in the context of examining national strategies against proliferation.

Nonpossession Instruments

Global Nonpossession Treaty Norms

The most visible instruments supporting the nonpossession approach to nonproliferation are universal normative affirmation pacts outlawing possession (i.e., BWC, CWC, NPT). Although these instruments are called universal, in practice they are not. They are universal only in that all countries that wish to do so may accede to them, and they aspire to universality.

Goodby (1993) makes a compelling case that, notwithstanding their evolving and multifaceted purposes, the primary nonproliferation function of these treaties is to create preventative norms against future possession. Although they also have a notional role in reversing proliferation, to date this has been limited to a pair of covert CW possessors unexpectedly declaring themselves following CWC entry into force in mid-1997.[7] Therefore, at least for now the main function of these instruments is codifying the intent of "have nots" to remain so.

The web of nonproliferation treaty norms is considered to be part of the U.N. system. Each of the these instruments explicitly invests the Security Council with ultimate enforcement authority (Lyons, 1995; United Nations Association, 1995). The effectiveness of a universal nonpossession instrument depends on a combination of factors, including breadth of subscription, particularly among countries with relevant capabilities (and especially those suspected of having covert programs); the effectiveness of its compliance provisions and the perceived track record of compliance over time; and its eventual recognition as embodying a truly universal norm under customary international law.

Regional or Targeted Nonpossession Mechanisms

Nonpossession mechanisms can also be developed and/or implemented on a region-specific basis. One reason to do this is the absence of a global norm. For example, the Mendoza Agreement created a CW–free zone in southern South America prior to the completion of the CWC (ACDA off., 1992). This rationale is especially applicable in the missile area, where there is no global norm against possession, and indeed there have been occasional proposals for missile-free zones. Another reason is to encourage regional participation in a pending or existing global norm by reassuring countries that all of their neighbors will also join. This is potentially an important function because proliferation tends to occur in regions where instability and mistrust are prevalent (Forsberg, Driscoll, Webb, & Dean, 1995). In addition, existing regional organizations (e.g., ARF, OAS, OSCE) can be recruited to assist in enforcement of compliance with global norms through complementary measures (Vachon, 1994). Finally, regional mechanisms can theoretically be used to augment global norms on a regional basis by providing for stricter measures among regional countries (Fergusson, 1995). The regional South Pacific Nuclear Free Zone, for example, has more demanding abrogation criteria than the global NPT. In practice, however, there have been very few examples of any of these types of regional mechanisms.

In addition to regional arrangements, nonpossession norms may be pursued on an ad hoc basis by cajoling or coercing a specific country to submit to disarmament arrangements outside the structure of a global norm. This targeted approach can be used either in the absence of a global norm or for possessors that refuse to accede to a global norm. The most well-known examples of this approach are the armistice conditions imposed on Iraq following the Gulf War and the U.S.–negotiated Agreed Framework reinforcing North Korea's NPT commitments in exchange for multilateral energy assistance, sanctions easing, and normalizing relations.

Compliance Mechanisms

Compliance mechanisms are key to the nonpossession approach. The types of instruments available are much the same as for supply-side nonproliferation, including verification, incentives, linkages, sanctions, and diplomatic pressure. The main difference is that these mechanisms are often implemented through treaty-affiliated multilateral organizations, making national enforcement actions comparatively less important (and stringent multilateral enforcement structures more so).

Verification plays the central role in nonpossession compliance. It is meant to inspire confidence that a treaty norm is being observed, deter cheating, and provide the data needed in order to resolve accusations of noncompliance. Verification is generally seen as so important that nonpossession instruments are usually evaluated based on perceptions of the extent and effectiveness of their verification provisions. As one veteran negotiator observes, "The verification provisions being formulated in any agreement are often seen as a barometer for assessing the seriousness of negotiators" (Vachon, 1997, p. 56). For instance, the CWC is perceived as more robust than the BWC. Therefore, at the national level support for (and confidence in) verification is a significant indicator of a state's commitment to the nonpossession approach.

Indirect Demand Reduction

Anything that reduces the demand for proscribed weapons indirectly bolsters the nonpossession approach to nonproliferation. Some analysts cite democratization and/or economic liberalization as among the most potent means to dampen demand for disreputable weapons (Bertsch, Cupitt, & Yamamoto, 1997; Sokolski, 1996; Solingen, 1995).[8] Others point to alliance relationships with a major nuclear power as a significant demand-reduction factor (Freedman, 1993; Gebhard, 1995; Rowen off., 1991). Still others see the creation of stability through regional security architectures as having a constitutive relationship with proliferation demand (Fergusson, 1995; Redick, 1995).

Promoting democratization, effectively managing and extending alliance relationships, or facilitating regional security cooperation may all indirectly contribute to nonpossession norms by reducing demand for proscribed weapons. But just as in the case of indirect capability-denial, only policies that have been pursued with proliferation in mind can properly be classified as national proliferation-response instruments. As another study observes, "Any effort to reduce regional tensions or solve long-standing disputes between nations can, of course, have a beneficial effect. . . . However, we are concerned with political actions aimed directly at stopping proliferation" (Flowerree, 1991, p. 69).

Consequence–Management Instruments

Counterproliferation

This concept refers to a range of military capabilities specifically designed to reduce or nullify any military advantage that a hostile proliferator might gain through using WMD; for example, by enabling conventional forces to continue to operate effectively in a WMD environment. This can involve passive or active defenses (e.g., missile defenses, CBW protection, CBW agent detection–avoidance, decontamination, vaccinations, medical treatment) or offensive counterforce capabilities, such as "bunker busting" munitions designed preemptively to destroy weapons stockpiles, that serve to reduce the detrimental impact of WMD in a wartime situation (OSD off., 1997a). Although counterproliferation is usually associated with protecting military forces against the tactical use of WMD, it can also be used to protect civilian populations, as in the U.S. National Missile Defense (NMD) program (Joseph & Lehman, 1998). The latter has received particular emphasis with the arrival of the new Bush administration, which has identified robust missile defenses as the centerpiece of its anti proliferation efforts.

Deterrence

Deterrence is preventing the use of proliferated weapons by convincing a possessor that the costs of using proscribed weapons would far outweigh any conceivable gains. Deterrence goes hand in hand with counterproliferation because "defense alone, with anti-missile and counterforce weapons, cannot make . . . forces and citizens entirely safe. . . . So deterrence is crucial" (Gompert, 1998, p. 3). At the same time, "Threats of devastating nuclear punishment seem increasingly less sensible than a deterrent strategy that also stresses defense against the spectrum of possible attacks with mass destruction weapons" (Goldfischer, 1998, p. 169). The bottom line is that deterrence and counterproliferation are mutually reinforcing elements of the consequence-management equation.

Deterrence is usually achieved by promising, and having the demonstrated capability to deliver, a vastly disproportionate military response. In the case of large-scale use of WMD, this in effect translates to inflicting massive retaliation in the form of retaliation in-kind, retaliation with another form of WMD, or possibly equivalent retaliation with overwhelmingly superior conventional forces (Utgoff, 1997). Such threats may also be used to deter limited use of WMD. However, this poses an obvious credibility problem, especially in response to small-scale CW use (which need not involve truly mass destruction). In such cases a combination of counterproliferation defenses and lesser disproportionate responses may be threatened instead. Conventional responses are therefore far more likely to be used to deter tactical use of WMD. In this sense, counterproliferation serves a deterrence purpose by demonstrating to an enemy that conventional forces will be able to inflict disproportionate responses even while operating in a

WMD environment (Gebhard, 1995; Wallerstein, 1998). The Bush administration, in particular, has taken pains to highlight the importance of a defensive element of deterrence.

Military instruments are the dominant but not the only basis for deterrence. Threats of punitive political, economic, or legal sanctions against any use of proscribed weapons are also instruments of deterrence. These instruments allow deterrence to be credibly extended beyond WMD use by adversaries in order to deter use in a conflict between third countries (e.g., India–Pakistan, Iran–Iraq). Normative prohibitions on use (e.g., 1925 Geneva Protocol, CWC Article I) at least technically could be classified as consequence-management instruments to the extent that they strengthen such threats, although they are not generally thought of as deterrence instruments.

NOTES

1. In the case of COCOM, the West had just such a consensus throughout the Cold War regarding the Soviet Bloc, but when the Soviet Union collapsed, so too did COCOM. Despite strenuous efforts by the United States to redirect COCOM from its original East–West Cold War orientation to a North–South "rogue state" orientation, its Western allies remained resolutely opposed (Wendt int., 1998). In the end, COCOM was replaced by the comparatively milquetoast Wassanaar Arrangement, which is little more than an information-sharing arrangement for conventional arms transfers to certain destinations. So while virtually all Western countries still operate de facto strategic trade controls, these are implemented strictly on a national basis, based on each country's perceptions of its own strategic interests.

2. Of course, the relative level of disapprobation can be affected by contingent factors. For example, while Washington must disapprove if it thinks that a friendly state like Israel has proliferated nuclear weapons, its reaction is sure to be stronger vis-à-vis similar programs in hostile states such as North Korea or Iran.

3. For example, taking 1990 as a snapshot year, BW proliferation was widespread, but with no acknowledged possessors; CW proliferation was widespread, with the United States and Soviet Union as acknowledged "status quo" possessors; missile proliferation was widespread, with numerous acknowledged possessors (but no generally accepted "status quo") and with the United States and the Soviet Union as the only formal nonpossessors (for intermediate-range systems banned by the INF Treaty).

4. However, since China does not have existing capabilities in some of these areas (e.g., long-range cruise missiles), it is unclear whether it should be considered a "have" in all instances.

5. That said, these two understandings of the concept are implicitly joined. Thomas and Thomas (1970) observe that there is a link between the traditional concept of customary norms and this type of legislated norm, in that the latter "may provide seeds from which international customary law springs"

(p. 44). From the opposite perspective, Price (1995) argues that there has been a longstanding taboo (i.e., traditional norm) against CW. This implies that the CWC, although a forced norm in one sense, nonetheless could also be seen as merely the culmination (or perhaps codification) of a full-blown norm that had already developed naturally over time. McElroy (1989) reinforces this latter point in his case study of the influence of norms on U.S. renunciation of CBW use.

6. This balance can get tricky in the case of states that are potentially both suppliers and proliferants (e.g., India, Israel). If countries that are seeking technology for programs of concern are allowed to join, then a regime faces the problem of needing to control internal proliferation.

7. India submitted an initial declaration on 26 June 1997 that refuted years of official denials that it had an offensive CW program, reportedly followed by South Korea on 17 August 1997 (*CBW Conventions Bulletin* 37, 1997). Britain, China, and France subsequently admitted to having had past programs (*Washington Post*, 10/28/97). It remains to be seen if this one unanticipated burst of candor heralds a growing rollback function for nonproliferation treaties generally.

8. Recent cases like South Africa and Argentina certainly support this theory. However, democratic proliferants such as India and Israel stand as cautionary examples that democratization is not necessarily a panacea for proliferation.

Chapter 2

Underlying Normative Perspectives on Competing Antiproliferation Strategies

The purpose of this chapter is to examine extant arguments about the relative strengths and weaknesses of the antiproliferation approaches spelled out in the preceding chapter as well as whether these strategies are naturally complementary. It does not seek to advocate a particular viewpoint, but rather to provide a balanced elucidation of the arguments on all sides of the normative debate. Understanding these underlying normative perspectives is important because they represent the abstract underpinning for any real-world differences in Western perspectives.

Theorizing on proliferation response is lamentably sparse. However, a lively normative debate is discernable in the more policy-oriented proliferation literature. Rather than a "great debate" of competing prescriptions derived from overarching theories, it comprises views on specific instruments (e.g., MTCR) or, very occasionally, classes of instruments (e.g., supplier regimes). But by applying the last chapter's conceptual framework, a variety of latent assumptions about each of the three major antiproliferation strategies can be culled from these discussions, yielding a set of broad normative perspectives on each approach.

CAPABILITY-DENIAL

Negative Perspectives

Technology Diffusion

The main argument against the capability-denial approach is that it is ineffective to the point of futility and, what is more, becoming increasingly so with each passing year. The reason for this is the inexorable diffusion of pertinent technologies within cognate civilian and permissible military sectors of the economies of developing countries (Bailey, 1993a, 1993b; Berkowitz, 1995; Forsberg, Driscoll, Webb, & Dean, 1995; Keeley, 1995; Moodie, 1995; Nolan, 1992; B. Richardson, 1993; Roberts, 1993, 1995; Sopko, 1996–1997). Given that, unlike strategic trade controls, supply-side nonproliferation generally does not target broad industrial bases, this problem is seen as virtually inescapable. As Robinson (1992) notes, it is impossible to erect truly effective barriers against the spread of low-technology dual-use capabilities without intruding on legitimate commercial activities.

This perspective is based on the supposition that CB/M capabilities are grounded in mature technologies, and that therefore their spread is a natural and inevitable consequence of economic development. The work of James Keeley has been influential in validating this already prevalent assumption by applying the well established model of industrial maturation to proliferation-related technology and production processes. Keeley (1994) finds that proliferation-related processes constitute mature "industries," particularly in the CBW areas, and that, consequently, scientific–technical and production–engineering barriers are rapidly diminishing. He concludes that this represents a generic factor affecting the dynamics of proliferation across the spectrum of WMD and missile areas: "The spread of basic technological capabilities with a weapons potential cannot be stopped," he asserts, because, "the maturation of such technology, and of specific weapons technologies, are merely part of a broader process" (p. 179). For Keeley (1995), the policy implications are obvious: "From a non-proliferation standpoint, technological maturation implies that more states may be better able to produce weaponry . . . and that the ability of 'supplier states'—the possessors of a technological edge in such weapons—to control their proliferation may consequently be eroding substantially" (p. 13).

Observers such as Bailey (1993b), Moodie (1995), and Roberts (1993, 1995) cite technology diffusion to draw damning conclusions about the long-term viability of supply-side strategies and, accordingly, to recommend giving higher priority to the norm-building approach. For example, Roberts (1995) states, "Broad diffusion of technology . . . and spread of the defense industrial base conspire to diminish the leverage of the industrial powers. . . . Thus, after years of trying to strengthen . . . [export-control] regimes, there is today a broader understanding that strategies of denial have only a limited . . . role to play in the nonproliferation project" (pp. 11–12).

Virtually all proponents of the technology-diffusion argument readily concede that its applicability varies considerably across the different proliferation areas. It is generally seen as least pertinent in the nuclear area, where a meaningful threshold continues to separate civilian technology and equipment from weapons programs. In the nonnuclear areas, it is seen as less applicable for missiles, more applicable for CW, and most applicable for BW. (It is no coincidence that many of the strongest supporters of the technology-diffusion argument are primarily CBW specialists, while observers giving it less credence often have nuclear or missile expertise.)

With a few exceptions, such as Nolan (1991) and Berkowitz (1995), most missile-proliferation experts do not see technology diffusion as highly relevant for missile proliferation. For example, Jones and McDonough (1998) offer a persuasive assessment that producing missiles remains a formidable challenge:

Missiles, especially ballistic missiles, are complex machines. For example, the medium-range U.S. Pershing II ballistic missile contained 250,000 parts—each of which needed to work right the first time under high levels of acceleration, vibration, heat, and cold. So the development of missiles is an expensive and time-consuming process, often resulting in an unreliable weapon system. Moreover, the development of ballistic missiles becomes particularly difficult at a range of about 1000km. Above that range, the missile must use two or more advanced technologies: staging (firing rockets in series, with the expended rockets reliably jettisoned from the missiles) and more sophisticated re-entry vehicles (to keep the warhead in working order during its fiery descent through the atmosphere). Longer ranges also put a premium on more efficient rocket engines, lighter and stronger materials, more advanced guidance systems, and lighter more advanced warheads (a considerable challenge when nuclear warheads are at issue). (p. 254)

Elleman and Harvey (1993) offer much the same assessment:

A high degree of technological competence is required to reverse-engineer and manufacture clones of simple systems, such as a Scud. Significant technical resources and arms manufacturing experience, as well as a relatively sophisticated industrial infrastructure, are needed for indigenous development and production of a first-generation missile. For this reason, many developing nations will, for the foreseeable future, be unable to produce even the most primitive missile system. (p. 27)

Karp (1996) observes that only a very few non–status quo states (e.g., India, Israel, North Korea) have produced ballistic missiles indigenously without outside assistance. He notes that "the importance of outside technical assistance creates tremendous opportunities for export controls to slow or even halt the proliferation process" (Karp, 1993, p. 256), leading him to conclude that "ballistic missile proliferation is probably more amenable to control than any other proliferation problem" (Karp, 1996, p. 9).

The situation is very different for CBW, which can be created using relatively unsophisticated equipment and technology. Indeed, for CW large-scale production, stockpiling, and use dates to World War I, and for BW to World War II (Larsen, 1995; Endicott & Hagerman, 1999).

Today, the technologies and industrial processes that are applicable to CBW are almost entirely dual-use (Erlick tst., 1989; King & Strauss, 1990). The technology-diffusion argument is therefore generally seen as highly germane. This is especially the case for proliferators that do not place a high premium on the safety of their own citizens, because some of the most technologically challenging facets of a CBW program involve environmental and worker safety (Forsberg et al., 1995). Bill Richardson (1993) gives a balanced and representative articulation of the prevailing view: "The range of technologies by which a nation might develop a chemical or biological warfare capability is very broad. A nation determined to have such a capability may be deterred by other means, may have its progress slowed, or may have to settle for agents other than those of choice, but it is unlikely to be stymied by a lack of technology" (p. 16). Even analysts who support supply-side strategies do not fundamentally disagree in principle with this assessment.

Technology diffusion is seen as a further order of magnitude greater for BW than for CW. The equipment and processes needed to produce BW are far less sophisticated than for CW, making the most common biological agents far easier to produce than their chemical counterparts (Erlick tst., 1989; Goldberg tst., 1989). In addition, "Biological agents reproduce themselves, and the same is true for the organisms that produce toxins. So, in contrast with chemical weapons, no large quantities of precursors are needed" (ter Haar, 1991, p. 51).

The dual-use nature of production is also far more pronounced for BW. As a result, "It is extremely difficult to deny help in terms of technology and material because it mimics almost exactly a pharmaceutical industry or some medically related . . . commercial facility" (Erlick tst., 1989, p. 37).

Noncooperative Suppliers

Some analysts argue that the problem with supply-side nonproliferation is not that the approach itself is necessarily flawed, but that it is difficult to implement effectively because too many significant suppliers opt not to participate (Müller, 1997). Other critics of denial strategies see the problem of rogue suppliers as merely making an already ineffective approach even more so (Bailey, 1993a, 1993b). In any case, all observers agree that Western countries cannot deny capabilities effectively when alternative suppliers undercut their efforts, either overtly or covertly. (Supporters of the capability-denial approach therefore put a high premium on enforcing the cooperation of all major suppliers.) Whether this factor completely eviscerates or merely complicates supply-side endeavors depends on the quantity and quality of the undercutting. The most serious challenges are posed by noncooperating first-tier suppliers (e.g., China, Russia), with second-tier suppliers (e.g., North Korea) representing a lesser problem.

Whether this problem has been worsening in recent years is an open question. A number of hitherto overtly noncooperating suppliers have been welcomed in one way or another into the supply-side fold in recent years, including Russia, China, Israel, South Africa, South Korea, Argentina, and Brazil. However, there is widespread belief that in some cases, notably Russia and China, noncooperation has continued covertly, and may even have increased. For example, U.S. Secretary of Defense Donald Rumsfeld has openly accused Moscow and Beijing of being active proliferators (*Washington Post*, 2/16/01). Moreover, many observers argue that activities undertaken by private entities may be beyond the control of these countries' governments. As Karp (1998) notes, "If the Chinese and Russian central governments no longer run non-proliferation policy, as increasingly appears to be the case, traditional non-proliferation mechanisms like the MTCR, sanctions and embassy demarches probably have passed their point of marginal returns" (p. 24).

It seems irrefutable that, at a minimum, eliminating instances of gross undercutting (i.e., large-scale, high-quality transfers) by first-tier suppliers like Russia and China represents a critical prerequisite for the viability of supply-side strategies.

Provoking Proliferation

A small handful of observers, such as Subrahmanyam (1993), charge that the coercive nature of the capability-denial approach may itself provoke states to seek proscribed weapons precisely in order to defy the will of outsiders. This perspective is extremely controversial. It views denial strategies as not merely ineffective, but as outright coun-terproductive. Many analysts concede that coercive supply-side non-proliferation may aggravate North–South tensions generally, as well as erode support for cooperative norm-building strategies specifically. However, the notion of an explicit causal relationship between the perceived heavy-handedness of the approach and a given state's deci-sion to seek proscribed weapons is widely seen as improbable or even disingenuous. The extensive literature on the causes of proliferation focuses instead on other factors, such as regional tensions, domestic politics, or national prestige. As Karp (1996) observes, it seems highly doubtful that a country would assume the high economic and politi-cal costs of pursuing proscribed weapons "just to show its contempt for others, childishly insisting on doing what outside powers say is forbidden" (p. 28).

Positive Perspectives

Continuing Foreign Dependence

A number of analysts argue that proponents of the technology-diffusion argument are too pessimistic, underestimating the extent to which many proliferators still depend on outside assistance. This school of thought does not dispute that technology diffusion exists and that it will continue to increase over time. However, it regards extreme pessimism about its consequences as overblown. The fact that nearly all proliferators in all of the proliferation areas continue to go to great lengths to obtain foreign assistance in pursuing their programs is seen ipso facto as proof that such outside assistance remains an important enabler. As a U.S. government advisory panel headed by then soon-to-be Secretary of Defense Rumsfeld concluded, "Foreign assistance is pervasive, enabling and often the preferred path to ballistic missile and WMD capability" (Commission to Assess the Ballistic Missile Threat off., 1998).

It has already been noted that the technology-diffusion argument is widely acknowledged to be less relevant in the case of missiles than for CBW. According to multiple open-source assessments, foreign as-sistance has played a critical role in the missile and/or SLV programs of countries as diverse as Brazil, Egypt, Iraq, Iran, Libya, Pakistan, Saudi Arabia, South Korea, and Syria. Even the few self-sufficient coun-tries, such as Israel and North Korea, could not have achieved that status without initial foreign assistance. A recent case study of the Condór II IRBM program—pursued jointly by Argentina, Egypt, Iraq, and Libya in the late 1980s before the advent of significant supply-side missile nonproliferation efforts and then shut down, apparently in large part due to the capability-denial efforts of the MTCR countries—reveals just how critical access to foreign assistance can be in enabling missile proliferation: "The technology was basically contraband from Germany, France and the United States, in some cases with the complicity of important and prestigious Western firms. A very advanced technical plant was built in . . . Argentina, almost entirely with smuggled technology" (Escudé, 1998, p. 57).

Beyond missiles, some observers argue that the relevance of technology diffusion is also often overstated in the chemical realm. For example, one comprehensive technical study states,

Conventional thinking is that chemical weapons (CW) are relatively easy to produce. Technically that may be true if produced in laboratory quantities, since the chemistry is well known and the chemical formulas are readily available in open literature. However, production beyond laboratory quantities requires materials, chemicals, process equipment, expertise, and some advanced technology. Additionally, the ability to produce chemical munitions alone does not assure a militarily viable option without other components. (Dunn et al., 1992, p. III-19)

Significantly, similar arguments are not heard in the case of biological items. Thus, proponents of the continuing foreign-dependence argument tend to see overall missile dependence as very high, CW dependence as lower but still significant, and BW dependence as negligible.

Adherents of this view see obvious prescriptive implications. "When we pick a target and stay focused," Sokolski argues, "it *does* work" (tst., 1991, p. 134). Bertsh, Cupitt, and Yamamoto (1997) assert that, technology diffusion notwithstanding, "export controls on dual-use items . . . can be critical tools for stemming proliferation well into the next century" (p. 408).

Choke Points

A variation on the continuing foreign-dependence argument is that supply-side nonproliferation can be fine-tuned to overcome the negative repercussions of technology diffusion by concentrating on key choke points for technology, equipment, and material. This argument is articulated frequently by U.S. officials among others. It is based on two premises. First, "Export controls can be effective when dealing with certain types of technology—such as advance guidance systems crucial to missile development—that are in the hands of only a few suppliers" (Keller & Nolan, 1997–1998). Second, it is not necessary to block all, or for that matter even most, equipment and technology; only a few essential areas need to be impeded in order for capability-denial to be effective (Sokolski tst., 1991). Thus, focusing on technology choke points can make denial strategies effective in stopping the spread of proscribed weapons, even CBW programs that use mature dual-use technologies (Eckert tst., 1994; Freedenberg tst., 1989; Tarbell tst., 1995; Wallerstein tst., 1997).

To a greater or lesser extent, choke-point technologies appear to exist in all of the proliferation areas. For example, although CW production equipment and technology is largely dual-use, it still requires at least some specialized equipment, particularly for the production of nerve agents (Goldberg tst., 1989). Moreover, a number of precursor chemicals have few civilian applications. Keeley (1995) himself notes that, even for mature technologies, there are always points in the dual-use production stream that involve exclusively military applications, and that the final stages of weaponization (i.e., systems integration and testing) are by definition exclusively military. This leads him to conclude in the end that, notwithstanding technology diffusion, supply-side efforts are not inherently ineffectual, but that they need to be honed to target military production streams and those civilian production streams with the most military utility.

Preventing Qualitative Deepening

Whether they adhere to the notion that technology diffusion makes it increasingly futile to try to prevent the spread of proscribed capabilities, many observers believe that this argument does not apply (or at least applies less) to efforts to impede the qualitative deepening of proliferation. They note that advanced programs remain beyond the reach of most developing countries, and that this is more or less true across the proliferation areas. This is viewed as important because there are significant differences between the threats posed by basic versus advanced capabilities in each of these areas. For example, one study asserts, "Across proliferation, acquisition of more advanced capabilities should be distinguished from possession of basic, entry-level capability" (Dunn et al., 1992, p. I-8).

Many analysts argue that even in cases where capability-denial tactics are unable to prevent proliferation in an absolute sense, they "still can help to contain the eventual scope and sophistication of existing programs, even in cases in which countries have crossed the NBC or missile threshold" (Dunn, 1998, p. 66). This argument is especially prevalent for missiles, where the general level of technology diffusion to begin with is relatively low. For instance, Elleman and Harvey (1993) note,

The diffusion of technologies and equipment . . . will enable some of the more advanced regional states to establish over the next decade a capacity domestically to produce short range (less than 500km) and inaccurate ballistic missiles, irrespective of export controls. Indeed, the MTCR alone will not halt missile proliferation. The regime, however, may be capable of limiting future threats by inhibiting countries from making qualitative improvements in range and accuracy. (p. 27)

An example that is often cited to illustrate the value of this is that during the Gulf War Iraq had only limited-range and inaccurate SCUD derivatives, rather than intermediate-range and highly accurate Condór II missiles. It may be recalled that Iraq tried to use radiological warfare of sorts by firing concrete-tipped missiles at an Israeli nuclear reactor, but was unable to score a hit.

Significantly, the same line of reasoning is also applied at the higher end of the technology-diffusion spectrum, including the overwhelmingly dual-use biological realm. For example, "A crude BW capability is within many countries' reach, but more sophisticated, militarily useable options—with less perishable agents, more sophisticated delivery means, and protection at home—are likely to be more difficult to obtain" (Dunn et al., 1992, pp. I-6–7). Specifically, "Nearly all proliferant states lack the sophisticated scientific and technical infrastructure needed to develop novel agents" (Forsberg et al., 1995, p. 57). Moreover, Western countries retain a virtual lock on the weapons potentiality afforded by genetic engineering, which is beyond the grasp of all but a few industrialized countries (Dunn et al., 1992). Even Keeley (1995) concludes that supply-side measures are effective, and probably will remain so, against the proliferation of high-end systems across the proliferation areas.

Proponents of supply-side strategies assert that preventing qualitative proliferation represents a profoundly important part of the overall antiproliferation enterprise. Sokolski (tst., 1991) notes that improvements in missile guidance accuracy can augment lethality by hundreds, thousands, or even many tens of thousands of casualties. As for CBW, he observes, "Although we can hope to cope defensively against current CBW threats, we may not have as much reason to be hopeful against advanced agents" (p. 127). Along the same lines, one study concludes, "The qualitative dimension of BW proliferation is now at least as threatening as the possible spread of BW programs to new states" (Dunn et al., 1992, p. IV-2). This last statement might well apply to the other proliferation areas, because many types of advanced capabilities in all areas are seen to greatly enhance the threat posed by these weapons.

Driving Up Costs, Slowing Down Progress

The vast majority of analysts believe that, regardless of whether denial tactics are able to prevent the spread of proscribed programs, these tools are almost always able to increase their cost and slow down their rate of progress (Lundbo, 1997; Simpson, 1998). Even the strongest promoters of nonpossession norms do not as a rule dispute this modest claim. For example, Evans and Grant (1991) offer the following assessment of the Australia Group: "The effectiveness of the system cannot be established in an absolute manner, but it has raised the cost of acquiring an offensive CW capability by drying up sources and diverting the delivery routes of CW proliferators. It may therefore have delayed the programs of countries seeking to acquire CW by forcing them into alternative and less efficient routes" (p. 88).

Although nonpossession enthusiasts do not usually extol such modest outcomes, defenders of the supply-side approach see them as extremely valuable. For example, Carus (1990), while expressing skepticism that export controls can prevent the spread of missile capabilities, nevertheless suggests that merely raising costs of individual programs in some cases can still serve to prevent proliferation. He explains,

It is likely that increasing diplomatic and economic costs will lead to the cancellation of some missile programs. If missile acquisition is made more expensive, other military requirements will compete for limited resources available for weapons procurement. Under such circumstances, missile programs are apt to be eliminated or given reduced priority. Higher costs also will affect the international trade in missiles by making purchases more expensive and less reliable. (p. 58)

Similar benefits are seen to be derived from delaying the progress of programs of concern. Bertsch, Cuppitt, and Yamamoto (1997) note,

Many analysts view export controls as a "second-best" form of policy. Effective export controls, however, can buy time for a host of alternative diplomatic, economic, and military policies, or a variety of events, particularly the advent of democracy, to further delay or even prevent proliferation, as well as raising the issue on the policy agenda and providing an important symbol of no "business as usual" with targets of the policy. (p. 408)

Lewis Dunn (1998) makes a similar point:

The importance of slowing programs and buying time should not be underestimated. Buying time is important to allow outsiders to try to influence countries' incentives to acquire NBC weaponry, sometimes beginning dialogues on nonproliferation that may bear fruit only years later. By slowing programs, export controls have on several occasions also made it possible for "other things to happen", not least new thinking by old leaders or new leaders rejecting old thinking. (p. 66)

In an interview, one veteran U.S. State Department official observed, "The classic examples of nonproliferation successes, Argentina, Brazil, South Africa, are really successes of keeping the lid on until more fundamental things change."

Some observers point out that even in cases where delay does not ultimately kill a program, it still gives Western countries breathing room to ensure that their defensive capabilities stay ahead of a proliferator's abilities to outstrip them (Hirsh, 1998; Sokolski tst., 1991). A U.S. Defense official summarized, "We think of our task as . . . slowing the proliferation of threatening technologies . . . in order to give ourselves more time to perfect other measures, active and passive defensive measures; of course, that includes also more time for diplomacy, for regional understanding and so forth to work" (Hinds tst., 1989b, p. 14).

The bottom line is that even the most modest claims for the capability-denial approach are seen by some to make a critical contribution to responding effectively to the threat of proliferation.

NONPOSSESSION NORM-BUILDING

Negative Perspectives

Breakout

As one senior ACDA official observed, the technology diffusion argument against supply-side strategies cuts both ways: "A norm has exactly the same problem in terms of the explosion of technology because there are then ways to work around the strictures of the norm" (Mahley int., 1998). This observation lies at the heart of the breakout argument, one of the main criticisms leveled at the nonpossession approach. Because relevant capabilities with dual-use and defensive applications typically are permitted under the nonpossession formula, to the extent that the line between these capabilities and proscribed weapons programs is narrow or blurred, a country can legally acquire capabilities just short of a prohibited program within the framework of treaty safeguards. In other words, the nonproliferation buffer is reduced to precisely the width and clarity of the line separating allowable civilian and defensive programs from proscribed weapons programs.

Proponents of the breakout argument note that participation in a nonpossession treaty norm does not merely allow this to happen, but indeed facilitates the process by explicitly legitimizing and even encouraging outside support for permissible cognate activities in exchange for such activities being subject to treaty safeguards against diversion to prohibited uses (e.g., BWC Article X, CWC Article XI). This is essentially the "atoms for peace" formula pioneered in the NPT, which has subsequently been transposed as a normative model in non-nuclear areas. Critics argue the nuclear-safeguards model is inappropriate for the other nonproliferation areas because meaningful thresholds do not exist between permissible and prohibited activities.

The technical overlap between civilian and/or allowable defensive programs and proscribed military programs in the CB/M areas is widely acknowledged. In the realm of ballistic missiles, Chow (1993) concludes definitively that there is no way to safeguard against converting a civilian SLV to an offensive ballistic missile. There is also extensive overlap between certain aspects of advanced civilian and military aircraft and unmanned air vehicle (UAV) technology and offensive cruise missiles (Defense Science Board off., 1995). Sokolski (1996) acerbically observes, "As for safeguarding 'peaceful' space launchers and drones, one might as well attempt to safeguard 'peaceful' nuclear explosives" (p. 93). Likewise, allowable missile-defense capabilities involve many of the most sophisticated aspects of missile technology.

We have already seen that CBW technologies are heavily dual-use. In terms of just how thin the breakout line separating civilian and military capabilities can be, then CIA Director Webster (tst., 1989a, 1989b) testified that certain civilian chemical-production facilities can be converted to CW production in less than a day. Erlick (tst., 1989) notes the line is even thinner for BW, asserting, "Most production facilities using microorganisms, including pharmaceutical plants or even breweries, can be converted to produce biological or toxin agents in a matter of hours, with modest prior provision" (p. 33), and thereafter can produce militarily significant quantities of agent in as little as ninety-six hours. In addition to this purely civilian overlap, the line between prescribed defensive and proscribed offensive military capabilities is also thin. Robinson (1992) notes, "In terms of what can actually be observed, a program of research into CW weapons may not be intrinsically different from a program of research into protection against CW weapons" (p. 62). Erlick (tst., 1989) makes the same point regarding BW: "The ultimate objective, be it vaccine or weapon, depends on the intent of the use" (p. 33). King and Strauss (1990) assert that when it comes to biodefense, "It is not that the programs 'appear' similar; it is that they have many of the same components" (p. 122). Moreover, unlike CW-related defensive research, in the case of agents used for biodefense research, "To go from legitimate 'laboratory quantities' to 'weapons quantities' is a matter of days or weeks, not years" (Larsen, 1995, p. 10). In addition, "The blurring of [BW] defensive and offensive programs is not limited to research, but extends to development, testing, production and training" (King & Strauss, 1990, p. 125). Even passive CBW defenses, such as mock suits and detection equipment, represent a key requirement of a useable offensive capability (Dunn et al., 1992; Findlay, 1993).

Acquiring breakout capabilities does not involve cheating. In fact, the actual act of breaking out is itself quite legal, since virtually all treaty norms include an abrogation clause allowing a party to withdraw after a brief specified period (e.g., BWC Article XIII).[1] Critics of treaty-based nonproliferation see this as a fatal flaw. Gray (1993), for example, argues, "States decline to be locked into regimes of arms control, or regime-compliance behavior, when it no longer serves their needs" (p. 342).

Cheating

The notion that technology diffusion can cut both ways also applies to the problem of cheating. The breakout problem exists even when a state fully complies with its obligations. But cheating can serve to aggravate the breakout problem. In a sense, cheating can be thought of as covert breakout-in-place. Needless to say, one's perspective on the seriousness of this problem depends on the perceptions that one has about the effectiveness of a given treaty norm's compliance-enforcement mechanisms. Put another way, if verification is seen to be effective, then covert noncompliance need not be a matter of concern. Ergo, differing assumptions about the importance of the problem of cheating tend to correspond to differing assessments of the effectiveness of verification.

Concern about cheating tends to be closely associated with the prevalence of applicable dual-use technology, which can provide effective camouflage for prohibited activities. Wallerstein (1998) comments,

Whereas traditional arms control techniques have utility in counting, monitoring and verifying munitions or munitions-related equipment, such as missile silos, artillery pieces or tanks, the arms control approach is less effective when the armament in question is produced substantially on the basis of *dual-use* technology. . . . This leads to the postulate that the more limited the probability of detection—or stated differently, the easier it is to mask or hide an NBC weapons capability—the less "deterrence" is gained from traditional measures such as mandatory declarations, and intrusive challenge inspections. (p. 2)

It therefore follows that verification problems will be least applicable for missiles, greater for CW, and greatest for BW. For example, it may well be impossible to safeguard a sounding rocket or SLV against breakout as a ballistic missile, but it is feasible to verify whether such systems are being tested as ballistic missiles (i.e., whether they come back down). By contrast, the dual-use nature of CBW provides ample scope for cheating. Kay (1995) elucidates, "The industrial base of many middle-size, developing countries is such that a modest chemical or biological weapons program could be easily accommodated within their open civilian infrastructure, without the construction of significant dedicated facilities and with only trivial and short fused adjustments associated with final weaponization" (p. 101).

There is considerable debate about the efficacy of CW verification. A vocal school of skeptics assert that CW verification methods provide little or no confidence against cheating (Bailey, 1993c, p. 15). On the other hand, numerous other experts take the position that even if not absolutely water tight, rigorous CW–related verification mechanisms can provide a high level of deterrence against cheating. However, a number of real-world events in the past several years seem to bolster the case for skepticism. For example, Russia has reputedly admitted that the Soviet Union developed a novel nerve agent called Novichok, specifically tailored to circumvent CWC verification provisions by using ingredients not listed on any of the CWC precursor schedules, and which is five to eight times more toxic than the most toxic common nerve agents (*CBW Bulletin*, 02/93). Negative perspectives were also greatly reinforced by high-level Iraqi defections in August 1995 revealing that, despite several years of the most intensive, intrusive verification efforts imaginable, significant elements of the Iraqi CBW program had remained undetected. As a senior U.S. intelligence official notes, in terms of CW–related items, UNSCOM failed to detect precursors amounting to 500 tons of VX agent (Oehler tst., 1996).

Even some of the most ardent verification optimists concede that it is impossible to achieve high confidence of detection when it comes to BW possession (Rosenberg, 2001; Smithson, 1998a; Wheelis, 1992), although most assert that imperfect verification is better than no verification. The cautionary lessons of UNSCOM are, if anything, seen as even starker in the biological field. As Wallerstein (1998) observes, Iraq was not only able to hide a large-scale offensive BW program, but in fact made significant technical advances (e.g., testing new aerosolization methods) despite UNSCOM's virtually constant presence. Furthermore, the program that UNSCOM failed to uncover in Iraq was larger and more sophisticated than most, and thus, in principle, more detectable (Kay, 1995). In addition to large stockpiles of standard agents such as anthrax and botulinus toxin, Iraqi military scientists were experimenting with novel agents—for example, aflatoxin, mycotoxin, ricin, and camelpox—all of which had been weaponized in munitions and/or missile warheads (Thraenert, 1997). Yet scholars like Wright (1993), prior to the 1995 defections—a political happenstance having nothing to do with UNSCOM's verification efforts—used the negative results of UNSCOM inspections to cast doubt on longstanding contentions that Iraq had violated the BWC. Indeed, according to the head of UNSCOM, at the time of the defections UNSCOM itself was within weeks of making a "serious mistake" by issuing a final report giving Iraq a clean bill of health (Butler, 1998). Putting it mildly, Oehler (tst., 1996) notes, "These revelations demonstrated the ability of countries to hide capabilities in the face of intrusive international inspection regimes" (p. 5).

Whatever the initial effectiveness of a verification system, its long-term utility as a deterrent against cheating is thought to decrease as participating target states become familiar with its weaknesses by receiving inspections and/or providing inspectors (Bailey, 1993c; Kay, 1995). Furthermore, the ability of individual countries to assist international verification efforts by providing vital intelligence likewise diminishes over time, because the very act of sharing intelligence multilaterally inevitably exposes sources and methods, which in turn enables the would-be proliferant to undertake countermeasures (Kay, 1995).

Finally, verification and compliance are closely related, but not synonymous. Whereas the former is a technical, institutionalized process to detect noncompliance, the latter is an overtly political, situational process to respond to evidence of it. Thus, even if verification points to cheating, any ambiguity short of a proverbial "smoking gun" may be insufficient to ensure the political will required to respond effectively to transgressions. In other words, imperfect verification can exacerbate and be compounded by political reluctance to enforce compliance.

Nonparticipating Proliferators

A final criticism of the nonpossession approach is that it only works for states that opt to participate, with the assumption being that many states pursuing proliferation programs will choose not to join. States that have no intention of proliferating thus bear the infringements on sovereignty and other costs of membership, while the "hard-cases" remain unaffected. As one observer states,

The BWC and CWC may have some useful provisions that will reduce worldwide stocks of biological and chemical weapons, but they cannot protect against regimes that do not join or governments that violate their provisions. The BWC and CWC will eliminate chemical and biological weapons in the U.S. and other law-abiding countries, while leaving such weapons in place in the countries that represent the greatest threat. (Hackett, 1996, p. 2)

India, Pakistan, and Israel, which as non–NPT members face no legal restrictions on nuclear weapons, stand as glaring examples of the opt-out problem.

Positive Perspectives

Changing the Milieu

Advocates of the normative approach argue that its value should not be judged narrowly in terms of the instantaneous impact of a specific treaty. Rather, they suggest that the greatest benefit to accrue from an interlocking web of nonpossession treaty norms is the long-term impact that such a network of instruments can have on the fundamental attitudes of states as well as the environment in which they operate. This notion is based on the tenet that normative treaties do not merely reflect and lock in place an existing consensus among states, but that in fact the identities, interests, and policies of states are changed over time by the new international norms that these instruments help to build (Jepperson, Wendt, & Katzenstein, 1996). In other words, norms shape change as well as vice versa. Therefore, even if a treaty norm is not universal today, it can gain momentum as more states join over time, until the critical mass is attained whereby the web of interlocking norms has altered the proliferation environment to such an extent that nonpossession will have become the genuine consensus. Fergusson (1994) explains that this process begins on the national level as states engage with external global norms over time: "This engagement and exposure will gradually result in learning through which states will begin to alter their thinking. . . . They will slowly integrate these global beliefs and norms, altering their national behaviour and creating the conditions for shifting the process itself to regional local, and dyadic levels" (p. 183). Roberts (1993) notes that this is a long-term strategy, and that accordingly there is no expectation for immediate results: "This is not to argue that norms can prevent ambitious and aggressive leaders from acquiring or using weapons of mass destruction; rather they work over the long term to shape the milieu in which leaders garner support domestically and internationally" (p. 13). Thus, success eventually will "rest on the voluntary renunciation of WMD by the overwhelming majority of the world community" (Müller, 1997, p. 69).

A corollary to this argument is that, unlike the capability-denial approach, the nonpossession approach sees no inherent danger in the spread of dual-use capabilities (Mutimer, 1998). For example, Müller (1997) asserts, "There is no linear, causal relationship between holding technology and abusing it for weapons purposes" (p. 66). This general argument is constitutively related to the proposition that technology diffusion makes capability-denial futile in the long term, and that therefore ultimately the only hope of preventing and rolling back proliferation is to change prospective proliferators' intentions to possess proscribed weapons. That is, if technology diffusion is inevitable, then it is more sensible to regulate it (i.e., ensuring it is not used for proscribed purposes) than to try to fight it.

Because this argument concentrates on the goal of building a consensus by changing perceptions over time, rather than blocking concrete instances of proliferation in the short term, it evaluates the strengths and weaknesses of specific instruments with primary reference to the long-term goal. For example, Butler (1998) argues that the purpose of verification for a nonpossession treaty norm should not be to detect actual instances of cheating, but instead to create a general climate of confidence. Likewise, most nonpossession advocates are not particularly concerned about the criticism that only "good guys" are affected by the rules, since their focus is on the future, when this description will apply universally.

Inherent Deterrent

A number of analysts argue that the inherent deterrent value of treaty norms, even in the short term, should not be underestimated. For example, Carus (1992b) concludes that, notwithstanding its limitations, the problem of CW proliferation would probably be worse without the CWC's codification and enforcement of a normative prohibition. Rosenberg (2001) makes much the same point about a less-than-perfect BWC compliance protocol. In a landmark study, Chevrier (1995) examines the original BWC as an example of an extremely weak treaty norm (i.e., one with no compliance mechanisms). She finds that the mere existence of a legal prohibition provides a meaningful disincentive for covert possession by participants, despite a very low probability of detection. This deterrent is based on the fact that even being suspected of violating any treaty brings into question a country's overall trustworthiness. Chevrier finds that there is even a deterrent for nonparties who act overtly or covertly in contravention of a widely subscribed nonpossession norm. She extrapolates that, this being the case, any strengthening of a norm's enforcement process can only serve to strengthen its basic deterrent value. Nor does it matter if this extra deterrence is only marginal, because, "from the point of view of a country concerned with the compliance of others, undetected possession . . . is not a more serious security threat if the weapons are outlawed, provided that the country maintains its . . . defenses and has no interest in having its own arsenal (p. 80).

Chevrier (1995) reinforces already prevalent assumptions among norm-building enthusiasts. Treaty norms are seen as valuable even in the short term by providing an inherent negative incentive against possession, and therefore any strengthening of the baseline norm through verification serves incrementally to augment this deterrent value. Thus, arguments that verification is less than perfect do not negate the need to make verification as strong as possible, and in any case do not detract from the inherent deterrent value of having a basic legal prohibition.

Narrowing the Problem

Even skeptics of the ability of norms to influence the behavior of proliferators often concede that they offer a useful means to narrow the scope of the problem to a relatively small number of "hard case" proliferators. That is to say, there is wide agreement that treaty norms are reasonably effective at their core prophylactic mission, and that this is extremely beneficial in preventing proliferation from begetting more proliferation. The figurative targets in this sense are not Libya and North Korea, but Japan and Sweden. One key U.S. official states this case as follows:

What a norm does, it helps you by limiting the problem. It's a way of keeping the vast majority of countries in the world that don't do this stuff from doing it in the future. By signing up, it makes it less likely they're going to go for it. By knowing that their neighbors have signed up, it makes them less worried that their neighbors are going to go for it. So that's the biggest thing that the norm does for you. ([State] int.)

This is in effect the flip side of the criticism that norms only affect the good guys, saying that even if this is true, it is important as a means to ensure that today's good guys stay that way.

CONSEQUENCE-MANAGEMENT

Negative Perspectives

The most significant criticism regarding the deterrence element of consequence-management in the CBW areas centers on refuting the assumption that this is best achieved through the threat of in-kind retaliation. Subsequent to all Western states renouncing in-kind deterrence in the early 1990s, however, this argument has largely been rendered moot by its own success. Recent criticism of antiproliferation deterrence considers whether nuclear deterrence is credible against limited use of CBW, or whether even overwhelming conventional superiority can provide an adequate deterrent against WMD. Another argument is that robust military deterrence capabilities may have the unintended consequence of provoking a sense of powerlessness and insecurity that could provoke weaker states to embark on proliferation as the only available asymmetric counterweight to Western military dominance.

Note that all but the last of these perspectives do not actually challenge the fundamental utility of antiproliferation deterrence, but instead merely question the particular methods by which best to achieve it. Indeed, Payne (1995) offers one of the few examples of a truly negative perspective on antiproliferation deterrence. He questions the efficacy of any kind of deterrence against rogue states, noting that such regimes are highly prone to misperception and miscalculation, and that deterrence concepts developed in the bipolar Cold War context do not readily apply to the multipolar antiproliferation mission. In general though, there is broad support for seeking to deter the use of WMD.

The counterproliferation element of consequence-management is largely uncontroversial, with one glaring exception. This is, of course, the hotly contested debate on U.S. missile-defense programs. Domestic critics question the high costs and technical feasibility of a full-blown National Missile Defense system. In addition, the new Bush administration's initiative to pursue a system that exceeds the boundaries set by the U.S.–Soviet Anti-Ballistic Missile Treaty raises concerns about damaging faith in arms control generally. This has also sparked a torrent of concern by many governments and analysts that such an ambitious system would undermine strategic stability, sparking a new global arms race among major nuclear powers. However, none of these concerns appears explicitly to target the notion of a relatively modest "counterproliferation" capability against the likes of North Korea and Iran—which along with accidental launches is Washington's main justification for NMD—but rather on fears that the United States is using the proliferation threat as an excuse to pursue a system that is really intended as a strategic shield to neutralize the nuclear forces of its closest peer rivals, Russia and China. In this sense, the NMD debate is not really about proliferation response. This is shown by the fact that there has been relatively little criticism of theater missile defense, which is the most applicable for all but the most advanced proliferations.

Beyond the raging NMD debate, even counterproliferation skeptics such as Turpen and Kadner (1997) do not challenge the principle that, in addition to prevention, it behooves Western countries to take at least some prudent steps to cope with mass-destruction weapons that manage to slip through the nonproliferation net. Some concern has been expressed that counterproliferation might be destabilizing. However, this seems to be based largely on understandable early confusion about what Washington had in mind when it launched its Counterproliferation Initiative in 1993—for the most part due to muddled, contradictory, and evolving U.S. explanations—with critics assuming (inaccurately) that Washington was proposing routinely to go to war with any country that had acquired proscribed capabilities (i.e., a systematic program of peacetime strikes designed to roll back proliferated stockpiles and production facilities). Therefore, although the notion of peacetime military responses to proliferation continues to be seen as highly controversial, regardless of whether they constitute preventative capability-denial or preemptive use-denial, these concerns have dampened as counterproliferation has come to be understood as a predominantly defensive and reactive concept.

Since few observers reject the notion of consequence-management altogether, particularly in terms of deterrence and latent military preparedness, the harshest critique ends up being not about the merits of the approach per se, but rather on whether it effectively complements the broader, preexisting nonproliferation project. This, in turn, is just one aspect of the complex question of complementarity among all three of the antiproliferation approaches (see next section).

Positive Perspectives

Aside from questions about whether NMD is really justified at present by a credible ICBM proliferation threat, most observers in principle accept the utility of having some means to deter and defend effectively against WMD attacks, if possible. All sides in the mainstream debate therefore in principle embrace a more or less positive perspective on consequence-management. The only debate is whether this is technically possible, and if so, at what cost.

The most categorically positive perspectives on consequence-management come from observers who are pessimistic about the utility of either approach to nonproliferation. These nonproliferation pessimists go further than advocating prudent deterrence and defense, suggesting that these tools should increasingly be seen as the most important element of proliferation response. For example, Bailey (1993a) asserts that the lack of effective policies to prevent proliferation means that defensive counterproliferation capabilities are needed. DeSutter (1997) and Utgoff (1997) make much the same point regarding the need for deterrence. However, even the most ardent proponents of consequence-management do not suggest that it should replace prevention (i.e., nonproliferation) altogether, but rather support it as a complementary response.

ARE THESE STRATEGIES COMPLEMENTARY?

General Perspectives

The capability-denial and nonpossession approaches to nonproliferation are customarily portrayed as mutually reinforcing, forming an integral two-tier structure (Fergusson, 1995; Karp, 1996; Mutimer, 1998;

Ozga, 1994; Rosenberg, 2001). Advocates of consequence-management likewise depict it as complementing both nonproliferation approaches (DeSutter, 1997; Gebhard, 1995; Wallerstein, 1998). Pearson (1993b) explicitly endorses all these viewpoints, calling for "a sustained effort by states to integrate various policy approaches with the goal of a strong and seamless web of deterrence against the production, possession, and use of these weapons" (p. 161). He argues that nonproliferation treaties, export controls, and applicable military capabilities are all equally important in responding to proliferation. A prominent academic conference draws similar conclusions, agreeing that a model nonproliferation system would effectively integrate robust nonpossession and denial tools (Stanley Foundation, 1996).

The implications of assertions of complementarity are considerable. If one accepts that the different approaches are complementary, it follows that, as Pearson (1993b) and others argue, they should all be pursued with equal vigor. If this is the case, then the protracted debate in the policy literature about their respective strengths and weaknesses would be, as one top Western official has suggested, largely irrelevant:

The argument about the relative effectiveness of global norms and export control regimes in containing the risk of proliferation is, I believe, essentially an academic and sterile exchange at the most which does no great credit to the protagonists of either viewpoint. It has all the flavour of fiddling while Rome burns. The plain, inescapable reality is that treaties and supplier group regimes must be complementary, and must *both* be effective if proliferation is to be stemmed. (Evans off., 1993a, p. 3)

Unfortunately, while pursuing parallel approaches with equal vigor is an appealingly simple prescription, it is not necessarily viable in the real world. The fact is that as much as scholars and policy makers might want to have their cake and eat it too, Western governments face inescapable tensions in choosing among the different antiproliferation approaches. A strong case can be made that there are inherent tradeoffs among some elements of these strategies.

In the first place, each antiproliferation approach entails significant costs.[2] The political capital, bureaucratic energy, and funding that countries have available nationally and multilaterally to address any policy problem are finite, and therefore priorities must be set on how best to allocate limited resources among available means. Even assuming that the approaches are fully mutually reinforcing, if one or another is seen to deliver only small benefits at considerable costs, it may simply be regarded as not worth pursuing, or only worth pursuing if these costs are strictly minimized. So even if the approaches do not impair one another directly, implicit tradeoffs between them may still exist.

Beyond such resource allocation considerations, to the extent that these approaches are not mutually reinforcing, then significant tradeoffs are inevitable. This brings us to the question of basic conceptual tensions. Zanders (1997) argues that while some elements of nonproliferation may be mutually reinforcing, others directly undermine one another. A study prepared for the U.S. Congress by the Office of Technology Assessment (off., 1993) sets forth similar conclusions: "Balances must . . . be struck between conflicting approaches to nonproliferation policy. . . . These approaches . . . do not represent diametrically opposed positions, but rather indicate opposing tensions that must be balanced against each other" (p. 29).

Even for analysts who ostensibly advocate a web of complementary strategies, a close reading usually reveals that they accord a marked priority to one approach, with the others relegated to supporting roles. In two contrasting, overt examples, Roberts (1998) argues that export controls complement norms, but gives clear priority to the latter, while Utgoff (1997) admits that nonpossession norms can be useful, but makes clear that they are worthwhile only if they are not too costly and do not interfere with supply-side nonproliferation and consequence-management efforts. Indeed, the few unequivocal claims of absolute compatibility apply specifically only to capability-denial and consequence-management strategies (Speier, 1999; Utgoff, 1997; Wallerstein, 1998). The bottom line is that, notwithstanding the many rosy exhortations that the strategies should coexist harmoniously, it is at least implicitly widely recognized that in fact there are specific incongruities that give rise to tensions between certain approaches.

Specific Incongruities between Approaches

Capability-Denial Undermines Nonpossession Norms

There is wide recognition in the literature that the aggressive use of the capability-denial approach creates tensions between participating supplier countries and both developing countries and noncooperating suppliers (Bailey, 1993b; Fergusson, 1995; Moodie, 1995; Roberts, 1998; Subrahmanyam, 1993). While we may be skeptical of claims that the discriminatory and coercive nature of supply-side nonproliferation directly provokes proliferation, it seems highly credible that denial strategies would foster resentment in their targets that would make these countries less inclined to work cooperatively with Western countries as partners in nonpossession arrangements. Moodie (1995) states,

From the South's perspective, the emphasis and approach of the U.S.–led industrialized states are hypocritical, selective, and discriminatory. Regimes such as the Missile Technology Control Regime (MTCR) and the Australia Group . . . are the objects of particularly intense Southern hostility. In the Southern view, these efforts to deny technology—especially because they deal with dual-use technology—have discriminatory implications well beyond the military realm. . . . Regimes such as the MTCR are seen as efforts to deny the developing world the advanced technologies needed not only for legitimate commercial purposes but as the foundation for sustained development. (p. 83)

He concludes that this has negative implications for cooperative strategies: "Continued reliance on denial strategies will undermine any progress . . . because the political support of developing countries is crucial" (p. 84). Müller (1997) warns that by continuing to pursue denial strategies, Western countries risk "dividing faithful [nonpossession] regime members between North and South and driving the well-minded non-aligned countries into a completely false and deleterious solidarity with a handful of wrongdoers" (p. 70). Logically, therefore, the only way for denial tools to not undermine cooperative nonproliferation is to apply them only to countries that do not participate in, or who have been unambiguously caught violating, the nonpossession regime. This is clearly a secondary role.

Consequence-Management Undermines Nonpossession Norms

Some observers affiliated with the U.S. Defense Department's Counterproliferation Initiative (CPI) (Gebhard, 1995; Miller tst., 1997; Wallerstein, 1998) have tried to argue that consequence-management might indirectly reinforce cooperative nonproliferation by providing a negative incentive for acquisition. More recently the same logic has been articulated by President George W. Bush in the context of touting the benefits of missile defenses (*New York Times*, 5/1/01). However, this line of reasoning is widely rejected in the academic literature, with analysts of various stripes agreeing that proliferation-management strategies tend to undermine cooperative nonproliferation (Keeny, 1994; Knoth, 1995; Kortunov, 1994; McColl, 1997; Pengelley, 1994; Turpen & Kadner, 1997). Indeed, even some senior career U.S. officials share this view (Gallucci int., 1998; ACDA int.). Certainly, the disincentive argument only makes sense to the extent that states are motivated to acquire WMD for the express purpose of using them against the United States and its Western allies, versus other motivations like regional rivalries. More to the point, even if proliferation management does offer some degree of disincentive, in terms of norm-building this is offset by other negative effects.

How specifically does consequence-management undermine the cooperative nonpossession approach? Virtually all of the consequence-management tools carry the latent threat of military coercion, and so a case could be made that this approach also might erode the willingness of developing countries to cooperate with Western countries on nonpossession norm-building. However, since in theory only those few states that actually acquire and use proscribed weapons are targets of mitigation strategies, it is debatable that such strategies should engender hostility among good-faith parties to nonproliferation treaties. Nonetheless, even improbable targets could resent its latent coerciveness and therefore might be less inclined to work cooperatively with governments pursuing use-denial strategies.

A more significant and pervasive concern is that robust Western preparations to cope with proliferation are defeatist about the overall effectiveness of any type of nonproliferation. This undermines the norm-building approach by signaling an unmistakable vote of no confidence in the efficacy of normative instruments. As a U.S. press report noted at the time that counterproliferation was launched, "Some analysts in the arms control community oppose the program because they believe it represents capitulation to arms proliferators—a collective throwing in the towel on efforts to prevent the spread" (*Washington Post*, 5/15/94, p. A11). According to one account, the nonproliferation bureaucracy in the Pentagon itself shared these concerns (*Washington Post*, 2/6/94).

This latter effect does not particularly undermine supply-side nonproliferation because denial strategies do not need to enjoy the confidence of their targets, and in any case do not claim to eliminate the problem completely. Furthermore, as Fergusson (1996) notes, counterproliferation can assist supply-side nonproliferation by raising the bar of effectiveness and forcing aspiring proliferants to seek more sophisticated programs, which are more costly, technically challenging, and vulnerable to supply-side disruption.

In marked contrast, the norm-building approach is premised on gaining the confidence of its targets in the effectiveness of the overall system, the aim of which is not merely to attenuate the problem, but to solve it. Nonpossession norms are constructed on a foundation of collective reassurance. Indeed, Robinson (1987) asserts that the main normative purpose of a nonpossession treaty is to inspire enough confidence in member states "for them to relax, or forgo adopting, measures of national self-reliance against that menace" (p. 21). By devoting vast resources and energies to proliferation management, Western countries are in effect visibly hedging their bets on whether treaty norms warrant such confidence. This overt signal of doubt cannot help but make other countries question whether it is wise to rely too heavily on nonpossession arrangements as the basis for their security (Keeny, 1994). Nor are security assurances—those frequently vague multilateral undertakings to assist participants who are attacked—likely to be sufficiently reassuring to offset these seeds of doubt.

On an even more direct level, given the overlap between defensive and offensive capabilities in the CB/M areas, defensive programs severely undermine the effectiveness of nonpossession norms by exacerbating the problems of breakout and cheating. A number of observers therefore argue that nonproliferation treaties could be greatly strengthened if some or all exemptions for defensive programs were eliminated (King & Strauss, 1990; Wright, 1993). This remains impossible, however, as long as key participants insist on the right to pursue counterproliferation strategies. Again, this problem does not especially affect supply-side strategies, since these tend to disregard intentions (e.g., defensive versus offensive) in the first place.

Nonpossession Undermines Capability-Denial

Nonpossession treaty norms reinforce supply-side efforts by legitimizing denial strategies that target nonmember proliferant states, but only at the price of undermining the legitimacy of similar efforts aimed at member states. Nonpossession treaty norms all to some degree explicitly authorize the provision and acquisition among their members of dual-use and defensive capabilities short of weaponization. In doing so, such treaties in effect define the proliferation problem as external (limited to nonmember states), notwithstanding intraregime problems such as breakout and undetected or unproven cheating. Burck and Flowerree (1991) epitomize this tendency when they state, "If all countries capable of making chemical weapons subscribed to the [CW] convention, the proliferation problem would disappear" (p. 568).

Denial efforts targeted against members of nonpossession treaty norms are therefore deemed unnecessary, or even inappropriate, because of the inherent assumption that the proliferation problem resides primarily outside the nonpossession regime. Ergo, denial strategies are delegitimized against treaty members. Stock and De Geer (1995) illustrate this syndrome by not even considering the possibility that the Australia Group should continue to operate once the CWC is fully up and running, despite the fact that the treaty's only explicit restriction on intramember transfers is a relatively weak one (on actual weapons agents).[3]

Eisenstein (1993) notes the consequences from a capability-denial perspective of this legitimizing effect on all internal dual-use capabilities: "Of concern is the prospect that some developing nations will sign the CWC with the intention of avoiding controls on export of chemicals to their countries while preparing themselves to break out rapidly from under CWC in times of national emergency" (p. ix). Chow (1993) makes much the same point in arguing against the creation of any type of global missile ban:

The problem is the illusion that such a safeguard regime would create. The MTCR members would then have to provide technical assistance to countries that are willing to join the regime. Some countries will join simply because they know the regime cannot stop them from transferring missile technology from space launchers to ballistic missiles. The creation of the regime would greatly reduce the likelihood of MTCR members joining forces in refraining from providing space launch assistance to others. (p. 65)

It is indisputable that a number of real-world cases have demonstrated that proliferators such as Iraq have been able to use membership in nonpossession treaties to provide a veneer of legitimacy to their efforts to secure ostensibly civilian equipment and technology for military programs (Burrows & Windrem, 1994) while at the same time lulling the international community into a false sense of confidence. The difficulty this poses from a capability-denial perspective is manifest when one considers that suspected proliferators such as Iran, Libya, and North Korea are parties in good standing to nonpossession treaty norms.

This effect may be magnified in the case of norms that feature verification provisions, since in such cases the legitimacy of denial efforts may be diminished even where suppliers suspect that a country has an illegal weapons program. Supply-side nonproliferation "has a positive verification bias . . . the parties are driven to deny technology transfer unless positive evidence of compliance exists," whereas the nonpossession approach "is driven towards a negative verification bias . . . the parties are driven to accept technology transfer in the absence of evidence of non-compliance" (Fergusson, 1995, p. 83). Consequently, unless a nonpossession verification system is foolproof, it runs the risk of undermining denial strategies by producing "false negative" results. (Recall Wright, who in 1993, prior to defectors proving otherwise, cited the failure of UNSCOM inspections to find evidence of an offensive BW program as the basis for challenging previous claims that Bagdad had violated the BWC.) Whereas for norm-building some verification is better than none, a poorly verified nonpossession instrument can be worse than no verification at all from a capability-denial perspective, because politically it becomes nearly impossible to target a facility that has received a clean bill of health. For example, in the absence of inspections uncovering a smoking gun, Iran's status as a CWC member is likely to undermine U.S. claims that it has an offensive CW program, making it harder for Washington to convince others to target Iran with robust supply-side efforts.

Nonpossession Undermines Consequence-Management

Universal nonpossession treaty norms eliminate the ability of members to manage proliferation by deterring the use or threat of use of the proscribed weapon through the threat of retaliation in kind. In addition, they may also implicitly erode defensive capabilities and alternative means of deterrence through what is sometimes termed the "lulling effect." Imperfect disarmament treaties can create false confidence that the specified threat has been eliminated, thereby undermining support for ongoing measures to deal with it (Bailey, 1993c; Lynn-Jones, 1987). This problem is seen as especially acute for democratic countries, where public support is needed for military spending. A frequently cited example of the lulling effect was the evisceration of Congressional support for U.S. biodefense programs following entry into force of the BWC in the 1970s. By contrast, because supply-side nonproliferation does not claim to eliminate the basic threat, it involves little or no lulling.

Summary Estimation of Complementarity

Capability-denial and consequence-management appear to be fully and mutually reinforcing on a conceptual level. Use-denial can even be seen as a logical extension or additional layer of capability-denial (i.e., capability-denial after the fact). In a sense these categories can appropriately be bundled together conceptually as two pieces of a common (i.e., complementary) approach.

In contrast, these approaches have a number of incongruous aspects with the nonpossession approach. This is not to imply that they are wholly irreconcilable, but in order for these approaches to be complementary, one or the other (here treating capability-denial and consequence-management together as a single extended approach) needs to be preeminent. Each has a potentially useful reinforcing role to play as a subordinate approach, but an implicit decision needs to be made regarding which takes precedence.

The conclusion seems virtually inescapable that, even if a state embraces all types of proliferation response simultaneously, it inevitably will be forced to prioritize between nonpossession norm-building on the one hand and capability-denial and/or consequence-management on the other. Whether this is based on a conscious strategy or is decided de facto by the accumulation of individual policy decisions, the point is that trade-offs are inevitable.

NOTES

1. In 1993 North Korea threatened to invoke just such a prerogative to withdraw from the NPT, leading to a major international crisis that was only resolved via the special arrangements of the U.S.–DPRK Agreed Framework. In the realm of traditional arms control, the Bush administration is threatening to withdraw from the ABM Treaty in order to pursue NMD, prompting

Russian officials to publicly threaten to retaliate by likewise withdrawing from START and INF.

2. To cite just a few obvious examples, export controls restrict profits from trade, intrusive verification jeopardizes sensitive proprietary and/or national security information, and CBW/M defense requires massive military investments.

3. Because the treaty has a general prohibition on assisting any state to acquire prohibited weapons, the case is often made that this represents a blanket obligation of supply-side restraint, including among parties. However, this is not reflected in the kinds of specific rules and implementation procedures that are needed for effective national implementation of a multilateral supply-side arrangement.

Chapter 3

U.S. Proliferation Response

This chapter provides a comprehensive account of the evolution of U.S. responses to chemical, biological, and missile proliferation over the past two decades. It opens with a chronological overview, including the general priority that Washington has accorded to proliferation response, and general initiatives encompassing all of the proliferation areas. It then examines U.S. proliferation response in separate case studies for each of the three subject proliferation areas. Finally, it summarizes common patterns that are discernible across these various sets of observations.

OVERVIEW

General Priority

Prior to the 1980s, the United States for all intents and purposes did not conceive of a proliferation problem in the CB/M areas. The threat posed by these weapons categories was seen almost exclusively in terms of the Soviet Union and its allies. The tiny nonproliferation bureaucracy of the time was concerned solely with the spread of nuclear weapons. The level of media and Congressional interest in nonnuclear dimensions of proliferation was correspondingly negligible. This almost total lack of attention, and even awareness, persisted into the early Reagan administration.

Awareness of the problem of horizontal CB/M proliferation did not occur evenly or all at once. The first glimmer was the realization among nuclear nonproliferation experts at ACDA and NSC that the spread of nuclear-capable missiles could envenom the risks associated with nuclear proliferation. This became the subject of interagency discussion beginning in early 1982 (Speier int., 1998). Awareness of the threat of CW proliferation occurred somewhat later, sparked by public allegations in 1983–1984 that Iraq had used poison gas against Iran. This was reinforced by the first signs of media interest in the wider issue of CW proliferation, based on a series of provocative intelligence leaks (Robinson, 1991). Awareness of BW proliferation was the last to emerge, sparked by the 1990 Gulf crisis (Mahley int., 1998).

Despite this growing awareness of the problem during the 1980s within the working-level bureaucracy, and the first tentative steps to formulate a cohesive set of policy responses, CB/M proliferation remained an extremely low priority until the 1990–1991 Gulf crisis. But that event, along with the near simultaneous elimination of the Soviet threat and the anticipation of greater regional instability in the post–Cold War environment, led to a sea change in the level of U.S. concern about proliferation. This was heightened when UNSCOM began to reveal the comprehensive scope of the failure of nonproliferation in Iraq, as well as how close Baghdad came to using CBW. Officials at all levels and across the interagency quickly came to conclude that the United States had only narrowly dodged the WMD bullet. The most serious threat that faced the newly lone superpower was seen as the asymmetric vulnerability of U.S. forces against a Third World enemy with WMD and missile capabilities. The catalytic impact of this perception at the highest levels was profound, putting antiproliferation at the very forefront of the American national security agenda.

In addition to increasing the executive branch focus on proliferation, the Gulf War also led to increasing public awareness of the issue, and particularly its CB/M dimensions. Media and Congressional interest in all aspects of proliferation surged, and has never abated since. Influential newspapers like the *New York Times*, *Washington Post*, and *Wall Street Journal* have carried hundreds of stories, editorials, and opinion essays on CB/M threats and responses. National security reporter Bill Gertz of the *Washington Times* has made a virtual cottage industry of splashing highly classified intelligence leaks about proliferation across the front page. On the Congressional front, more than a dozen House and Senate committees and subcommittees have issued scores of reports and held hundreds of hearings, receiving testimony from nearly 700 witnesses relating to CB/M proliferation since the Gulf War.

The Clinton administration came to office at the bow wave of this intense public and Congressional concern about proliferation. The new president arrived in Washington with an election mandate (and personal inclination) to focus on domestic rather than foreign policy and national security issues. However, his newly assembled national security team took pains to indicate that proliferation was at the top of their priority list. For example, Defense Secretary Les Aspin's much touted Bottom Up Review of U.S. strategic priorities identified the proliferation of WMD and missiles as the single most urgent and direct threat to the security interests of the United States (Pilat & Kirchner, 1995). By the middle of President Clinton's first term, antiproliferation had become firmly established at the center of a new national security orthodoxy. What just a few years before had been the concern of a small clique of lowly bureaucrats had now become a major day-to-day focus of the most senior officials.

It must be noted that there are many knowledgeable observers who assert that, in spite of its declared commitment to the cause of antiproliferation, the Clinton administration's deeds did not match its antiproliferation rhetoric. Specifically, they note that it was unwilling to sacrifice diplomatic, economic, and other interests to achieve antiproliferation goals. Because the administration was seen regularly to subordinate antiproliferation goals to competing interests, these observers infer that President Clinton was dishonest about the priority that he and his administration attached to fighting proliferation. For example, a former mid-level official from the Bush administration charged, "As a policy matter, nonproliferation is being taken less and less seriously" (Sokolski, 1996). Likewise, a Congressional report on nonproliferation charged, "By speaking loudly but carrying a small stick the Clinton Administration risks its credibility and America's security" (U.S. Cong. Senate off., 1998, p. 1). This sentiment is echoed in interviews by several former mid-level and senior officials from various agencies (including at least one who served in both the Bush and Clinton administrations), as well as career bureaucrats ([ACDA] int.; [DOD] ints.; [State] int.).

The Clinton administration for its part publicly rejected suggestions that it downgraded its commitment to proliferation response, insisting that this remained second to none. Moreover, a former senior White House official who served in both the first Bush and Clinton administrations explicitly refutes claims to the contrary, insisting, "There was absolutely no diminution of efforts to implement the nonproliferation regimes forcefully and effectively in the Clinton Administration" (Poneman int., 1998).

What is to be made of these conflicting accounts? Perhaps the Clinton administration overstated its commitment. On the other hand, the administration's critics may have exaggerated its deficiencies. It is even conceivable that both perspectives are valid; that proliferation response was the administration's top national security priority, but that at the same time it put even its highest national security interests behind competing political and economic interests. Whatever the truth of the matter, there is no question that the priority given to proliferation response has dramatically and steadily risen since the mid-1980s. The only difference of opinion is by precisely how much in recent years. This question seems impossible to resolve definitively in the face of starkly conflicting claims by those in positions to know. At the very least, this controversy suggests that Clinton administration statements should not necessarily be trusted at face value.

The new Bush administration has not had time fully to articulate where and how proliferation response fits within its nascent new strategic framework, but statements by President Bush and his senior officials, particularly in the context of missile defenses, suggest that the proliferation threat is likely to be seen as among its highest priorities.

General Doctrine and Policy Initiatives

The United States did not have any overarching antiproliferation strategy until the final months of the Bush administration (Fitzgibbon int., 1998). Prior to that, proliferation-response policies were ad hoc. However, even in the absence of a cohesive doctrine, there were consistent themes in the policy initiatives of the day.

During the early to mid-Reagan period, the main focus was on strengthening national export controls on relevant items. OSD and State led an ongoing effort to push the interagency to adopt systematic nonproliferation export controls. This process continued throughout the 1980s. It culminated in July 1990 (coincidentally, just days before Iraq invaded Kuwait), when a target list of thirty-six countries with projects of proliferation concern was instituted. Even as East–West trade controls were being eased, this list ensured that licenses would be required for relevant dual-use exports to countries posing proliferation risks (LeMunyon tst., 1990). In a sense, this represented the juncture at which the main goal of U.S. export controls shifted from strategic trade control to nonproliferation.[1]

Parallel to getting its own house in order—and not unrelated, since the Commerce Department as a rule would only go along with new U.S. export controls if other Western countries followed suit ([ACDA] int.)—the Reagan administration early on began to bring sustained bilateral pressure to bear on allies such as Germany to create or tighten relevant national export controls (Perle int., 1998). By the mid-1980s, with these tasks well along, U.S. focus turned to the more ambitious project of creating and then strengthening a system of multilateral supplier regimes to formalize and harmonize Western nonproliferation export controls ([State] int). This would remain the locus of U.S. proliferation-response efforts through the early 1990s.

Beginning early in the Bush administration, even as it concentrated on bolstering export controls, Washington began modestly to expand its conception of proliferation response, tentatively looking beyond traditional supply-side tools. It began to consider the antiproliferation utility of global nonpossession treaties (hitherto viewed primarily as East–West arms control tools). In addition, the Pentagon quietly took steps to counter proliferation militarily. On 18 October 1989, the undersecretaries of defense for policy and acquisition established the DOD-wide Proliferation Countermeasures Working Group, with a mandate to assess and address emerging proliferation threats from a military perspective (Rowen off., 1991; Wolfowitz off., 1991). The group's chairman described its purpose as follows: "We need to start working on how to deal with proliferation we may not be able to control. Because our efforts may not be 100 percent successful, DOD has begun a parallel effort to assess new military threats and promote appropriate military countermeasures to them. . . . The group hopes to learn what specific operational or program changes might be desirable" (Sokolski tst., 1990a, p. 172). Although this internal DOD initiative did not receive much attention at the time (despite being notified to Congress and covered in the specialized defense press), it marked the official addition of consequence-management as an explicit element of U.S. proliferation response.

The first public reference to an overall proliferation response strategy was articulated in the 1990 *National Security Strategy*: "Our comprehensive approach to this problem includes stringent controls and multilateral cooperation designed to stop the spread of these technologies and components" (Bush off., 1990, p. 66). Although rather nebulous, this formulation suggests that, even as the United States was stepping up efforts to negotiate the CWC and strengthen the BWC as well as taking the first steps to introduce military countermeasures, it continued to see supply-side denial tactics as the main pillar of its ad hoc antiproliferation strategy.

However, only a year later, in the aftermath of the Gulf War, a senior official publicly articulated a much wider formulation: "Of necessity, we have a multifaceted approach to non-proliferation. This approach includes vigorous arms control measures, encouraging regional confidence building, export controls, multilateral supplier group efforts, focused intervention in specific cases, and sanctions" (Clarke tst., 1991, p. 82).

The abrupt end of the Cold War, together with the sudden leap in concern about proliferation sparked by the Gulf War, had brought about a swift evolution in U.S. nonproliferation doctrine, embracing a much more expansive approach. In part this involved publicly reorienting and redefining existing East–West activities, such as CBW disarmament and strategic trade controls, to serve this new North–South role.[2] Nonetheless, officials from the State and Defense departments continued to make it clear that denial strategies remained the primary focus of the evolving U.S. nonproliferation strategy. The main goal was to strengthen the existing multilateral supplier regimes as much as possible (at the time explicitly defined as making them more like COCOM, with rigorous restrictions targeting specified proliferants and improving coordination between the supplier regimes), while going beyond these multilateral frameworks using additional unilateral and bilateral measures such as interdiction, sanctions, and the like (Clarke tst., 1991; LeMunyon tst., 1991; Smoldone int., 1998; Sokolski int., 1998, tst., 1991; Verville tst., 1990). Indeed, even today this remains the basic U.S. supply-side strategy. According to one official, unilateral or bilateral measures over and above the requirements of the various multilateral regimes account for probably up to 90 percent of U.S. nonproliferation activities, with participation in the regimes therefore representing just a small fraction of overall U.S. denial efforts (Smoldone int., 1998).

President Bush launched the first sweeping nonproliferation initiative, the Enhanced Proliferation Control Initiative (EPCI), on 13 December 1990. This was a wholly supply-side venture, comprising a web of regulations under various existing legislative authorities (Clarke tst., 1991; OSD off., 1997b). Its effect was to duplicate the full scope of longstanding regulatory authorities for nuclear nonproliferation in the CB/M areas. In addition to dramatically expanding the number of specific items requiring export licenses (i.e., beyond the AG and MTCR lists), EPCI introduced so-called catch-all controls, requiring licenses for any item (i.e., items not on national control lists) known to be destined for a project of proliferation concern. The licensing role of the nonproliferation-minded departments of Defense and State was also expanded, for the first time including them in decisions on all Commerce Department licenses deemed to be relevant to proliferation (Clarke tst., 1991). Prohibitions were also enacted against so-called off-shore procurement, allowing the government to deny government and commercial purchases that would provide financial support to proliferation programs (Clarke tst., 1990; McNamara tst., 1995; Smoldone int., 1998; Sokolski tst., 1990a). Finally, the president was given discretionary authority to impose punitive economic sanctions on any foreign supplier or receiver of proliferation-related items, and automatic sanctions were put in place for proliferation-related transfers to Iran, Iraq, and Libya (OSD off., 1997b).

Following the pattern established in the 1980s, having strengthened its own denial instruments, the United States pressured its Western partners to follow its lead. Even before EPCI was announced, a State Department official told a Congressional hearing, "We believe that such steps need to be taken, but not only to block U.S. exports from going to different countries and projects. They are also needed so the United States can continue to take the lead in building up the existing international consensus to establish such effective controls on a multilateral basis" (Verville tst., 1990, p. 36). Sure enough, a few months after announcing EPCI the administration reported, "We have been vigorously seeking to convince other countries to adopt controls comparable to EPCI. . . . We have pursued EPCI through existing multilateral mechanisms and in our bilateral dealings" (Clarke tst., 1991, p. 89).

The president then announced what was ostensibly a second major supply-side nonproliferation venture in May 1991, the Arms Control Middle East (ACME) initiative. The White House envisioned a targeted suppliers cartel made up of the five permanent members (P-5) of the Security Council. Its primary intended purpose was to curb the spread of WMD and missiles to the Middle East, and secondarily to prevent destabilizing conventional buildups (White House off., 1991). However, the United States was forced to deviate from the president's original vision during the ensuing negotiations. ACME turned out to have little or nothing to do with nonproliferation. According to an official involved throughout the process, almost as soon as the talks began their focus shifted to conventional arms transfers rather than WMD and missile proliferation.[3] Although a set of "Interim Guidelines Related to Weapons of Mass Destruction" was adopted at the third session in May 1992, this merely reiterated commitments that all the participants had already undertaken elsewhere, because China was unwilling to go any further on nonproliferation ([DOD] int.). Thus, despite U.S. efforts at the highest level, the enterprise never got off the ground as a nonproliferation regime.

In the final year of the Bush administration, having aggressively pursued a wide range of antiproliferation efforts following the Gulf War, the White House finally moved to craft a comprehensive, formal antiproliferation strategy. In addition to codifying existing efforts, the White House wanted the United States to propose a grand bargain to recast the nature of Western nonproliferation efforts in the new post–Cold War environment. Specifically, National Security Adviser Brent Scowcroft wanted the United States to propose to agree to dramatically loosen the COCOM strategic trade control system, including giving up the U.S. veto, in exchange for agreement by Western countries to abide by stricter rules in the nonproliferation export-control regimes. But according to an interview with a former White House official, elements of the deeply entrenched strategic trade bureaucracy successfully blocked this initiative, arguing (incorrectly) that COCOM was still needed and would endure long after the Cold War. As a result, this official describes the presidential directive that eventually emerged as "thin gruel" that merely confirmed existing approaches.

President Bush signed the resulting National Security Decision Directive-70 on 13 July 1992, for the first time laying out a comprehensive set of internal antiproliferation guidelines. It embraced four basic tenets: (1) the United States would seek to strengthen and broaden existing global norms against proliferation, (2) the United States would seek to focus additional efforts on regions of acute proliferation concern (i.e., Middle East, South Asia, Korean peninsula), (3) the United States would seek to foster the broadest possible multilateral support for supply-side prevention efforts, and (4) the United States would use a range of tools to address the problem, including political, economic, intelligence, regional security, and export controls (L. Dunn et al., 1992). In other words, Washington would do more of everything that it had already been doing for at least the past year.

A few months and one presidential election later, a new administration set about taking a fresh look at the U.S. proliferation-response strategy that it had inherited. Following an intensive interagency review, President Clinton signed Presidential Decision Directive-13 in September 1993 to supersede NSDD-70 (White House off., 1993). Although PDD-13 parted ways with NSDD-70 on a number of specific policy issues, as well as on nuances of emphasis, the general theme of the new strategy nevertheless was to do more of the same, essentially reaffirming the fundamental tenets so recently codified by its primogenitor. PDD-13 has not been replaced by the new Bush administration and so remains the operative guidance for U.S. proliferation response today.

Consistent with PDD-13, the Clinton administration instituted several major policy initiatives. The first and highest profile of these was the Pentagon's December 1993 counterproliferation initiative, adding a third major approach to the U.S. antiproliferation quiver.[4] This would go beyond the already massive U.S. missile defense program to address every manner of proliferation threat. Even before the formal announcement, a senior State Department official noted that counterproliferation would play an important role in the overall U.S. response to proliferation (Davis tst., 1993).

This initiative was a natural outgrowth of the direction charted by the prior administration. As one study notes, "Although the Bush administration . . . began an exploration of proliferation countermeasures, the Clinton administration has expanded the scope and raised the priority of counterproliferation" (Pilat & Kirchner, 1995, p. 156). The guiding principle was to apply longstanding Cold War concepts of WMD defense and deterrence to regional conflicts (Carter int., 1999). According to former Deputy Assistant Secretary of Defense Mitchel Wallerstein (tst., 1998), the elevation of defense and deterrence strategies to the status of an independent approach to proliferation response was the direct result of the pessimism about all aspects of nonproliferation that had been engendered by the unfolding lessons of Iraq:

It became clear that Iraq had successfully evaded the provisions of virtually every extant non-proliferation regime. . . . The Administration's response to these lessons was to pursue a two track approach: On the one hand, seek to prevent proliferation wherever possible through bilateral and multilateral diplomacy; and on the other hand, be prepared to deter and defend against states possessing nuclear, chemical and biological weapons and missile delivery systems. (p. 2)

In announcing the initiative, Secretary of Defense Les Aspin explicitly stated that, while prevention remained the primary goal, the United States had concluded that "efforts to prevent, stop, or reverse proliferation may not always succeed" (quoted in OSD off., 1997a, p. 53). Therefore, relying solely on nonproliferation represented an incomplete response to proliferation (Carter int., 1999).

Total funding for counterproliferation acquisition for fiscal year 1996—the second budget following the launch of the initiative—was a staggering $3.8 billion (*CWC Bulletin* [30], 1995). In early 1995 the new defense secretary, William Perry, gave the program a further boost by creating the Counterproliferation Council to ensure that counterproliferation was treated as a priority by all elements of DOD (Miller tst., 1997). This high-level steering committee, headed by the deputy secretary, added additional funding for coordinating various acquisition programs, bringing total funding to almost $4 billion annually (*CWC Bulletin* [30], 1995). As its primary architect notes, in just a few short years, "Counterproliferation is now established and recognized" (Carter int., 1999).

Parallel to its own counterproliferation program, Washington aggressively sought to multilateralize the approach, urging its allies to participate in coordinated efforts. Despite marked European reluctance, the January 1994 NATO Summit acceded at the behest of the United States to establish a high-level NATO committee to coordinate an Alliance military response to proliferation (*CWC Bulletin* [23], 1994). The United States also pushed hard for similar cooperation with non-NATO allies such as Australia and Japan ([DOD] int.).

Another major initiative of the Clinton administration, conducted through quiet, ad hoc diplomacy, was to try to add a robust targeted dimension to multilateral supply-side efforts. Specifically, the United States wanted the countries that it identified as "rogue states" to be subject to the type of draconian Western denial efforts that previously had been reserved for Communist countries. Just months into office, at a meeting with his Western European counterparts, Secretary of State Warren Christopher pushed for a total embargo on dual-use equipment and technology to Iran. He pleaded for a collective policy to contain Iranian WMD and missile programs. Despite a tepid response to this and subsequent proposals along the same lines, the Clinton administration continued to stringently apply a targeted denial strategy against rogue states, and relentlessly urged others to do the same.

A final major initiative of the Clinton period was to reform nonproliferation export controls by narrowing their scope. The goal was to focus on key technologies that were not readily available elsewhere (i.e., choke points).[5] The administration announced this plan on 31 March 1994, in connection with the renewal of the Export Administration Act, which was set to expire in a few months (Bowen & Dunn, 1996).[6] This initiative sparked heated controversy, with critics charging that it amounted to loosening nonproliferation controls, presumably in the interests of facilitating foreign trade (U.S. Cong. Senate off., 1998). The administration fiercely denied such contentions, responding that its reforms were in fact designed to strengthen the effectiveness of nonproliferation export controls by building higher fences around fewer items. As one senior Commerce Department official explained at the time,

Our challenge is to identify specific "choke point" items that can be effectively denied. . . . By focusing on items that are truly sensitive and would enable would-be proliferators to make significant advances, we ensure that our scarce licensing and enforcement resources are properly deployed. By narrowing our control lists to choke point items we are more likely to gain meaningful cooperation of our allies in the various nonproliferation regimes. Concentrating our resources in this fashion is most likely to result in actually halting transactions of true importance, which after all is the real objective of our nonproliferation export controls. (Eckert tst., 1994, p. 7)

Former Deputy Assistant Secretary of Defense Wallerstein (int., 1998) likewise insists that streamlining export controls was intended to strengthen rather than weaken them, noting that this was a necessary consequence of reorienting strategic trade controls to the nonproliferation mission. He recalls, "We had to take a hard look at what was in fact controllable." He also points out that the reform package resolved a long-standing bureaucratic turf battle between Commerce and the more nonproliferation-minded agencies by establishing a regularized high-level interagency review and appeal process through which any agency could challenge any licensing decision (Wallerstein tst., 1998).

The new Bush administration is apparently still reviewing its overall proliferation response strategy as a part of its larger ongoing strategic review. PDD-13 therefore remains the basis of U.S. antiproliferation efforts until and unless President Bush promulgates a revised strategy. Although the outcome of the strategic review and its possible impact on proliferation response is not yet known, there has been no suggestion that the new administration will repudiate major Clinton initiatives that cut across the different proliferation areas, including counterproliferation, targeting rogue states, and export-control reform. That said, it remains to be seen whether it plans to launch any significant initiatives of its own. Its stated intention to transform the nature of deterrence may well qualify in this regard. The one thing that is certain at this juncture is that responding to proliferation remains a major element of the new administration's foreign and national security focus.

CASE STUDY: CHEMICAL WEAPONS

Capability-Denial

National Export Controls

The United States has consistently applied relatively strict export controls on CW-related items over the past two decades. These have evolved primarily as unilateral measures, with an admixture of national implementation of multilateral arrangements (i.e., AG rules). The United States first imposed export controls on three dual-use precursor chemicals in the early 1960s as part of its system of strategic trade controls. The first nonproliferation controls as such were instituted in March 1984 in response to Iraqi CW use. These foreign policy controls were applied to the export of the three chemicals already controlled, plus an additional five precursors, to either Iraq or Iran (Burck & Flowerree, 1991; Adelman tst., 1984; Olmer tst., 1984). These very limited, targeted controls were modestly expanded in June 1986, soon after the beginning of the process that became known as the AG, to include exports of these same eight precursors to Syria, on the basis of intelligence that Syria was assisting Iran's CW program and pursuing one of its own (*New York Times*, 6/6/86). This left Washington controlling more than the AG's five Core List chemicals, but unlike some other AG countries, only applying these controls to a very limited number of destinations. It therefore controlled more items to fewer destinations than some other AG partners during this period.

In the final two years of the Reagan administration, the United States moved to apply CW-related export controls nearly universally (with an exemption for exports to AG countries). By this time the AG list had caught up with U.S. national controls. U.S. implementation went beyond AG requirements, however, in that as a matter of national policy the United States automatically denied all export-license applications to Iran, Iraq, Syria, Libya, Cuba, Vietnam, Cambodia, and North Korea (LeMunyon tst., 1989a). The United States thus implemented targeted controls beyond AG requirements. As a retiring senior Commerce Department official testified at the close of the Reagan administration, "The U.S. currently maintains much stricter controls on these chemicals than the rest of the Australia Group" (Freedenberg tst., 1989). Moreover, most agencies had wanted to go even further, but were thwarted by the Commerce Department, which generally opposed expanding the scope of dual-use nonproliferation export controls, particularly on a unilateral basis ([ACDA] int.).

Incited by revelations of Iraqi use of CW against its own Kurdish population and Libya's CW program, the incoming Bush administration moved to further strengthen CW-related export controls within days of taking office. This moved U.S. controls well beyond AG parameters. Whereas the AG only specified controls on nine chemicals, in February 1989 the United States imposed controls on a total of eleven precursors to all destinations (except AG countries), and an additional twenty-nine precursors to more than a dozen specified destinations.[7] The policy of automatic denial to specified destinations was extended to all forty of these various chemicals. At the same time, implementation was strengthened by assigning interagency licensing deliberations for the first time to a dedicated CBW nonproliferation group, rather than East–West oriented strategic trade control processes (Bartholomew tst., 1989b; Holmes tst., 1989a, 1989b).

The Bush administration further strengthened CW-related export controls in early 1990. Mandatory controls were applied to twelve additional chemicals for exports to Libya, Iran, Iraq, and Syria, bringing the total to fifty for these sensitive destinations (Clarke tst., 1990). Washington at this juncture controlled more items than the AG required for all non-AG destinations, and more than five times as many items for targeted destinations, the latter also being subject to a strict blanket policy of automatic denial.

As part of the EPCI initiative announced in late 1990 following Iraq's invasion of Kuwait, the United States extended export controls on all fifty chemicals that it controlled to sensitive destinations to all non-AG destinations. It also placed restrictions on U.S. firms' involvement in the development or construction of any chemical plant manufacturing any of these chemicals in any non-AG country. Finally, it added new controls on dual-use production equipment to twenty-eight destinations. And, of course, EPCI's general catch-all provisions applied to virtually any export to any project of chemical proliferation concern (Clarke tst., 1991; LeMunyon tst., 1991). At the time these sweeping new restrictions went into effect on 13 March 1991, the AG Core List provided for controls on just thirteen chemicals. Thus, in early 1991 the United States controlled nearly four times the number of chemicals to all non-AG destinations, plus equipment and other forms of assistance not covered at all by the AG.

AG controls once again caught up with U.S. export controls by the end of 1991. U.S. national controls and the AG Core List subsequently have remained roughly in balance, although in mid-1997 the United States expanded its national controls to include additional dual-use equipment not covered by the AG (*Disarmament Diplomacy* [17], 1997). In addition, the AG still does not require catch-all controls.

Multilateral Export-Control Regime: Australia Group

Washington has been far and away the most active Western proponent of robust CW-related export controls. The United States first proposed a multilateral ban on exporting CW and "all analogous liquids" during the negotiations that led to the 1925 Geneva Protocol, but was unable to garner sufficient international support for the concept (Burck & Flowerree, 1991; Thomas & Thomas, 1970). There the matter of multilateral CW-related export controls rested, both for the United States and the international community generally, until the U.N. secretary general in 1984 issued a report concluding that Iraq had used poison gas against Iranian troops. In response, Washington imposed controls on exports of five precursor chemicals to Iraq and Iran, and urged other industrialized countries to do likewise (Adelman tst., 1984; Olmer tst., 1984). Most Western countries quickly heeded the American call. This modest, pragmatic initiative represented the first attempt to multilateralize chemical export controls in the Cold War era. It also marked the genesis of the first nonproliferation suppliers regime outside the nuclear area, the Australia Group.

What happened next is a subject of some contention. In June 1985, Australia hosted a meeting of the Western countries that had already implemented export controls in response to Iraqi use in order to try to harmonize these national efforts. The Department of Foreign Affairs official responsible maintains that, although Washington had been considering similar initiatives and was consulted before Australia took any action, the idea for this specific meeting originated in Canberra (Walker int., 1998). Another Australian official corroborates that this was how the initiative was characterized to other Australian agencies (int.).

However, there is some circumstantial evidence to suggest that the idea actually may have been suggested by American officials. One lower-level DFA official involved recounts in an interview that there were certainly rumors to this effect at the time. A U.S. official specifically recalls having been told that the United States had informally approached Australian officials to ask them to undertake such an initiative. According to this official, Washington calculated that Australia's experience with poison gas in World War I would give it both the interest and the moral leadership to get the job done ([ACDA] int.). The clear implication is that Washington thought that the idea would be less likely to get a receptive hearing from some countries if it was seen as a U.S. initiative. At least one published account also refers to declassified U.S. documents that appear to support the notion that it was Washington that approached Australia, rather than vice versa (Findlay, 1993).

Whether or not the Australian initiative per se emanated from Washington, there is no doubt that the United States had been considering the idea well beforehand. In June 1984, a full year before the meeting called by Australia, a top U.S. official testified that the Reagan administration planned to pursue the following new steps to combat CW proliferation: "Greater cooperation among countries, especially in the West, who have chemical industries in order to share export controls . . . and to also share information. . . . There can be consultations and intelligence sharing, and anticipation of the kind of problems that we could have in the future and how to deal with them" (Adelman tst., 1984, p. 35). There is also no doubt that when Australia formally approached the United States bilaterally to propose calling a meeting to coordinate export controls among suppliers, it received Washington's enthusiastic backing (Walker int., 1998).

Even before the first meeting, the United States worked actively to nurture what was to become the Australia Group. That said, U.S. policy makers initially did not envision a global regime, but rather a narrower mechanism to target the belligerents in the Iraq–Iran War (Feith int., 1998). However, the Washington interagency gradually came to the view that the emerging regime could be used to target CW proliferation on a broader scale.

From the very first meeting, the United States worked to widen the scope and deepen the institutional structure of the process. The United States pushed hard for all of the precursors that it controlled to be included on a harmonized list, and worked to ensure that the regime-building process did not end there. At three subsequent meetings over the next few years, the United States pressed to add additional chemicals to what became known as the Core List (items requiring export controls), to create what became known as the Warning List of less-sensitive chemicals (not subject to automatic licensing requirements), and to regularize meetings. However, the United States resisted suggestions by Australia and others that membership should be widened to include Third World states, fearing that this would erode the group's cohesiveness as a cartel of like-minded suppliers (Walker int., 1998).

Notwithstanding its activist role during this early period, the United States had not pressed as hard to expand the scope of coverage as Defense, State, and ACDA had wanted. This was due to resistance by the Commerce Department bureaucracy to creating additional dual-use export controls ([ACDA] int.). But the Commerce bureaucracy was forced to relent under an onslaught of publicity about CW proliferation beginning in mid-1988. For the first time, policy decisions on AG issues began to attract the attention of more senior policy makers. Under these circumstances, Commerce essentially agreed to go along with any new AG controls, although it continued to resist new unilateral measures ([ACDA] int.). Defense, State, and ACDA therefore had free rein to push as hard as possible to strengthen the regime, particularly with the advent of the Bush administration.

Following almost two years of German and Japanese refusal to agree to broaden the Core List, U.S. press leaks in January 1989 revealed that German and Japanese companies were assisting Libya's CW program. AG countries widely assumed this had been a deliberate U.S. tactic to pressure these governments to go along with strengthening the AG. Intentional or not, the result was achieved. AG partners agreed in May 1989 to expand the Core List to nine precursors, and the Warning List to forty-four additional chemicals (ACDA off., 1997b). Partners also agreed to U.S. proposals to share information on license denials, and to pledge not to undercut one another's denials. The United States also began to sound out the prospects for getting partners' support for steps to make the regime less ad hoc; for example, establishing a permanent secretariat and making decisions politically binding on members (Bartholomew tst., 1989a).

At the following meeting in June 1990, the United States successfully sought to expand the Core List to ten precursors, to expand the Warning List to fifty chemicals, and for the first time to add dual-use production equipment to the Warning List. In addition, it succeeded in having notification guidelines expanded to include license approvals (ACDA off., 1997b; Clarke tst., 1990).

Iraq's invasion of Kuwait in August 1990 was a watershed in U.S. efforts to strengthen the AG. It led to uniform agreement in the famously fractured interagency process—especially discordant in the nonproliferation, export-control, and arms-control spheres—on the need to build and maintain as robust an AG as possible. Indeed, according to virtually all interview subjects, this has since then been among the least contentious issues in the relevant interagency processes. Moreover, particularly in the immediate aftermath of the Gulf War, the issue for the first time attracted the interest of top administration officials and influential members of Congress.

U.S. efforts to strengthen the AG reached a fever pitch in the immediate aftermath of Iraq's invasion. At the December 1990 plenary meeting, the United States pushed the AG to adopt controls analogous to its new EPCI regulations. In effect, the United States was asking the group to subsume the entire Warning List (including equipment items) into the Core List, as well as to add catch-all controls (Clarke tst., 1991). An Australian official who worked closely with the United States on behalf of the AG chairman confirms that the United States brought intense and sustained pressure to bear on partners who resisted these stalwart reforms ([DFAT] int.).

The United States did not get its way immediately. For example, the December 1990 meeting saw agreement on only a modest addition of three new chemicals to the Core List, bringing the total to thirteen. However, by the December 1991 meeting, after a year of intense bilateral and multilateral activity, the Core List had indeed grown to fifty chemicals plus dual-use equipment. Several months later four more chemicals were added, representing the last major addition to date (ACDA off., 1997b). A mid-level State Department official directly involved at the time makes clear in an interview that the dramatic development of the AG in the early 1990s in very large measure was driven by U.S. policy initiatives. As another U.S. participant recalls, the United States had achieved virtually everything it set out to do in the two years following the Gulf War, and Washington was extremely pleased with the outcome (Donadio int., 1998). Since this burst of post–Gulf War expansion, the United States has viewed the scope of AG controls to be mature, satisfied that all relevant items are covered ([State] int.). Again, this perspective is for the most part shared by all the various agencies, and so there has not been any serious interagency disagreement in recent years on the structure and operation of the regime (Donadio int., 1998; Fitzgibbon int., 1998; Rybka int., 1997; Smoldone int., 1998; Wallerstein int., 1998).

Even as it labored to strengthen the AG after the Gulf War, the United States was forced to fight a simultaneous rearguard action not only to maintain these gains, but to preserve the very existence of the regime. As the CWC negotiations in the Conference on Disarmament (CD) entered the crucial endgame phase beginning around 1991, many nonaligned movement (NAM) states became more insistent in questioning the need for the AG once the CWC was completed. What claim to legitimacy did an insular, self-appointed club of states have to continue to target CWC parties with discriminatory controls? Some CD members (e.g., Iran) threatened to build a coalition against the CWC unless Western countries agreed to disband the AG, or at least severely curtail its activities vis-à-vis CWC members. Faced with the prospect of the CWC negotiations unraveling, some AG partners were inclined to capitulate on the key issue of whether the AG had an indefinite future, or to at least compromise significantly on its future structure and operations (Donadio int., 1998). By contrast, Washington never seriously considered the option of compromising the AG to secure the CWC.

U.S. negotiators had been alert to the prospect that the CWC could undermine capability-denial efforts from the very beginning. Article X, providing for technical cooperation and assistance among States Parties, was a source of particular concern, the fear being that this could impose legal obligations on suppliers to assist dual-use programs in developing countries. Therefore, the United States had taken the lead during the CWC negotiations to resist anything but extremely weak assistance and cooperation provisions (Nelson int., 1998). As one key official recalls, "We would not have agreed to a Convention that would have had a 'poisons for peace' provision; just wouldn't have happened. And naturally, as we now know, the Senate would not have ratified such a Convention" ([State] int.). As for NAM attacks on the related AG issue—short of technology entitlements, at least trying to eliminate or curtail AG restrictions—the Pentagon had anticipated pressure along these lines once the CWC negotiations began to show progress in the late 1980s. Consequently, long before the issue had surfaced as a serious point of contention in the Geneva negotiations, Defense had successfully made the case in the interagency that the United States would have to be prepared to fight aggressively any attempt to trade the AG for the CWC (Fitzgibbon int., 1998; Rostow int., 1998). According to an ACDA official (int.) intimately involved in interagency deliberations at the time, there was never any dispute on this point. Thus, when the issue surfaced during the CWC endgame, there was already a long-standing interagency consensus on how the United States should respond. All agencies agreed that in seeking to conclude the CWC the United States should not agree to narrow or relax AG controls ([OSD] int.; Donadio int., 1998; Mahley int., 1998). In addition to repeatedly reaffirming this position, both at AG meetings and in the Geneva negotiations, the United States brought sustained bilateral pressure to bear on wavering AG countries to shore up their resolve (Donadio int., 1998). Indeed, the ACDA official directly in charge of coordinating interagency policy for the CWC negotiations at the time confirms in no uncertain terms that Washington had been fully prepared to let the CWC negotiations reach an impasse rather than accede to nonaligned countries' demands regarding the Australia Group (Mahley int., 1998).

In the event the quarrel between the NAM and AG countries was nimbly sidestepped, if not resolved, albeit in a way not entirely to Washington's liking. This was accomplished through a statement read into the record at the Geneva negotiations on 6 August 1992 by the Australian ambassador, speaking on behalf of the AG members collectively. It appeared to promise that AG controls would be eliminated or relaxed for CWC parties, but on close reading, and as interpreted by Washington, promised no such thing.

As far as many U.S. officials were concerned, this tactic was problematic, coming too near to casting the future of the AG in doubt. Indeed, it seems highly doubtful that the interagency would have gone along with the so-called O'Sullivan Statement but for the fact that Washington had been skillfully maneuvered by its own chief negotiator into a position where it was left with little choice.

The genesis of the O'Sullivan Statement still touches a raw nerve among many of those involved, particularly on the Washington end. A former top member of the U.S. delegation (int.) concedes that the statement was conceived entirely by negotiators in Geneva. This initiative was led by U.S. Ambassador Stephen J. Ledogar and his Australian counterpart, Paul O'Sullivan, but without Washington's authorization or knowledge. The ambassadors took the brash step of negotiating without a mandate from their governments out of concern that the AG controversy, and in particular the intransigent U.S. position, would derail the CWC negotiations at a crucial juncture. Having finalized a draft among themselves, the Geneva delegations of the AG members sent this to their respective capitals as an agreed text. Moreover, they did so on a take-it-or-leave-it basis. Relevant agencies, including ACDA (which had the interagency lead on CWC), had been kept completely in the dark (Mahley int., 1998).[8] The agreed text, when it landed, caught the interagency utterly by surprise.

Ambassador Ledogar argued that the statement was consistent with U.S. policy because it had been carefully worded so as not to put the AG in any real jeopardy. However, the entire interagency was unhappy with the formula, since it certainly conveyed the impression that the status of the AG would be put on the table at some future date. Even ACDA, which had the highest stake in successfully completing the CWC, was wary that the O'Sullivan Statement went too far (Mahley int., 1998). The Pentagon in particular was up in arms. Former Deputy Assistant Secretary of Defense William Inglee (int., 1998) recalls, "The problem with it to me was that it was disingenuous bordering upon dishonest. I really felt it was contriving to create a rationale for doing something that I felt was very harmful . . . to give [CWC] signatories a blank check on export control regulations, or to lead them to believe that that would be the outcome."

However, in reality, Washington had been left with no viable option but to go along with the strategy. Because the U.S. ambassador had already given his agreement to the other AG delegations ad referendum, and furthermore had ruled out any modifications as part of this agreement, the interagency concluded that it had been handed what amounted to a fait accompli. A mid-level State Department official recalls, "The O'Sullivan Statement was put together by . . . the Australian CD Representative, and worked on by the Geneva delegations of the AG countries, and at the last minute foisted upon their capitals as a take it or leave it proposition. And so we basically took it . . . but a lot of people back in Washington . . . were not exactly pleased with the evolution of that statement" (int.). The Pentagon protested vigorously at the very highest levels, but in the end was forced to concede that it would be impractical to attempt to walk back from something that had already been circulated so widely (Inglee int., 1998).

Having reluctantly gone along with the O'Sullivan Statement— which accomplished what it was supposed to accomplish (i.e., dodging the dispute long enough to wrap up the CWC negotiations)—Washington cleaved to a minimalist interpretation of the commitment therein implied. As far as the United States was concerned, the AG countries had merely agreed to review their export-control practices. Having done so, and finding nothing inconsistent with the CWC, Washington considered the matter to be closed. Since then, there has been unwavering agreement among agencies that a robust AG will be needed indefinitely irrespective of the disposition of the CWC (Fitzgibbon int., 1998; Mahley int., 1998; Smoldone int., 1998; [State] int.; Wallerstein int., 1998) This consensus that the AG needs to be maintained and strengthened was formalized by presidential directive within days of the completion of CWC negotiations, and again the following year. Finally, the U.S. Senate cemented this policy into law by making it an explicit condition of its consent to ratify the CWC (U.S. Cong. Senate off., 1997). Moreover, the Clinton administration made no effort to oppose this condition, since it was consistent with the president's standing guidance (Wallerstein int., 1998).

Far from contemplating scaling back or eliminating the AG now that the CWC has entered into force, the United States presently sees this as an opportunity to expand the scope of its activities. A mid-level State Department official (int.) familiar with current interagency deliberations notes that, inasmuch as the CWC is now up and running, the United States believes that the AG can afford to abandon its "defensive crouch" of recent years. Consequently, the United States wants to see the group become more outward looking. Specifically, it plans to push the AG to move beyond just controlling exports by its members, and to begin as a regime to undertake efforts to curtail transfers between nonmembers (i.e., a corporate interdiction program).

Wider Export-Control Norms

The United States worked almost from the advent of the Australia Group to promote wider application of CW-related export controls. In November 1985, just months after the inaugural AG meeting, the United States initiated a regular bilateral mechanism with the USSR to persuade Moscow to implement CW-related export controls, and to work with Washington to encourage others to do the same (Gordon tst., 1990). This process yielded a joint statement at the June 1988 Reagan–Gorbachev summit calling on all countries capable of producing CW-relevant chemicals to institute stringent export controls in order to prevent CW proliferation (*CWC Bulletin* [2], 1988).

Following Iraq's use of poison gas against the Kurds, President Reagan called for a meeting of the world's foreign ministers to reaffirm support for the 1925 Geneva Protocol's prohibition on CW use. However, the real U.S. purpose was to use this conference as a venue to promote global support for CW export controls. The conference took place in Paris in January 1989, serving as the multilateral debut for incoming Secretary of State James Baker III. Although the United States pushed hard to have the conference call on participating states to institute controls on relevant exports, this initiative was blocked by a number of developing countries. In the end, Washington had to settle for a vague statement endorsing restraint in matters relevant to the subject of the conference, but with no explicit reference to CW-related transfers (Burck & Flowerree, 1991). This outcome was a far cry from the broad multilateral pledge to support export controls that Washington had envisioned when President Reagan had called for the conference.

The United States had no intention of allowing the matter to rest with this failure. It immediately set about organizing a follow-up meeting that would have promoting export controls as an explicit goal. Since Australia was the permanent chair of the Australia Group, it was seen as a natural host. Secretary Baker therefore telephoned his Australian counterpart and convinced him to sponsor a high-level meeting of governments and representatives of their chemical industries (Evans int., 1998).

A major U.S. goal for inviting industry participation was "enabling the chemical industry to contribute to . . . helping us to better control the burgeoning trade in CW precursors and technology" (Holmes tst., 1989a, p. 13). Indeed, senior U.S. officials indicated that, although other issues such as the CWC negotiations might also be addressed, the U.S. saw promoting export controls as the primary objective. For example, a senior State Department official testified several months beforehand, "We believe that this will be an excellent opportunity to involve industry and governments worldwide in the common effort to control the trade in chemical weapons precursors, as well as to gain industry support for the Geneva negotiations on a CW ban. We hope that the Conference will focus particularly on government and industry cooperative efforts to control the movement of precursors in international commerce" (Bartholomew tst., 1989b, p. 16). A senior Commerce Department official identified similar priorities: "The idea for this conference came from the United States, and I think its the best hope we have for beginning to effectively control the means to produce chemical weapons. Perhaps the most important goal of this type of multilateral conference would be better enforcement coordination" (Freedenberg tst., 1989, p. 155).

However, U.S. efforts to use the conference to promote wider export-control norms were thwarted, this time not by developing countries, but by none other than the Australian hosts (see Chapter 4). The agenda of the Government–Industry Conference Against Chemical Weapons, held in Canberra in September 1989, was limited exclusively to fostering support for the CWC negotiations. The most that the United States was able to do was to urge in its national statement, "Those who have not yet implemented export controls with teeth, should do so" (Clarke off., 1989b, p. 409).

In the wake of these successive high-profile failures to forge broad multilateral adherence to CW-related export controls, the United States set out to bolster the role of the emerging CWC in this regard. In August 1991, the United States introduced draft treaty language requiring CWC members to limit exports of scheduled chemicals, equipment, and technology to nonmembers through export controls (*CWC Bulletin* [13], 1991). Although this proposal excluded intraparty transfers, it nevertheless succeeded in establishing a broad multilateral obligation to establish national export-control systems. In addition, Washington continued to promote wider adherence to AG norms through bilateral means. Deputy Assistant Secretary of State Elizabeth Verville toured former Warsaw Pact countries in the summer of 1991 to urge them to adhere to Australia Group rules unilaterally (Clarke tst., 1991). As a carrot, Washington agreed to relax its CBW-related export restrictions to some of these countries once they had export controls in place (LeMunyon tst., 1991). The following year, the United States began to provide funds under the Cooperative Threat Reduction (CTR) program to assist Russia, Ukraine, Belarus, and Kazakhistan to develop effective export-control systems, explicitly including the CBW areas

(Duffy tst., 1994; Eckert tst., 1994; State off., 1999). Washington also pressed China to implement CW export controls, although it was unable to secure a satisfactory commitment from Beijing until 1998 (*CBW Conventions Bulletin* [41], 1998).

National Enforcement Mechanisms

The intensity of U.S. commitment to supply-side nonproliferation is vividly shown by the energy that it has expended to enforce export-control norms. As in all of the proliferation areas, this commitment to enforcement begins with its own CW-relevant dual-use exports in the form of long-standing programs run by the State and Commerce departments to verify the end use of items that have been exported subject to end-use assurances. However, most U.S. enforcement efforts target transfers by other countries. Australia Group norms, as well as the blanket nonassistance obligation incorporated in the CWC, provide the general framework for these efforts. However, Washington has had no compunction about taking action against transfers from or to countries that are not members of these regimes, and/or involving items not covered by them.

Washington began to use diplomatic démarches to interdict chemical transfers to countries of proliferation concern in the mid-1980s ([ACDA] int.; Harrison tst., 1989). In 1989 a top official testified that these démarches over the previous few years had made a significant material impact on the number of companies assisting CW proliferators (Burns tst., 1989a). The most concerted such effort during the Reagan period targeted transfers to Libya's Rabta plant. Beginning in late 1988, Secretary of State George Shultz sent personal envoys to pressure the governments of countries with companies assisting the Rabta project to cut off any and all further assistance (Holmes tst., 1989a; Webster tst., 1989a).

One of the first nonproliferation initiatives of the Bush administration was to regularize such ad hoc efforts by creating an interagency group to coordinate CBW interdiction: "The group monitors intelligence, coordinates proposed *demarches*, and provides a centralized mechanism for obtaining clearance to downgrade and release intelligence information [to other countries] and ensure necessary follow up" (Bartholomew tst., 1989b, pp. 13–14).

SHIELD (originally known as Operation Shield) systematically identified problematic commercial activities on an ongoing basis to raise with both AG and non-AG governments. In cases involving non-AG members, Washington often tried to get other AG countries to support its efforts by undertaking their own parallel démarches (Donadio int., 1998). Since the SHIELD group was formed the United States has sent out approximately 80 to 130 démarches annually through regular diplomatic channels (not counting bilateral meetings) regarding specific CBW-related transfers, or up to more than ten interdiction démarches per month ([State] int.). In 1991, a senior official testified, "Our USG [U.S. government] interdiction groups for CBW . . . have . . . proven effective. These groups seek to identify illicit proliferation-related shipments and stop them through cooperation with foreign governments. We have succeeded in a number of cases" (Clarke tst., 1991, p. 93).

Interdiction efforts continued under the Clinton administration. It focused particular attention on problematic Chinese exports. Former Assistant Secretary of State Robert Gallucci (int., 1998) recalls repeatedly raising concerns about specific transfers during his meetings with Chinese officials. Indeed, interdiction issues were raised with the Chinese even at the presidential level (Davis tst., 1996). Former Deputy Assistant Secretary of Defense Mitchel Wallerstein (int., 1998) indicates that bilateral efforts to stop ongoing Chinese transfers of pertinent equipment and materials constituted the single key focus of the Clinton administration's CW nonproliferation policy until at least 1996. He recalls, "They saw the export of chemical precursors or the export of chemical equipment . . . as a way of earning foreign exchange, end of story." Moreover, he recollects that Washington did not receive very much help from its AG partners in responding to this problem: "There were attempts at coordinating démarches. I was never convinced that many other countries were approaching China with the degree of seriousness and perspicacity that was needed for China really to get the message." A mid-level State Department official (int.) likewise confirms that the United States has had to go it alone in its interdiction efforts. He notes that, although some AG partners do undertake outreach to explain the regime to nonmembers, they have provided very little help interdicting transfers by nonmembers.

CW-related interdiction efforts have largely been confined to démarches and other diplomatic tools. However, early in the Clinton administration the United States flirted with a more muscular approach. In the late summer of 1993, the U.S. military for nearly three weeks shadowed the Chinese cargo ship *Yin He*, suspected of carrying CW-related chemicals to Iran. China refused to permit the U.S. Navy to conduct a search on the high seas. However, under intense diplomatic pressure from Washington, China consented to divert the ship to Saudi Arabia to be inspected. When the search turned up nothing, China demanded a public apology, monetary compensation, and a pledge that no similar incidents would occur again. Washington rejected all of these demands (*Washington Post*, 9/5/93), but has never since sought seizure of a suspected CW-related shipment.

Beginning in the early 1990s the United States supplemented its interdiction program with unilateral CBW nonproliferation sanctions tied to the proliferation behavior of foreign firms and governments. Such sanctions had first been proposed by a presidential commission in 1985, although the recommendation was not taken up (Webster tst., 1989a). However, beginning in late 1988 Congress began considering a flurry of CBW sanctions bills, which attracted bipartisan support. The Bush administration took an equivocal position on these legislative initiatives. On the one hand, it strongly supported giving the president the authority to sanction foreign firms for providing CBW-related assistance to proliferators. For example, CIA Director William Webster (tst., 1989a) testified in February 1989, "Legislation authorizing the President to impose sanctions on . . . companies which contribute to CBW proliferation, would address an inadequacy in existing law and would be an important step to deter the proliferation . . . of CBW" (p. 25). At the same time, the administration felt that such sanctions should not be automatic, since this would infringe on the president's flexibility to conduct foreign policy (Bartholomew tst., 1989b; Executive Office of the President off., 1989b; Webster tst., 1989a).

The administration negotiated with Congress on different versions of sanctions legislation throughout 1989 and 1990. Ultimately, sanctions advocates in Congress felt that the administration was seeking too much flexibility. They therefore used a common Congressional tactic for avoiding a presidential veto by attaching sanctions legislation to a bill that the administration would be loath to veto, in this case the November 1990 extension of the Export Administration Act of 1979. However, the president outmaneuvered Congress by vetoing the bill but then extending its provisions by executive order. The only difference between the vetoed legislation and the simultaneous executive order was that the CBW sanctions provisions provided greater presidential discretion (Congressional Research Service off., 1991). In a sop to Congress, however, the executive order provided automatic sanctions for transfers to Iran, Iraq, and Libya (OSD off., 1997b).

Less than a year later, Congress reintroduced legislation requiring automatic sanctions on CBW transfers to all state sponsors of terrorism in the Chemical and Biological Weapons Control and Warfare Elimination Act. This time, President Bush did not use the veto, and mandatory CBW sanctions became law on 28 October 1991 (CRS off., 1997; OSD off., 1997b). According to an official (int.) involved at very senior levels, while the White House formally opposed automatic sanctions as a matter of constitutional principle, the State Department and other agencies had viewed automatic sanctions as a useful tool. Another official involved at the time recalls that the working-level bureaucracy had no objections to automatic sanctions ([ACDA] int.).

U.S. CBW sanctions are not explicitly tied to the AG, but rather apply the standards set by U.S. national export controls (CRS off., 1997; OSD off., 1997b). The United States sought unsuccessfully to have the AG adopt a similar multilateral measure. When this failed, it resorted to urging AG governments to adopt comparable sanctions on a national basis ([DFAT] int.).

U.S. CBW sanctions apply only to transfers to countries that are deemed to have used or prepared to use CBW since 1 January 1980, and to all of the countries on the State Department's list of state sponsors of terrorism. There is no exemption for entities from AG or CWC member countries, and in fact actions that are allowable under these instruments nonetheless may be subject to sanctions (e.g., Schedule 1 transfers among certain CWC parties) ([State] int.; [ACDA] int.). However, the president can waive sanctions if the government of jurisdiction undertakes specific and effective enforcement actions to prevent or punish the sanctionable activity. A sanctioned entity is barred from exporting to the United States for at least a year, and thereafter until the president certifies that it is not longer aiding or abetting foreign CBW programs, or that providing a waiver is in the national security interests of the United States (CRS off., 1997; OSD off., 1997b).

Responsibility for identifying potentially sanctionable activity has been assigned to the existing interagency interdiction group since the mandatory sanctions law came into effect (Clarke tst., 1991). Presidential authority to make sanctions determinations was devolved formally to the cognizant undersecretary of state. The law has been invoked on a number of occasions in the intervening years. For example, three Thai companies were sanctioned in March 1994 for supplying workers to Libya's Rabta facility, following several months of diplomatic warnings by Washington (*CWC Bulletin* [24], 1994). Two Swiss firms were sanctioned later that same year for providing construction machinery to the same project (*CWC Bulletin* [26], 1994). Most recently, Washington imposed sanctions on two Chinese companies, five Chinese persons, and a Hong Kong firm in May 1997, and another Chinese company in June 2001, for assisting the Iranian CW program (*Disarmament Diplomacy* [15], 1997; *Washington Post*, 6/28/01).[9]

Other Capability-Denial Responses

Other than general targeted initiatives such as ACME, there have been no apparent cases where the United States has tried to foster such arrangements specifically against CW programs.

Although Washington has not frequently taken, or even threatened, preemptive attacks against nascent CW programs, it has done so on occasion. The first such instance occurred in late 1988, when President

Reagan stated during a television interview that he was considering ordering a military attack on a suspected CW factory under construction in Libya. Two weeks later, the United States moved an aircraft carrier to international waters just off Libya, provoking a response that resulted in the downing of two Libyan fighters (CWC Bulletin [3], 1989). Following this incident, however, the United States denied that it had ever had any concrete plans to attack Rabta (CWC Bulletin [4], 1989). But when the Rabta plant mysteriously caught fire during the 1990 Gulf Crisis, press reports suggested that the fire had been an intentional act of sabotage. Indeed, the Washington Post (4/18/90) editorial page went so far as to welcome the "intriguing mystery" as "perhaps the best news on the nonproliferation front since Israel bombed Iraq's nuclear reactor a decade ago" (p. B6).

Several years later, with nonproliferation efforts having prevented Libya from completing Rabta, Secretary of Defense William Perry told the press that, if and when Libya neared completion, the United States would consider a preemptive military attack. "If you would like to consider that a warning to Libya," he stated, "you can so consider it" (as quoted in Disarmament Diplomacy [4], 1996, p. 44). Oddly enough, the only overt attack on a suspected CW facility (other than in the unique case of the Gulf War) happened with no warning or prior diplomatic initiatives, when the United States attacked an alleged CW factory in the capital of Sudan in August 1998.[10]

Nonpossession Norm-Building

Global Nonpossession Norm: Chemical Weapons Convention

For all but the final two to three years of the CWC negotiations, the United States did not regard the process as a means to respond to horizontal proliferation. Rather, until about 1990, Washington saw the Geneva talks almost exclusively in terms of addressing the strategic threat posed by massively asymmetric Soviet capabilities. From the U.S. perspective, Third World proliferation simply did not enter into its CWC equation ([OSD] int.; Hinds int., 1998; Mahley int., 1998; Nelson int., 1998; [State] int.). Although U.S. agencies had different perspectives on the efficacy of a CW ban, they all saw it as part of the larger bilateral U.S.–USSR arms-control process, multilateral trappings notwithstanding. Not surprising, then, to the extent that there was any real attention given to CW disarmament up until 1990, it occurred in bilateral channels behind the scenes.

Given that the United States initially saw the CWC talks primarily as an East–West disarmament process rather than a vehicle for non-

proliferation, strictly speaking only the final few years of the negotiations should be considered as being part of U.S. proliferation response.
That said, U.S. positions during this final phase were extensively
shaped by its earlier disarmament agenda. As a longstanding mid-
level State Department official comments, "The CWC really started
out as a Cold War instrument to try to deal with the huge Soviet CW
program. . . . If we had created a CWC from the beginning that was
focused more on the proliferation threat, it would probably be a lot
simpler and less elaborate than the CWC that we ended up with" (int.).
Accordingly, U.S. positions on the CWC as a nonproliferation instrument can only be properly understood in the context of the bilateral
arms-control agenda from which they evolved.

The United States came to the CWC negotiations with a long track
record of skepticism about CW disarmament. It had rejected a proposal to ban poison gases put forward by Fascist Italy and Imperial
Japan at the multilateral 1921 Washington Conference, arguing that
such an instrument could not adequately protect against covert CW
acquisition by unscrupulous powers (Thomas & Thomas, 1970). Washington likewise rejected a 1969 Warsaw Pact proposal in the United
Nations to negotiate a global ban on CW, asserting that the inherent
limitations of such a ban necessitated retaining deterrence through
the ability to retaliate in kind. The first meaningful U.S. willingness to
consider CW disarmament occurred in a U.S.–USSR bilateral working
group established by the Carter administration in 1977. These bilateral talks reached agreement on the scope of a notional treaty, but rapidly deadlocked on specific modalities. With no further progress being
made, and bilateral relations deteriorating generally, this bilateral process was formally disbanded by the Reagan administration in 1981,
with the two superpowers agreeing to remand the issue to the CD in
Geneva (Burcke & Flowerree, 1991). According to one official involved
in the bilateral talks, once it had become clear that the Soviets were
not serious, the United States lost any interest in trying to pursue CW
disarmament. Washington therefore referred the issue to the CD—
which it regarded as "a place to get things done slowly, if at all"—
specifically as a way to preclude further progress ([OSD] int.).

The failure of the bilateral talks, and the subsequent putting of CW
disarmament out to the multilateral pasture, did not displease most
elements of the U.S. government, particularly in the new Reagan administration. Senior officials at the Pentagon actively opposed pressing ahead with serious negotiations—believing that the Soviets could
not be prevented from cheating, and a treaty would undercut support
for defensive and retaliatory programs—while senior officials at other
agencies were at best indifferent, with the notable exception of a single

individual. As a White House aide recalls, "In the Reagan Adminis-tration the only person who cared about chemical weapons [disarma-ment] was George Bush, the Vice President" (Mahley int., 1998).

Washington effectively blocked any chance of progress in the multi-lateral talks by refusing to agree to give the relevant working group a mandate to actually try to negotiate a treaty. This straightforward strat-egy of declining to negotiate, and likewise preventing others from doing so, prevailed throughout the administration's first term. Al-though the United States went through the motions of participating in Geneva—for example, tabling a paper spelling out its broad objec-tives for a CW treaty in February 1983 (Emery tst., 1984)—in reality it did nothing that would allow any real progress.

This changed abruptly when Secretary of State George Shultz an-nounced in January 1984 during an unrelated speech to his counter-parts in the Conference on Security and Cooperation in Europe (CSCE) that the United States soon planned to table a draft CW negotiating text at the CD. What accounted for this dramatic turnaround? Not, it appears, a consensus within the administration.

According to senior officials involved at the time, the decision to announce tabling a draft treaty was made without interagency con-sensus or White House approval (Feith int., 1998; Gaffney tst., 1989; Perle int., 1998). Moreover, it was not merely a case of an initiative that had not been properly vetted by the interagency beforehand, but rather one that had been vigorously and explicitly rejected. Based on a formal intelligence assessment that a CW ban could not be effec-tively verified, even regarding militarily significant violations, the in-teragency had weeks before overwhelmingly rejected a proposal by a mid-level State Department official to allow the CD to begin formal negotiations. It was this official who slipped the draft text initiative into Shultz's speech, without telling him that it was an unauthorized initiative. Afterward, the Pentagon went directly to President Reagan to demand a retraction. However, after consulting with Shultz, the president decided that he could not undermine his Secretary of State's credibility by reversing a high-profile public initiative (Feith int., 1998).

As one Defense official later testified, "Having no choice but to act upon the initiative of the Secretary of State, we did the next best thing, which was to try to limit the damage" (Gaffney tst., 1989, p. 98). By all accounts, the Pentagon sought to accomplish this by inserting a clause for "anytime, anywhere" challenge inspections into the draft treaty as a nonnegotiable provision that the Soviets were certain to reject. A former non-Defense official recalls,

Anytime, anywhere with no right of refusal was a formula that was generated by [Assistant Secretary] Richard Perle at the Department of Defense. And it was generated by Richard Perle with the plain statement within the inter-agency when he generated it that this is something the Russians will never agree to so therefore it's a means we will block negotiation of the treaty, and we will be able to sit there with that demand on the table and we will not have to make progress on this silly treaty and will still at the same time be able to say that we're doing everything we can. (int.)

Members of Perle's staff at the time provide similar accounts ([OSD] ints.). One recalls,

He deliberately forced into the treaty this article with the intention of killing the Convention, assuming . . . that this made it non-negotiable; the Soviet Union would never accept it, and the Europeans wouldn't accept it either for different reasons. So he . . . told the Joint Chiefs that the chemical weapons treaty was a bad idea, but Shultz had made a public statement promising its being presented by the United States, and that he had fixed it by putting this poison pill into it and that they had nothing to worry about. ([OSD] int.)

Perle (int., 1998) himself readily acknowledges that "anytime, any-where" was his brainchild. However, he remains circumspect about whether his overt intention was to sabotage the negotiations. He states only that he saw it as a minimum requirement for a useful agreement, and that he preferred no agreement to a bad agreement. "So yes," he concludes, "I plead guilty, but not to making sure there wasn't any agreement, but rather that there wasn't a bad agreement."

At the time the United States tabled its draft treaty in 1984, there was virtually no interagency interest in obtaining results. Instead, the consensus was to be seen to be trying to negotiate such a CW ban. So why negotiate at all? The simple answer is that the administration needed to be seen to be negotiating in order to satisfy a Congressional requirement that the acquisition of a new generation of reliable binary CW occur as part of a two-track approach, in parallel to arms-control talks.[11] Then White House aide Donald Mahley (int., 1998) asserts, "From the standpoint of the Defense Department, from the standpoint of the National Security Council, from the standpoint of the State De-partment, putting the new draft treaty that [Vice President George H. W.] Bush put down on the table at the Conference on Disarmament was done purely because—not mostly because, but purely because—that was a Congressional requirement in order for the Congress to vote for binary production funds."

This Congressional requirement was reinforced by Vice President Bush, who privately let Army officials know that he would only sup-port the binary program as a means to force the Soviets to the negoti-ating table ([DOD] int.). Richard Perle (int., 1998) confirms that the only reason that he went along with tabling the draft treaty, even with the "anytime, anywhere" provision, was the need to garner support for the binary program.

The first attempt to interject an explicit nonproliferation element into the CW disarmament process came from the new Soviet leader, Gorbachev, following the tabling of the U.S. draft treaty in Geneva. Since Moscow adamantly refused to consider the type of intrusive verification that the United States was seeking for the CWC, and Washington refused to show any flexibility in its position, Gorbachev suggested that the two superpowers sidestep this stalemate. During a 1985 summit meeting he privately proposed a joint U.S.–USSR initiative to create a CW nonproliferation treaty analogous to the NPT—with the United States and the USSR remaining haves and the rest of the world signing on as have-nots—as an interim arrangement pending future progress on superpower disarmament. This proposal was explored in a series of clandestine bilateral meetings, which the United States kept secret even from its closest allies (Nelson int., 1998). However, in the end Washington rejected the proposal, concluding that the appearance of arms-control progress would jeopardize Congressional support for the U.S. binary weapons program, thus locking in a Soviet advantage. Since U.S. priorities focused on the Soviet threat rather than proliferation, any potential nonproliferation benefit was not considered worth this price (Mahley int., 1998). When Moscow subsequently raised the idea publicly, the United States rejected it out of hand, stating that it preferred to support the CWC negotiations.

Notwithstanding this declaratory support, Washington had little enthusiasm for the Geneva talks over the next several years. Having agreed to negotiations largely to garner Congressional support for the binary weapons program, and subsequently perceiving no signs of movement in behind-the-scenes bilateral talks with the Soviets, there was no political will within the interagency to negotiate in earnest. The Pentagon worked aggressively to ensure that the administration's overriding objective continued to be preserving the binary program, rather than making progress in Geneva. Although Vice President Bush managed to keep the issue from being completely relegated to the sidelines through personal interventions, and a few ACDA officials pressed at the working level for flexibility, the key agencies favored an uncompromising negotiating posture. In addition to holding firm on "anytime, anywhere" verification, the United States continued to insist that the CWC should only enter into force if and when all CW-capable states had joined, effectively killing any realistic prospects for an operative treaty.

Interagency ambivalence and/or opposition was grounded in successive intelligence assessments concluding that even the most rigorous possible verification would provide at best low confidence to detect cheating. Indeed, far from considering greater flexibility, the interagency in 1987 agreed unanimously at very senior levels that, given the unverifiability of a CW ban, and with the binary weapons program well on its way, the United States should withdraw its formal support for the CWC negotiations. This recommendation was forwarded to President Reagan for approval, but was derailed by the personal intervention of Vice President Bush (Gaffney tst., 1989; Hinds int., 1998). Nevertheless, as a former senior Pentagon official later testified,

It frankly would be hard to overstate the significance . . . that every involved agency including . . . the Office of the Secretary of Defense . . . the Joint Chiefs of Staff, the Arms Control and Disarmament Agency, the State Department . . . and the National Security Council itself had arrived—reluctantly, but nonetheless had arrived—at a recommendation that we must change our position in favor of . . . pursuit of a chemical weapons ban. (Gaffney tst., 1989, p. 79)

Only a few months later, a blue-ribbon government panel cochaired by former ACDA Director Fred C. Iklé reached virtually the same recommendation in a public report delivered to the White House, concluding that it was unrealistic for the United States to continue to pursue an inherently unverifiable ban (*CWC Bulletin* [1], 1988).

Then, suddenly, everything changed. Less than a year after the interagency had unanimously recommended abandoning even the pretext of trying to negotiate a CW ban, and just months after the Iklé panel publicly made the same recommendation, the only ranking official who had ever ardently supported chemical disarmament was elected president of the United States. Whether the interagency liked it or not, all at once the CWC negotiations had to be taken seriously.

From the very beginning of his term, President George H. W. Bush made it clear to his senior political appointees in the different agencies that the CWC negotiations represented a personal priority (Alessi int., 1998). Moreover, due to the dramatic thaw in U.S.–Soviet relations, and an upsurge in concern about Third World programs in 1989, elements in ACDA and State began to promote using the CWC as a tool to fight proliferation. This simultaneous boost in priority and reorientation in purpose led to a dramatic reassessment of long-standing U.S. negotiating positions. This, in turn, led to sharp discord among agencies. With the president vigorously supporting CWC (and the traditional bilateral arms-control agenda looking increasingly less relevant), senior ACDA and State officials started to promote the negotiations. In other agencies, however, senior officials taking their first close look at the draft text discovered that they did not like what they found.

Taking CWC seriously for the first time, some agencies realized that "anytime, anywhere" challenge inspections could seriously imperil sensitive programs that had nothing to do with CW. In light of the interagency consensus that even intrusive inspections could not provide high-confidence verification, agencies with defensive equities unrelated to CW concluded that doubtful verification gains were not worth the high adjunct costs associated with intrusive "anytime, anywhere" inspections (Alessi int., 1998; Donadio int., 1998; Inglee int., 1998; Rybka int., 1997). The upshot was that in the first half of 1989, three agencies—DOD, DOE, and the IC—laid down markers at very senior levels that they could not live with "anytime, anywhere" challenge inspections (Alessi int., 1998; Donadio int., 1998; Inglee int., 1998; Mahley int., 1998).

The White House secretly convened a high-level review of the U.S. negotiating position in the summer of 1989.[12] This revealed deep divisions within the new national security team about the merits of pursuing a global CW ban. Although ACDA and State favored moving forward with the Geneva negotiations, OSD strenuously argued against pursuing the CWC. It insisted that, at a minimum, the United States should insist on a package of changes, including being allowed to continue producing binary weapons after entry into force in a "build-down" arrangement, being allowed to indefinitely and unconditionally retain a small CW stockpile, and adding an explicit "firebreak" clause that would allow the United States to halt reductions and reevaluate the treaty's merits at a specified point during implementation. The Joint Staff refused to support even this proposal, arguing that the United States should withdraw from the CWC talks altogether, and instead negotiate reductions bilaterally with Moscow (*Washington Post*, 9/10/89).

Faced with stiff opposition within his cabinet to key elements of the draft CWC, the president opted to compromise across the board. He signed a secret directive authorizing the continuation of binary production during negotiations, committing the United States to negotiate the right to retain a small "security stockpile" within the CWC framework until all CW-capable states had acceded to the treaty and leaving the door open for the United States to seek to continue "build-down" production even after the CWC came into force (*Washington Post*, 9/10/89). He also moved to detach the ongoing bilateral talks from the multilateral process and to bring them to swift closure, in order to ensure that the increasingly promising bilateral agenda did not become hostage to the more dubious prospects for multilateral progress (Mahley int., 1998).

This bilateral process occupied Washington's attention for the next ten months, effectively superseding the debate on CWC. On 23 September 1989, Washington and Moscow concluded an intense round of high-level negotiations, signing a bilateral agreement in Wyoming to exchange and verify data on their respective stockpiles. This involved not only detailed data exchanges, but on-site inspections at declared facilities (ACDA off., 1998). Two days later, President Bush used a speech to the United Nations to propose a bilateral disarmament agreement, whereby each country would immediately begin to reduce its stockpile to an amount equivalent to 20 percent of the current U.S. stockpile, with a further reduction to 2 percent within eight years after eventual CWC entry into force. At the 2–3 December 1989 Malta summit, the president sweetened this offer by agreeing to drop plans to insist on continuing binary production after CWC (*CWC Bulletin* [7], 1990). After several rounds of high-level negotiations, the Bilateral Destruction Agreement (BDA) was signed on 1 June 1990. In a final concession, the United States had agreed to immediately halt binary production. However, the agreement gave each party the right to retain a "security stockpile" equal to 2 percent of the current U.S. stockpile until at least eight years after eventual CWC entry into force, at which point the continued retention of security stockpiles would be reviewed.

Securing a bilateral disarmament agreement with Moscow allowed Washington for the first time to treat the Geneva talks primarily as a nonproliferation vehicle. This nearly total shift in objectives served to increase the internal pressure to modify long-standing U.S. negotiating positions, which had been designed with the Soviet stockpile in mind. Advocates of the multilateral treaty, starting with the president himself, had to find a formula that would satisfy critics within the administration, particularly Defense Secretary Richard Cheney.

Pursuant to the president's earlier compromise, the United States tabled a joint proposal in Geneva with the Soviet Union several weeks after signing the BDA, calling for the security stockpile provisions in the BDA to be incorporated into the draft CWC. The United States followed this with statements on 24 July and 16 August noting that it intended to continue to reserve the right to use its security stockpile to retaliate in-kind (*CWC Bulletin* [9], 1990). A short time later, Washington also changed its long-standing position on verification. In August 1990 the United States formally notified the Western Group (WEOG) caucus in Geneva that it was withdrawing its support for "anytime, anywhere." It tabled a new negotiating position reserving the ultimate right of a States Party to refuse challenge inspections (Cousins off., 1991a).

By adopting a position on retention and use that was anathema to the Third World and a position on verification that was unacceptable to the WEOG, the revised U.S. negotiating position presented obstacles to progress on all sides (Ledogar, 1991). The bottom line was that without U.S. concessions on these issues the negotiations would not be going anywhere anytime soon. This left the Geneva process to stagnate, while the interagency argued about whether to show greater flexibility, and if so, how much. This debate became so rancorous that even the smallest technical issues were elevated to the cabinet level ([State] int.).

The most divisive issue remained multilateral (i.e., non-Soviet) challenge inspections.[13] Having dropped "anytime, anywhere," Washington needed to offer a detailed proposal to flesh out its new position. The Geneva delegation and ACDA pushed to return to a tough stance on verification. DOD, DOE, and the IC insisted on protecting non-CW-related U.S. facilities against intrusive verification. State and Commerce occupied the middle ground, with State leaning toward ACDA and Commerce leaning toward the rest, while NSC remained neutral (Donadio int., 1998). This lineup left verification supporters very much in the minority. As the former U.S. chief negotiator bitterly recounts, the interagency was dominated by the defensive concerns of DOD, DOE, and the IC (Ledogar int., 1998). A prominent State Department participant likewise recalls, "You had everybody except State and ACDA very much wanting to protect almost at the expense of being able to detect" (int.).

In the end, the "defensive" coalition prevailed decisively. A participant recalls that at the end of a series of meetings chaired by the NSC staff the Pentagon and its interagency allies emerged with almost all of the defensive provisions that they had sought in order to ensure that multilateral inspections would be relatively toothless (Bushong int.).

In the spring of 1991, the United States dispatched a delegation to various Western countries to preview its new position on verification, which it characterized as reflecting a British approach known as "managed access" (Cousins off., 1991a). As one observer notes, "It was such a retreat from 'anytime, anywhere' as to amount to a neutering of the challenge inspection concept" (Findlay, 1993, p. 33). Among its defensive features, the proposal allowed the inspected party to establish a delay of inspectors for up to a week to negotiate a perimeter around the site, gave the inspected party the final say in setting the perimeter if these negotiations failed, allowed the inspected party to forbid inspectors access on the ground within this perimeter, and strictly forbade searching exiting personnel and private vehicles (Findlay, 1991a). The United States also supported limiting routine inspections to facilities that had actually in the past produced at least 100 tons of CW precursors annually, rather than all facilities capable of doing so (Findlay, 1992a). Ironically, this proposal moved the United States closer to the verification preferences of China and the NAM countries than to most of its Western allies (Donadio int., 1998; [State] int.). Having persuaded Australia, Japan, and the United Kingdom to reluctantly sign on as cosponsors, the United States formally tabled this proposal in the WEOG in July 1991.

At this juncture, the White House changed the interagency balance by effectively abandoning its role as a neutral arbitrator of interagency disagreements. Sensing that the post–Gulf War environment offered a narrow window of opportunity, and fearing that U.S. inflexibility could derail the negotiations at this critical juncture, President Bush stepped in to reverse his earlier decisions on retaining a security stockpile and the right to retaliate in-kind. This change, of course, was not agreed in the interagency. Rather, it was handed down as an edict from the White House. While Defense Secretary Cheney and others objected vigorously, in the end they had no choice but to defer to the president's decision ([ACDA] int.; Moodie int., 1998; Nelson int., 1998; Rostow int., 1998). As one senior negotiator recalls, the reaction among many senior officials in Washington was, "It may be a rotten treaty and we hate it, but you know this is what the President decided" (int.).

These major concessions left the ongoing stalemate in the WEOG on challenge inspections as the lone key obstacle.[14] The Pentagon and its interagency allies consequently drew a line in the sand on this issue, ferociously resisting any compromise on challenge inspections. As a result, the United States spent months debating a single adjective in its proposal with other Western governments (Donadio int., 1998; Moodie int., 1998).

However, when Australia took it upon itself to try to bilaterally broker a compromise behind the scenes (see Chapter 4), the White House once again abandoned neutrality, pressing for flexibility as these secret bilateral talks unfolded. A former senior ACDA official recounts, "At that point there was enormous [White House] pressure to get the thing done" (Moodie int., 1998). A former mid-level Defense official ruefully recalls that, as a result of the pressure brought to bear by the White House during the bilateral talks with Australia, "As we got into it, basically we discovered that we had no friends . . . and so whenever we looked for cover we suddenly found that we were alone, and none of our traditional allies . . . came out to help us" (Rostow int., 1998).

In the end, the United States accepted a formula that, while not going as far as most of its Western allies would have liked, went much farther than many U.S. agencies would have accepted absent sustained and irresistible pressure from the president and his NSC staff. Most officials involved readily admit that the United States almost certainly would never have accepted the treaty that it signed in January 1993 but for the personal interventions of President Bush.

U.S. ambivalence toward the CWC did not end with the conclusion of the negotiations. It was now up to a new president to carry forward U.S. support for, and participation in, the new treaty regime. In the absence of close management by senior White House officials, simmering divisions in the interagency reasserted themselves in relation to implementation issues being negotiated in the Preparatory Commission (PrepCom) of the Organization for the Prohibition of Chemical Weapons (OPCW). With CWC skeptics once again able to exert influence, the United States sought to put limits on intrusive verification; for example, by restricting the equipment used by inspectors (int.).

The Clinton administration failed to act quickly and decisively to secure Senate ratification. In part, this was due to becoming mired in a bitter interagency dispute over a decision by the NSC staff to change Washington's unilateral interpretation of the CWC's restrictions on the use of riot control agents (RCAs). This self-inflicted controversy not only delayed the ratification process, but raised concerns by the powerful and nearly universally respected chairman of the Senate Armed Services Committee, Democrat Sam Nunn, and would remain a major source of contention between the administration and the Senate.[15] Meanwhile, consistent with long-standing IC assessments, top intelligence officials testified that the treaty's verification provisions would not provide high confidence to detect cheating (Landry tst., 1994; Woolsey tst., 1994). Along similar lines, then Deputy Secretary of Defense John Deutch (tst., 1994) admitted, "We recognize that the CWC may not be universal or universally complied with" (p. 34).

In response to the concern such statements generated in the Senate, the Clinton NSC staff exerted pressure on the IC and DOD to adopt a more positive assessment of the CWC's effectiveness. As a result, "At the end of the day the Intelligence Community and . . . DOD reluctantly said that CWC was marginally verifiable" (Wallerstein int., 1998). However, the damage had been done. This was compounded by the administration's ongoing failure to promote the treaty aggressively. As one observer notes, "All told, by the second anniversary of the Convention's signing, the President had publicly uttered fewer than 100 words about it" (Smithson, 1995, p. 174), concluding, "The NSC's insistence that ratification of the CWC was a central element of the administration's nonproliferation policy rang false without the involvement of Clinton, Gore, Christopher, Aspin, or his successor, William Perry" (p. 177).

With ratification going nowhere fast, its prospects took a series of blows in 1995. First, the Republicans gained control of both houses of Congress, and Senator Jesse Helms, an avowed CWC opponent, assumed leadership of the main committee responsible for ratifying treaties. Then, a few months later, existing doubts about verification were enhanced by dramatic revelations that Iraq had been able to conceal significant elements of its CW stockpile from UNSCOM inspections (int.). Shortly after these revelations, a senior intelligence official went out on a limb by bluntly telling Congress, "Some chemical weapons-capable countries, such as Iran, have signed the CWC but show no signs of ending their programs" (Oehler tst., 1995). The administration also was forced to admit that it suspected Russia might be cheating on the BDA, by extension casting doubt on whether it would comply in good faith with the CWC (ACDA off., 1998; OSD off., 1997a; *Washington Times*, 8/8/96). Even Secretary of Defense William Perry (tst., 1996), sent along with Secretary of State Warren Christopher to reassure the Senate that the CWC was effectively verifiable, admitted under questioning that this assessment applied only to the destruction of *declared* stockpiles, and that verification of covert production and stockpiles remained uncertain.

At the same time that the Clinton administration was undertaking this tepid ratification campaign, a slew of high-ranking former officials was publicly speaking out against it. Former Reagan administration officials Frank Gaffney and Kathleen Bailey had been actively attacking the treaty in editorial articles almost from the moment it was signed. However, the campaign against the Convention reached new heights in an extraordinary open letter sent to Senate Majority Leader Trent Lott on 6 September 1996 from numerous former top officials, including many involved in negotiating the CWC, urging the Senate to reject ratification. This devastating letter was signed by, among others, seven former cabinet officers (including three secretaries of defense), two former national security advisors, twelve retired senior generals and admirals, and dozens of other former senior officials from NSC, State, Commerce, Defense, and other agencies (Cheney et al., 1996). Judging that it would lose a Senate vote, the administration was forced to withdraw the CWC from Senate consideration.

Faced with this humiliating foreign policy defeat, the Clinton administration made CWC ratification a high foreign policy priority as it entered its second term. Believing that the Senate would be compelled by the prospect of the CWC entering into force without the United States as an original States Party, the administration tacitly precipitated this crisis by discretely encouraging Hungary to start the six-month countdown to entry into force by depositing its instrument of ratification in late 1996 ([ACDA] int.).[16]

The United States very nearly did not ratify CWC, just as, subsequently, it would decline to ratify the Comprehensive Test Ban Treaty (CTBT). In the immediate run-up to the ratification vote, key Senate Democrats anticipated that passage was doubtful (*Washington Post*, 4/19/97). As one observers notes, "The CWC's fate really did hang in the balance until the very last moment" (Smithson, 1997b, p. 250). Senate concerns about the CWC focused on its potential negative impact on capability-denial and consequence-management efforts. The administration took pains to point out that during the negotiations the United States had successfully denuded Article X (providing for technical cooperation and assistance) and had circumvented restrictions on the Australia Group. Moreover, the administration stressed that it did not place undue faith in the treaty, repeatedly characterizing it as a marginally useful tool that would make an incremental contribution by "making clandestine weapons production and stockpiling more difficult, more risky, and more expensive" (Clinton off., 1998, p. 4). However, the Senate remained unconvinced.

Facing an uphill battle, the administration desperately scrambled to keep prospects for ratification afloat. It took the unusual step of decoupling ratification from the associated implementing legislation, concluding that the latter had no chance of passing, and in failing could drag ratification down with it ([ACDA] int.).[17] It also fell back on the argument of last resort, that the international reputation of the United States was at stake and that therefore the Senate should ratify regardless of its views on the merits of the treaty. Indeed, Senate Majority Leader Trent Lott, in explaining his eleventh-hour support for ratification, made it clear he did so only to preserve "the credibility of commitments made by two presidents of our country" (as quoted by *Arms Control Today*, 10/97).

In the end the White House was forced to agree to a number of major substantive concessions in order to narrowly scrape by with ratification. Some of the most onerous were unrelated to the treaty (e.g., abolishing ACDA). Others sought to address specific concerns about the CWC itself. For example, President Clinton provided Senator Lott with a written commitment that the president, in consultation with the Senate, would withdraw from the CWC if other States Parties put U.S. interests at risk by abusing Article X or Article XI (providing for cooperation and assistance) (*Arms Control Today*, 10/97). The White House also agreed to allow the Senate to embed twenty-eight separate conditions within the ratification legislation.[18]

Some of these conditions were designed to ensure that the CWC would not undermine other antiproliferation efforts. These included securing assurances from all AG countries that AG controls would be maintained in their current form against all non-AG countries (i.e., regardless of whether they are parties to CWC), and continuation and expansion of U.S. chemical defense programs. Other of the conditions served to abridge the treaty itself, including giving the president authority to refuse a challenge inspection on national security grounds, prohibiting OPCW inspectors from removing chemical samples from U.S. territory, interpreting restrictions on the use of RCAs so as to preserve the then current U.S. guidelines, narrowing the number of U.S. industrial facilities required to provide declarations, and prohibiting U.S. contributions to the OPCW voluntary fund for defense assistance under Article XI (U.S. Cong. Senate off., 1997).[19]

Taken together, U.S. ratification conditions amounted to the most grudging approval imaginable, designed to send an unmistakable signal of no confidence. As one analyst points out, if other countries opt to match these conditions, the treaty in effect will be eviscerated (Tucker, 1998a).

Although ratification occurred in time to allow the United States to become a charter member of the OPCW, it still had no national implementing legislation. As a result, the United States was unable to meet its obligations to provide commercial data declarations, putting it in "technical violation" of the CWC a month after it had joined. This state of membership limbo lasted for nearly two years. One observer, commenting on this period, concludes, "The United States has been the malignancy in the midst of the CWC" (Smithson, 1998a).

Congress and the Clinton administration finally agreed on implementing legislation on 21 October 1998. However, the administration failed to persuade Congress to soften the ratification conditions, which were codified in the implementing legislation (*CBW Bulletin* [42], 1998). Thus, while the United States faces the future as a full CWC member, it can hardly be characterized as a maximalist participant. Nor is it likely that Washington's enthusiasm will increase during the new Bush administration, particularly considering that in the past Vice President Cheney was among the Convention's most prominent critics.

Other Nonpossession Responses

The United States never promoted regional CW nonpossession instruments prior to the advent of the CWC. The Reagan administration flatly rejected a proposal by the East German SED party and the West German SPD party for a CW-free zone in Central Europe in September 1985 (Burck & Flowerree, 1991). A similar proposal a few months later by Senator Albert Gore, Jr., likewise garnered no meaningful support in Washington. The only successful CW-free zone, the Mendoza agreement, negotiated by Argentina, Brazil, and Chile prior to completion of the CWC, does not appear to have involved Washington. Likewise, the United States has not participated in or promoted regional instruments to complement the CWC.

Consequence-Management

Counterproliferation

CBW counterproliferation, like other elements of proliferation response, evolved from concepts that were originally oriented toward the Cold War–era Soviet threat. The United States maintained an extensive chemical defense program throughout the Cold War. These efforts were bolstered significantly during the first Reagan administration (L. Dunn et al., 1992). From the mid-1980s through the Gulf War, DOD maintained a steady annual budget of $500–600 million on its CBW defense program (U.S. Cong. House off., 1993). The first explicit reorientation of these capabilities to countering the proliferation threat occurred prior to the Gulf War, under the aegis of the Pentagon's working group on proliferation countermeasures. However, it was the Gulf War that prompted a significant focus on so-called regional CW programs. In 1992 the Pentagon announced a coordinated effort to develop active and passive CBW defenses to counter proliferation threats. The first active-defense element of this program came in a solicitation for bids by the Air Force in August 1992 for development of a warhead that could destroy or disable CBW and bulk agents (*CWC Bulletin* [17], 1992).

Expenditures on CBW counterproliferation have risen dramatically since the launch of the Defense Counterproliferation Initiative in late 1993. The total non-missile-related counterproliferation annual budget for the 1998 fiscal year was $4.9 billion. Moreover, the Quadrennial Defense Review augmented this by an additional $1 billion through to the 2003 fiscal year for CBW protective equipment (*Disarmament Diplomacy* [17], 1997). Counterforce programs now include the Air Force's Agent Defeat Weapon program and Deeply Buried Target Defeat Capability program. Defensive programs now include development and acquisition of numerous systems to improve capabilities in contamination avoidance, protection, and decontamination and treatment (OSD off., 1997a). The Pentagon has also trained and assigned National Guard units in ten states to assist civilian authorities in the event of a CBW attack, effectively the first civil defense program in decades (*Washington Post*, 5/23/98). In sum, proliferation-oriented chemical defense has become a major military priority, toward which the United States has increasingly directed significant resources.

Deterrence

In-kind deterrence was the mainstay of the U.S. response to the Soviet CW threat during the Cold War. As concern about non-Soviet CW programs emerged in the late 1980s, deterrence in-kind was explicitly extended to cover these threats. As already discussed, President Bush's decision to renounce retaliation in-kind shortly after the Gulf War had been bitterly opposed by the Pentagon. However, the incoming Clinton administration asserted that the CWC did not obviate the need for effective deterrence against CW attacks. It was willing to forgo retaliation in-kind, but only because the Pentagon believed that it could attain effective and credible deterrence by other means (Slocombe tst., 1994).

Washington was extremely mindful that its implied threat of nuclear retaliation may have been the primary reason that Iraq did not use CBW against coalition forces during the Gulf War (Wallerstein int., 1998). Consequently, it began inching steadily toward an explicit policy of nuclear deterrence against all forms of WMD. As often happens, the first suggestion along these lines came from a quasi-official advisory panel, chaired by former Air Force Secretary Thomas Reed, which in January 1992 recommended that, following implementation of START II, residual U.S. nuclear forces should be assigned the new mission of deterring CBW attacks by Third World countries (*CWC Bulletin* [15], 1992).

In the first year of the Clinton administration, Secretary of Defense Les Aspin directed his agency to conduct an official review of U.S. nuclear doctrine, including whether to act on the recommendations of the Reed panel (*Washington Post*, 10/19/93). According to press reports, this issue led to a rift in the interagency, with some agencies worried that threatening nuclear retaliation against CBW attacks would violate existing U.S. assurances that it would not threaten to attack NPT states with nuclear weapons. Because of this internal dispute, the United States adopted an intentionally ambiguous CBW deterrence posture. For instance, when Aspin's Nuclear Posture Review was finally released, it did not mention CBW deterrence. However, at the attendant press conference, Deputy Secretary of Defense John Deutch stated that, despite the document's silence on the issue, countries contemplating CBW use would have to take into account the possibility of a U.S. nuclear response (*CWC Bulletin* [26], 1994). When pressed by Congress to clarify this posture, another senior Defense official offered the following equivocal testimony: "For obvious reasons, we do not choose to specify in detail what responses we would make to a chemical attack. However, as we stated during the Gulf War . . . the response will be 'absolutely overwhelming' and 'devastating'" (Slocombe tst., 1994, p. 3). Former Assistant Secretary of Defense Ashton Carter (int., 1999) notes that while having the option of nuclear retaliation, the Pentagon also concentrated on developing a range of intermediate nonnuclear responses, in order to provide a credible deterrent to the full range of CBW threats.

In recent years the United States has moved toward a more explicit nuclear deterrence posture. When the United States signed the African Nuclear-Weapon Free Zone Treaty on 11 April 1996, the Clinton White House issued a statement reaffirming testimony by Secretary of Defense Perry the month before asserting that the United States did not interpret this obligation as limiting its options to respond to a WMD attack by another party (*Disarmament Diplomacy* [4], 1996; Schwartz, 1998). In 1997 the issue was formally revisited in a second review of U.S. nuclear strategy. In the context of this review, a senior Defense official bluntly testified, "The knowledge that the U.S. has a powerful and ready nuclear capability is, I believe, a significant deterrent to proliferators to even contemplate the use of WMD" (Slocombe tst., 1997, p. 5).

An explicit shift to nuclear deterrence was formalized in November 1997 by Presidential Decision Directive-60, revising U.S. nuclear doctrine, which reputedly authorizes nuclear weapons to be used against rogue states in retaliation for WMD use (Schwartz, 1998). "The new circumstances associated with the spread of chemical and biological weapons," a subsequent study notes approvingly, "have expanded the role of nuclear weapons to deter such use" (Joseph & Lehman, 1998). Interestingly, one of the authors of this study is now President George W. Bush's chief White House aide for proliferation response issues. Not surprising, the Bush administration has stressed the need to transform deterrence in order to refocus it on proliferation threats, including CBW attacks (*New York Times*, 5/1/01).

CASE STUDY: BIOLOGICAL WEAPONS

Capability-Denial

National Export Controls

Restrictions on biological agents and associated dual-use equipment were considered as early as 1984, when the United States instituted export controls on CW precursors (Olmer tst., 1984). However, it was not until 1989, the first year of the Bush administration, that any BW-related nonproliferation controls were put in place, covering just a few organisms. These modest unilateral controls applied to all destinations except Canada, with a policy of automatic denial for exports to Cuba, Vietnam, Cambodia, North Korea, Iran, Iraq, Syria, and Libya ([ACDA] int.; U.S. Cong. OTA off., 1993).

The Gulf War, and subsequent revelations that Iraq had obtained pathogens from U.S. companies, prompted the first serious effort to establish comprehensive BW-related nonproliferation controls. In addition to creating catch-all controls, President Bush in November 1990 ordered the Commerce Department to expand unilateral controls on BW-relevant items and to coordinate licensing decisions on these with State and Defense. In response, Commerce added controls on exports of dual-use production equipment to twenty-eight destinations. After 1991, the United States expanded these controls in line with agreed AG requirements. U.S. controls have by and large remained stable since the final expansion of the AG lists in June 1993 (ACDA off., 1997b; GAO off., 1992).

Multilateral Export-Control Regime: Australia Group

As soon as the United States instituted its own unilateral BW-related controls in early 1989, it sought to multilateralize this effort, proposing to widen the scope of the AG to include BW nonproliferation. As one key official states, "We were the ones who played a big role in pushing for biological controls" ([State] int.).

The AG agreed to add BW nonproliferation to its basic mission in June 1990, although no specific rules were adopted (ACDA off., 1997b; Clarke tst., 1990). However, following the Iraqi invasion of Kuwait several weeks later, Washington significantly intensified its push for concrete measures. At the December 1990 meeting, the United States proposed specific BW-relevant controls, as well as CBW catch-all controls (Clarke tst., 1991). Following intense intersessional lobbying by Washington (Fox off., 1991), the Group adopted controls on biological agents, toxins, and associated equipment in December 1991. These controls were expanded further in June 1992, including the addition of animal and plant pathogens (ACDA off., 1997b). The following month, President Bush directed the interagency to seek to expand AG controls further on BW-related items (L. Dunn et al., 1992). In June 1993, the AG again expanded its lists of biological agents and dual-use equipment, fully meeting U.S. expectations for comprehensive controls (ACDA off., 1997; [State] int.).

The United States was satisfied after 1993 with the scope and operation of AG activities against BW proliferation (Smoldone int., 1998; Fitzgibbon int., 1998; [State] int.). However, Washington soon faced a new challenge to the status quo. Just as some NAM states had used the CWC negotiations to attack the AG, it again came under fire in the negotiations to create a new BWC compliance regime. Moreover, believing themselves to have been misled in the CWC context by the 1992 O'Sullivan Statement, opponents of the AG were determined not to again allow their demands to be sidestepped with vague assurances. Ergo, the United States and its AG partners came under intense pressure to agree to eliminate or weaken the regime as a condition for achieving a BWC protocol.

Washington, for its part, categorically maintained that it would not brook any compromise on the AG in order to strengthen the BWC. The chief U.S. negotiator for the BWC talks indicates that the interagency was wary of this tradeoff all along, and that the United States had always been fully prepared to stand alone to break consensus. He amplifies, "The idea that this becomes a free shot at restricting our national sovereign right to work anti-proliferation is . . . an issue . . . on which we have absolutely no flexibility" (Mahley int., 1998). Acting Undersecretary of State John Holum echoed much the same thing to the press on 6 October 1998: "We will not, in the name of strengthening compliance with this treaty, allow an undercutting of the regimes that presently limit proliferation of biological weapons. We think those are indispensable and need to be continued" (*CBW Bulletin* [48], 1998, p. 42).

A number of officials privately observe that the Clinton administration was not in a position to soften this stance even if it had wanted to, because the Senate would almost certainly have refused to ratify any agreement that undermined the AG. Provisions thought to undermine the AG were, in fact, one of the significant factors that led the new Bush administration to reject the outcome of the protocol talks (*Washington Times*, 7/25/01).

Wider Export-Control Norms

In the wake of the Gulf War, the United States started to promote wider application of BW controls in conjunction with its standing CW-related efforts. At the September 1991 Third BWC Review Conference—even before the AG had incorporated biological controls—the United States urged BWC members to implement national export controls and sanctions along the lines of its own, pursuant to implementing the treaty's general prohibition on assisting BW programs (Fox off., 1991; Wright, 1993).

Once the AG adopted comprehensive BW-related controls, Washington folded its efforts to widen biological controls into its ongoing campaign to promote universal adherence to AG rules. The Bush administration placed particular emphasis on the need to persuade FSU states, especially Russia, to enact strict BW-related export controls (L. Dunn et al., 1992).

The United States has continued to use the BWC as a legal justification to urge non-AG countries to adopt applicable export controls. Moreover, unlike in the case of the CWC, Washington has refused to concede any special exemptions for transfers between BWC members. For example, at the 1996 RevCon the United States stated,

Some would weaken the Convention by twisting Article III into a mandate to let all equipment and material transfers presumptively run free to States Parties. But surely we know, based on experience, that membership in a regime is no guarantee of compliance. The Article III prohibition on proliferant transfers and assistance is and must remain absolute. Its duty as to vigilance cannot be suspended as to members, but rather demands constant attention as to all. (Holum off., 1996, p. 2)

National Enforcement Mechanisms

The United States was constrained in undertaking national efforts to prevent BW-related transfers in the 1980s by its own lack of export controls (Holmes tst., 1989b). However, since adopting export controls in 1989, the United States has extended virtually all of its national enforcement mechanisms for CW to also cover BW, including interdiction, sanctions, and incentives.

Other Capability-Denial Responses

Besides general initiatives like ACME, there have been no apparent cases where the United States has tried to foster targeted arrangements specifically against BW programs. There also have been no apparent cases of sabotage or destruction targeting BW programs, other than in the unique case of Iraq.

Nonpossession Norm-Building

Global Nonpossession Norm: Biological Weapons Convention

Throughout the Cold War, for all intents the United States saw the BWC solely as a means to outlaw Soviet BW capabilities. It had agreed to the Convention in this context during détente in the early 1970s. Although the treaty made no pretext at verification, Washington was not concerned about this weakness, regarding BW disarmament as inherently unverifiable and, in any case, having nothing to lose having unilaterally renounced BW already (Chevrier, 1995; Harris, 1987). The BWC attracted scant notice from American policy makers after entering into force. Although the United States supported adding a few anodyne transparency declarations at the first BWC Review Conference in 1980, it otherwise neglected BWC implementation.

In the wake of gathering information about what increasingly seemed like a suspicious 1979 outbreak of anthrax in the Soviet Union, the incoming Reagan administration grew convinced that Moscow was pursuing a large-scale offensive BW program in flagrant violation of the BWC. Soviet noncompliance represented virtually the only U.S. concern going into the 1986 BWC Review Conference. But, unlike some Western governments, Washington stoutly rejected trying to strengthen compliance by adding verification measures. The interagency unanimously agreed that, since meaningful verification was deemed impossible, it was better to have this clearly understood by the rest of the world (Feith int., 1998; Mahley int., 1998). This position was bluntly articulated in a press leak well in advance of the Review Conference (*Washington Times*, 6/9/86).

As an alternative to verification, the United States sought to get the Review Conference to mandate national declarations on prior BW stockpiles and production facilities and whether and how these had been destroyed or converted (Sims, 1990a).[20] Although this initiative was blocked, U.S. proposals to enhance the existing transparency declarations were adopted as a modest package of voluntary CBMs.[21] However, the United States was so focused on Soviet cheating, and so convinced that the Convention was irredeemably flawed, that it actually blocked proposals to widen the BWC's normative nonproliferation role by having the Review Conference issue a statement encouraging new states to join (DFAT off., 1990b).

By the next Review Conference in 1991, while remaining deeply concerned about Soviet noncompliance, the United States also wanted to strengthen the Convention's nonproliferation role as a global nonpossession norm. Compliance was also a key factor in this regard, since the United States believed that several other States Parties were violating the BWC; for example, China and Iran. In light of this new nonproliferation imperative, the interagency conducted a major review of the verification issue. However, this process merely served to reaffirm for all agencies that the BWC was inherently unverifiable, and that ineffective verification would be worse than no verification.

Despite pressure from other Western governments at the 1991 Review Conference, Washington refused to budge on verification, insisting that enhancing existing CBMs was the only practical way to strengthen the treaty (Mahley int., 1998; Moodie int., 1998). The chief U.S. delegate recalls "much of the rest of the world saying some verification is better than none, and the U.S. position being bad verification is worse than none" (Moodie int., 1998). In addition, in the absence of verification, the United States ruled out any type of multilateral organization to assist in implementing the treaty (ACDA & State tst., 1990). It likewise opposed proposals by many Western governments to develop indicative lists and associated quantitative thresholds to clarify what items and activities were prohibited in order to facilitate verification (GAO off., 1992; Moodie int., 1998).[22]

As a compromise, Washington agreed to go along with creating an intersessional working group of verification experts (VEREX) to study the technical feasibility of verification. However, it did not intend for this process to lead to anything: "VEREX from the Unites States standpoint . . . was something which we were prepared to allow . . . on the presumption that it would demonstrate the futility of the exercise" (Mahley int., 1998). Accordingly, Washington insisted on an extremely restrictive mandate for VEREX; for example, limiting its duration, precluding it from developing draft provisions (or even recommending options), excluding nongovernment participants, and most important, requiring consensus on its final report (Australia off., 1991; DFAT off., 1991e; GAO off., 1992).

Not surprising, at the first VEREX session in early 1992 U.S. scientists categorically averred that they knew of no way to make the BWC verifiable. The U.S. delegation also stated that it would oppose any measures that could impinge on either proprietary commercial information or military biodefense programs (GAO off., 1992).

Soon after VEREX began, Russian President Boris Yeltsin unexpectedly confirmed that the former Soviet regime had maintained an offensive BW program in violation of the BWC, which he pledged to terminate. Consistent with the pattern set in the CW area, the United States opted to address this disarmament opportunity bilaterally—or in this case trilaterally with the British—in order to allow the type of intrusive on-site compliance measures that it was opposing multilaterally (Goodby int., 1998).[23] However, some agencies had opposed this process, arguing that it would give ammunition to proponents of BWC verification (Rostow int., 1998).

Notwithstanding this trilateral flirtation with verification, Washington held firmly to its opposition to any BWC verification. NSDD-70, signed at the end of the Bush administration, committed the United States to maintaining the status quo on the BWC (L. Dunn et al., 1992). At the penultimate third round of VEREX talks in May–June 1993, the new Clinton administration reaffirmed this position, stating that it would block consensus on any positive assessments in a final report (DFAT off., 1993f).

Just as it seemed that VEREX would wind down to an inconclusive finish—which of course had been the U.S. plan from the start—a dramatic policy reversal was hatched by a junior member of the new NSC staff. PDD-13, signed by President Clinton in September to replace NSDD-70, contained language supporting new measures to help deter violations of the BWC (White House off., 1993). As a senior official explained to Congress, "To strengthen the Biological Weapons Convention (BWC), we are parting company with the previous administration and promoting new measures designed to increase transparency of activities and facilities that could have biological weapons applications, thereby increasing confidence in compliance with the Convention" (Davis tst., 1993, p. 60). This change stood as the only major shift in the new Clinton administration's nonproliferation strategy.

By all accounts, the White House took this step over the vigorous, unanimous objections of the interagency (Alessi int., 1998; Mahley int., 1998; [NSC] int.; Wallerstein int., 1998; [State] int.). "They simply said 'we're going to do it,'" recalls one official, "and then turned around to the operating parts of the government afterwards and said 'now you guys make it work'" ([ACDA] int.). In explaining this unprecedented action, officials from different agencies point to the personal agenda of a single low-level political appointee on the still inexperienced Clinton NSC staff, as well as a general desire by the White House to take credit for an innovative nonproliferation initiative ([ACDA] int.; [State] int.; Wallerstein int., 1998).

Stuck with the virtual certainty of a new negotiating process, the interagency launched a vigorous rear-guard effort to stall and rein in the entire endeavor. Almost immediately, under intense interagency pressure, the NSC was forced to clarify that the administration still unambiguously considered the BWC to be unverifiable ([ACDA] int.; [NSC] int.; Wallerstein int., 1998; [State] int.). Accordingly, at the final VEREX meeting and subsequently, whereas the United States agreed to support a generally positive report, it nonetheless insisted that the goal for any future negotiations should be "transparency" or "compliance enhancement" rather than "verification." It also insisted on a formal reservation stating that it would insist on protecting proprietary and national security information, and noting that this might prove infeasible (*CWC Bulletin* [22], 1993, [26], 1994; DFAT off., 1993i). It reiterated this stance at the 1994 BWC Special Conference that provided the mandate for an Ad Hoc Group (AHG) to negotiate a legally binding compliance protocol (Dando, 1995).

The United States embarked on the BWC protocol negotiations in 1995 without a consensus on a desired outcome. The NSC staff remained isolated in seeking support for highly intrusive measures, with the interagency continuing to resist anything resembling a verification regime ([NSC] int.; Wallerstein int., 1998). For example, the Commerce, Defense, and Energy departments adamantly opposed any type of routine inspections, and insisted that initiating challenge inspections should require a high standard of evidence (Tucker, 1998c).

Revelations soon after the start of AHG talks regarding the wholesale failure of UNSCOM to detect significant parts of Iraq's BW program or even to prevent its further development profoundly reinforced interagency skepticism about the AHG process ([State] int.; Wallerstein int., 1998).

In May 1996, the NSC staff was further isolated when the Pharmaceutical Research and Manufacturers of America (PhRMA), representing one of the major domestic BW-relevant industries, announced its formal opposition to measures that would jeopardize confidential business information, including routine inspections of commercial facilities (Woollett, 1998). In November PhRMA took this position directly to the Fourth BWC RevCon (Thraenert, 1997).

The lack of agreement between the entire interagency bureaucracy and industry on one hand and the NSC staff on the other led to the United States having no negotiating flexibility during the first three years of the AHG process. In practice, this left the United States with a minimalist stance. For example, in a speech to the UNGA in September 1996, President Clinton stated that the United States supported on-site inspections in cases of suspected BW use or unusual disease outbreaks (*CWC Bulletin* [34], 1996), conspicuously omitting any mention not only of routine inspections, but even challenge inspections of suspicious production or storage facilities. Many observers attribute the almost total lack of momentum in the AHG during this period to U.S. unwillingness to consider compromises on key issues such as routine inspections (Chevrier, 1995, 1996; Dando, 1997; MacEachin, 1998; Smithson, 1998a; Tucker, 1998c).

In a bid to salvage the AHG process, the NSC staff in late 1997 put high-level pressure on the interagency to adopt a more forward-leaning position ([State] int.; Wallerstein int., 1998). In the face of stiff resistance from key agency heads, a compromise was finally reached at a January 1998 meeting attended by Secretary of State Albright, Secretary of Defense Cohen, and Secretary of Commerce Daly, just in time to be announced in President Clinton's State of the Union speech *(Washington Post,* 1/28/98). However, this hard-won deal embraced only modest concessions, and, more important, remained explicitly contingent on approval by private industry.

Under the January 1998 initiative, the Clinton administration pledged to ask relevant U.S. industries to consider a package including voluntary visits (i.e., by industry's invitation) at declared facilities, reasonable clarifying visits at declared facilities to address specific problems arising from national declarations, and challenge inspections at undeclared facilities based on the approval of a simple majority of the protocol implementing organization's Executive Council. Significantly, this tentative negotiating position did not include any type of mandatory routine (i.e., random) inspections at any declared facilities, including even high-risk facilities (*CBW Bulletin* [39], 1998; Tucker, 1998c). It also did not alter Washington's implacable view that the BWC was not verifiable, and its resultant unwillingness to permit references to verification (or even the looser term "evaluation") in the draft text (Mahley int., 1998; [State] int.). One independent assessment at the time concludes that the Clinton package "will prevent the erection of any meaningful system and thus make the protocol a void document" (Müller, 1998).

Even this relatively modest package of concessions failed to ever become the U.S. negotiating position. Industry continued to object to key parts of virtually every element of the president's January 1998 initiative, as well as aspects of the existing U.S. negotiating position. For example, PhRMA opposed routine inspections even on a voluntary basis. It also insisted that challenge inspections require approval by a supermajority of the Executive Council, that mandatory declarations not be expanded beyond those required in the present voluntary CBMs, and that additional definitions were needed to clarify what items were to be prohibited (Tucker, 1998c; Woollett, 1998).

Almost a year after his January 1998 initiative, because of continuing opposition by industry, President Clinton could only repeat that "the United States will work closely with U.S. industry to develop

U.S. negotiating positions and then to reach international agreement on: declarations, nonchallenge clarifying visits, and challenge investigations" (Clinton off., 1998, p. 5). This agenda remained essentially unchanged for the remainder of Clinton's tenure, with little apparent progress or flexibility on core issues in Geneva despite the looming target of completing a protocol by the 2001 BWC Review Conference.

As for the attitude of those responsible for carrying out the negotiations under these circumstances, one key State Department official interviewed at the time lamented, "The bureaucracy is not very happy with the whole thing, and the issue is plagued by major disconnects between the working-level bureaucracy and the working-level [Clinton] White House." Summing up the mood that prevailed in the final two Clinton years, this official noted that while the United States remained willing to consider measures that might usefully enhance transparency and deter violations, it believed that the exercise had at best marginal utility, and therefore Washington was unwilling to pay any high costs, especially since the Senate had no interest in ratifying an overly ambitious compliance instrument.

Given the legacy of staunch interagency opposition in the Clinton administration, together with the fact that the first Bush administration had opposed ever having entered BWC-related negotiations in the first place, it is no surprise that the incoming Bush administration quickly decided to cut its losses. Having inherited a rolling text that remained peppered with hundreds of brackets reflecting fundamental disagreements, along with what it saw as an irredeemably flawed compromise from Ad Hoc Group Chairman Tibor Toth, and with a negotiating deadline looming that in practical terms made the Toth text a take-it-or-leave-it proposition, the Bush administration decided to walk away from the Ad Hoc Group outcome. With a new NSC team leading the review, it took just a few months to decide that the Toth text was unacceptable, and probably unsalvageable (*New York Times*, 7/25/01; *Washington Post*, 7/25/01, 7/26/01; *Washington Times*, 2/25/01).

Other Nonpossession Responses

The United States has never attempted to supplement the BWC with regional–targeted nonpossession arrangements.

Consequence–Management

Counterproliferation

The United States all but abandoned biodefense after the BWC entered into force. Although the Reagan administration revived the program in response to a perceived Soviet threat, it remained a far lower priority than chemical defense (Hinds tst., 1989a).

This heritage of inattention left a gap in U.S. biodefense capabilities when priorities shifted from Russia to counterproliferation in the early 1990s. A 1992 study notes that in contrast to robust CW-related capabilities, "Reliable BW agent detection technologies do not yet exist, current stocks of U.S. vaccines and medicines are inadequate, and U.S. forces and civil defense personnel are completely lacking in training and other forms of preparedness for biological warfare" (L. Dunn et al., 1992, p. IV-2).

That same year, the Pentagon designated BW defense as a priority acquisition requirement for the first time, increasing BW-related programs to over 40 percent of the overall CBW-defense budget (*CWC Bulletin* [16], 1992). In its final budget request, the Bush administration the next year sought a significant additional increase in biodefense funding (*CWC Bulletin* [20], 1993).

The Clinton administration accorded highest priority to BW in its counterproliferation efforts (Carter int., 1999). In recent years the Pentagon has developed new detection and protective technology and equipment. It also has invested massively in programs to develop up to eighteen new vaccines for BW-related diseases, as well as prophylactic and therapeutic treatments for nerve agents. In May 1998, President Clinton approved a DOD program to vaccinate all 2.4 million U.S. military personnel (i.e., active duty and reserve) against anthrax, and to begin stockpiling BW-relevant vaccines and antibiotics for civilians, at a projected cost of billions of dollars (OSD off., 1997a; *Washington Post*, 5/21/98, 5/23/98; *CBW Convention Bulletin* [41], 1998).

Its commitment to BW counterproliferation has also led the United States to shoulder a high-profile, controversial dispute within the U.N. system. In December 1994, Washington and Moscow agreed to suspend plans to destroy the world's last known samples of the smallpox virus, which each held, contravening a consensus recommendation by the World Health Organization (WHO) (*CWC Bulletin* [23], 1994).[24] Over the objections of the Pentagon (as well as the British government), the Clinton NSC staff opted to compromise, agreeing to merely defer destruction for several years in order to allow further defensive research (int.; *CWC Bulletin* [27], 1995). However, as the June 1999 deadline loomed, the White House had second thoughts. A scientific advisory panel was convened to review the issue, concluding that the United States needed to retain its smallpox as a hedge against covert BW programs (*Washington Post*, 3/15/99, 3/16/99). Citing this defensive requirement, the United States announced in April 1999 that it was again shifting position to oppose destruction, compelling a special WHO conference to agree to suspend destruction indefinitely (*Washington Post*, 4/23/99, 5/25/99).

Deterrence

Unlike in the CW case, the United States was willing during the Cold War to forgo in-kind deterrence against BW. That said, as an unnamed official in the Reagan administration stated to the press, "The thought that you could deter the use of biological weapons through the threat of U.S. strategic nuclear weapons being used was an important argument behind President Nixon's unilateral renunciation of biological weapons in 1969" (*Washington Times*, 6/9/86, p. 3).

Throughout the post–Cold War period, CBW deterrence has evolved as a single doctrine, but it seems likely that nuclear retaliation would be deemed more credible in the case of BW, given its far greater capacity as a mass destruction weapon.

CASE STUDY: MISSILES

Capability-Denial

National Export Controls

The first de facto export restrictions on nuclear-capable missiles were instituted as far back as 1964 by National Security Action Memorandum-294, "U.S. Nuclear and Strategic Delivery System Assistance to France," prohibiting transfers of strategic missiles even to close allies (Speier, 1995; State off., 1997). This was indirectly reinforced in 1972 by National Security Decision Directive-187, prohibiting technical assistance to foreign space-launch projects, in part out of concern about contributing to foreign missile capabilities (Speier, 1995). This resulted in a system of case-by-case licensing decisions. However, these were not really nonproliferation controls. Instead, they were intended chiefly to protect the commercial interests of U.S. space-launch providers, as well as to extend strategic trade controls to what had become recognized as a militarily relevant technology (Karp, 1989; Ozga, 1994; Speier, 1995).

Unilateral missile nonproliferation controls as such were instituted in 1982 as part of the missile nonproliferation policy conceived by President Reagan's NSDD-70. These regulations required case-by-case licensing on a comprehensive array of equipment and technology relevant to ballistic and cruise missiles and SLVs. Individual licensing decisions were governed by a policy to deny exports that would make more than a marginal contribution to any foreign missile program, although waivers could be considered for friends and allies (Reagan off., 1982).

Once the MTCR became operative in 1987, the United States continued to implement missile technology controls universally, with no automatic exemption for MTCR members (except Canada) (U.S. Cong.

OTA off., 1993). At the same time, Washington maintained a strict policy of denying exports of MTCR items to specified countries of concern, as well as to specified projects of concern in other countries (LeMunyon tst., 1989b).

Washington has been among the most rigorous of the MTCR partners in its national interpretation and implementation of the regime's guidelines.[25] For example, it has been reasonably consistent in denying exports that would contribute to space-launch programs, from the outset refusing to distinguish such civilian projects from military missile programs (Holmes tst., 1989c). As a Bush administration official testified in 1991, "While launch *services* must be available on the world market, launch *vehicles* must not" (Sokolski tst., 1991, pp. 126–127). That said, in late 1992 the Bush administration relaxed this policy for some close allies within the MTCR (Speier int., 1998; [State] int.). The Clinton administration soon after specified that, while the United States would not encourage any SLV programs (including within the MTCR), an absolute prohibition on transfers would apply only to new SLV programs outside the MTCR, thus permitting space cooperation with Russia and Ukraine (White House off., 1993). Nonetheless, the United States retained among the strictest national prohibitions on assisting SLV programs.

The scope of U.S. export controls generally has tracked with the MTCR since it was established, with changes first being negotiated multilaterally. However, the Bush administration instituted some unilateral restrictions beyond MTCR requirements. For example, on 5 June 1989 it instituted a ban on exports of satellites and associated components to China as part of wider human rights sanctions in the response to the Tiananmen Square massacre. This ban was expanded a few months later to prohibit Chinese launches of U.S. satellites without a case-by-case presidential waiver. On 27 May 1991, the White House further strengthened this prohibition for nonproliferation reasons, announcing that as a matter of policy it would no longer provide such waivers, and that henceforth it would deny licenses for exports of high-speed computers that could be used to assist Chinese missile development (Rennack off., 1996). In addition, catch-all controls were introduced in 1990 under EPCI regulations. Finally, the United States began to use export controls and other tactics to block U.S. companies from purchasing missile- or SLV-related goods or services from foreign entities involved in proliferation, in order to cut off proliferators from indirect financial support (Smoldone int., 1998).[26]

The Clinton administration sought to ease a few of these unilateral measures to some extent. In 1993 it loosened restrictions on mid-range computers (i.e., under 1,500 MTOPS), and in 1996 again lowered this threshold, citing wide international availability due to rapid advances in commercial technology. However, Congress partially rolled back these reforms the following year because of proliferation concerns (U.S. Cong. Senate off., 1998). Also in 1996, the administration eased restrictions on civilian access to the most accurate version of the Defense Department's Global Positioning System (GPS) (*Washington Post*, 3/30/96). Case-by-case presidential waivers to allow U.S. companies to launch their satellites on Chinese SLVs were also reinstated early in the administration. Again, responding to evidence that some inappropriate technology transfers may have occurred, Congress in 1998 imposed a total ban on Chinese launches of U.S. satellites, and reclassified all types of satellites as weapons licensed by the State Department rather than dual-use items licensed by the Commerce Department (*New York Times*, 5/21/98, 9/18/98; *Washington Post*, 7/18/98, 5/12/98).

The United States on balance retains stringent unilateral controls well beyond MTCR requirements. These are especially rigorous regarding specific countries of concern.

Multilateral Export-Control Regime: Missile Technology Control Regime

The November 1982 presidential directive establishing unilateral missile nonproliferation export controls also mandated simultaneously trying to multilateralize this effort (Reagan off., 1982). Beginning with Britain, the United States put out feelers to its G-7 Economic Summit partners almost immediately to sound out their willingness to participate in an export-control regime (Ozga, 1994). As one U.S. participant explains this choice of interlocutors, "The group was large enough to influence the rest of the world with its policies but small enough to try to keep the talks under wraps" (Speier, 1995, p. 19). The unambiguous U.S. objective going into this process was to get the most stringent regime possible, explicitly using COCOM as a model (McNamara int., 1998; [State] int.).

In March 1993 the United States initiated what would prove to be a long and rancorous multilateral negotiation by circulating a confidential paper called "Missile Technology Control" proposing common G-7 export-control guidelines for ballistic and cruise missiles and associated technology. These would include provisions for consultations and revisions, and would be implemented nationally using a detailed annex of equipment and technology to be updated yearly, with national participation codified by the exchange of confidential diplomatic notes. Although vague on details, this proposal laid out the basic structure and procedures of what eventually would become the MTCR (Speier, 1995).

Prior to the first round of secret multilateral negotiations in June 1983, the United States supplemented its guidelines paper with a detailed technical proposal, which defined nuclear-capable missiles as systems capable of carrying a 500-kilogram payload to a range of 300 kilometers with an accuracy of 10 kilometers circular error of probability. It explicitly stated that civilian SLVs would be treated the same as offensive missiles under this definition. It also provided a specific "short list" of key items to be controlled, including missiles, major subsystems, and complete production facilities. Finally, it proposed developing a "watch list" of less-sensitive dual-use items. At the meeting, Washington obtained agreement in principle on this technical package (Speier, 1995).

Despite this promising start, the interagency had been unable prior to the inaugural meeting to agree on specific guidelines for controlling listed items. The Pentagon wanted to propose an absolute prohibition on transferring "short list" items to nonmembers other than by unanimous consent. But State and ACDA wanted a more flexible system. After intensive interagency debate at senior levels, a compromise formula was agreed that leaned heavily toward the Pentagon's position: Category I items would require unanimous consent for export to nonmembers, Category 2 items would be subject to consultations prior to export to nonmembers, and all license applications would be prenotified to all members (Speier, 1995).

Washington encountered fierce resistance when it tabled these draft guidelines at the second round of talks. There was widespread resistance to COCOM-style consensus rules for Category I, prior consultations for Category 2, and prior notification of any license applications. In addition, two countries remained implacably opposed to including civilian SLVs in Category I. The session ended in a tense deadlock that was destined to last almost two years (McNamara int., 1998; Speier, 1995).

Throughout this period, senior Defense officials successfully resisted interagency suggestions to consider flexibility in the U.S. negotiating position. Instead, in an all out bid to sell its position, the United States launched an intensive series of bilateral meetings beginning in mid-1984 (Speier, 1995). As the chief U.S. negotiator recalls, "We had to basically badger the Europeans and push them into doing things . . . which required political and bureaucratic measures that were difficult for them to take" (McNamara int., 1998). In November 1995, bowing to this diplomatic offensive, the last allied government resisting the U.S. position on SLVs relented, allowing Category I to be finalized at a multilateral meeting the following month.[27] However, Washington had been unable to convince some countries to go along with requiring consensus approval on Category I transfers (Speier, 1995).

Faced with seemingly no possibility of getting multilateral agreement on a consensus rule, the State Department requested another interagency review. In a compromise hammered out at senior levels, the Pentagon reluctantly comprised: The interagency would harden its proposal on transfers of Category I production facilities to an absolute prohibition, but soften its position on other Category I transfers to a "strong presumption of denial" except on rare occasions. Moreover, no explicit restrictions would be put on interregime trade. The United States tabled this package in February 1986. It warned that this represented a major concession, amounting to weaker rules than Washington had wanted, and that it was absolutely unwilling to compromise further. Although negotiations continued for another year, this compromise ultimately was accepted, with minor modifications (McNamara int., 1998; Speier, 1995). In the end, Washington by and large had succeeded in fashioning a multilateral instrument in the image of its own national policies.

The fundamental tensions between Washington and its European allies did not end with the successful culmination of the MTCR negotiations. Indeed, friction surfaced almost at once over how to divulge the existence of the new regime, with the Europeans objecting to U.S. plans for a high-profile announcement by President Reagan. Washington was forced to scale back its announcement to a nonetheless well-publicized statement issue by the White House press secretary in the president's name, along with a State Department press conference (*New York Times*, 4/17/87; Speier, 1995; *Washington Post*, 4/18/87, 4/20/87). This discord foreshadowed a struggle within the fledgling Regime, with the United States fighting to assert its interpretation of the compromises embodied in the sometimes vague and contradictory language of the Guidelines and Annex.

In the MTCR's first years, the United States worked to solidify its interpretation that the Guidelines applied to all Category I programs, regardless of whether these were civilian SLVs or the country concerned did not have a nuclear weapons program. However, some partners, in particular France, resisted this strict interpretation (Holmes tst., 1989c; Sokolski tst., 1990a, 1990b; Verville tst., 1990; Zimmerman int., 1998).[28] The United States also sought to strengthen implementation by proposing that the Regime adopt a common list of programs and countries of concern. Again though, some partners refused, leaving Washington to circulate its own such list, which it urged partners to consider in their national implementation (LeMunyon tst., 1989b; Zimmerman int., 1998).

In addition to continuing to work to build support for U.S. interpretations of the Guidelines, the Bush administration pressed to strengthen and expand the Regime's institutional scope. In October 1989, Vice President Dan Quayle publicly called for all European Community (EC) states to join. The administration soon expanded on this proposal, suggesting that membership should include all EC, NATO, European Space Agency, and ANZUS countries (Clarke tst., 1991).

The Gulf War provided both impetus and opportunity for Washington to renew its efforts to strengthen the MTCR, leading to a flurry of U.S. proposals at the March 1991 plenary. These reflected "U.S. determination to impose progress on the Regime and gather multilateral action in conformity with its own tightened non-proliferation regulations" (DFAT off., 1991i). For instance, having tried since 1989 to widen the Regime's scope to encompass CBW- as well as nuclear-capable missiles (Holmes tst., 1989c), the United States was finally able to obtain agreement (Ozga, 1994).[29] At the same meeting, the United States asked the Regime to adopt catch-all controls comparable to its new EPCI regulations (LeMunyon tst., 1991) Although it failed to get such controls added to the Guidelines, it continued to push in subsequent meetings and through bilateral diplomacy, with the result that a large majority of MTCR states now implement catch-all controls nationally. Finally, in order to implement these reforms within just nine months, the United States proposed, and offered to host, an unprecedented second plenary meeting later that same year (DFAT off., 1991f). By the end of the Bush administration, the Annex and Guidelines had been strengthened, membership had been expanded to include virtually all Western states, a regularized intersessional consultative mechanism had been established, and major internal differences regarding interpretation had been resolved in Washington's favor.

Satisfied that the MTCR had become a mature export-control regime, the incoming Clinton administration set out to prod it to take collective action against proliferation between nonmembers. It also sought to expand membership to include significant non-Western supplier countries, in order to expand its reach as a supply-side cartel. Since this latter policy entailed bringing hitherto targets of the Regime into the fold (e.g., Argentina, South Africa), Washington sought to institute safeguards to prevent the MTCR from becoming a "technology supermarket" for incoming members. These included seeking to bolster the rules constraining interpartner trade, only admitting countries that were already significant potential suppliers of missile technology, and only welcoming states "that subscribe to international nonproliferation standards, enforce effective export controls and [except Russia and China] abandon offensive ballistic missile programs" (White House off., 1993).

Modest membership expansion went forward, but the United States failed to win support within the Regime for any of these countervailing safeguards. It therefore was forced to resort to the extremely contentious practice of imposing its restrictive membership criteria unilaterally by exercising its consensus veto on membership applications, imposing these requirements on new members such as Argentina, Brazil, Hungary, and South Africa. Washington also delayed approving

Russian membership for several years until it was satisfied that Moscow had established a track record of responsible export behavior (although in the event this seems to have failed in ensuring Russian compliance). It also delayed applications by a number of other candidates, such as South Korea (Karika int., 1998; [State] int.).

At the same time that the United States was chastised by many of its MTCR partners for unilaterally imposing restrictive membership criteria (Karika int., 1998), the Clinton administration faced the opposite criticism from Congress and others, that these requirements were too lax in that countries could retain SLV programs (Davis tst., 1993; Bertsch & Zaborsky, 1997; Bowen, 1997; Jones & McDonough, 1998; Sokolski, 1995a, tst., 1996; Speier, 1999; *Washington Post*, 3/23/98).[30] Such skepticism apparently was shared internally by DOD, which had vigorously opposed the policy of allowing new members to retain SLVs (Speier int., 1998; Wallerstein int., 1998). Moreover, the decision to exempt Ukraine from having to forgo offensive missiles (*Arms Control Today*, 3/6/98) raised concerns that the administration was backing away from even these requirements, although it contended that Ukraine was a unique case. Nonetheless, Washington indisputably has remained the leading advocate of retaining stringent membership requirements to ensure that the Regime remains an effective supply-side cartel (Karika int., 1998; Smoldone int., 1998; [State] int.).

Washington's main focus in recent years has been to enforce strict compliance and otherwise maintain the status quo. One new U.S. initiative that is still being negotiated, however, has been to try to strengthen MTCR controls on stealthy cruise missiles (Gormley, 1998; Khromov, 1997). It is uncertain whether the new Bush administration will continue to push for this improvement in the face of determined resistence from some partners. Otherwise, however, it seems likely to try to maintain as robust a Regime as possible.

Wider Export-Control Norms

Persuading outside suppliers to implement export controls in line with MTCR norms has consistently been a critical priority for the United States. Indeed, even as it initiated the MTCR talks with the G-7, Washington was mindful of the need to secure cooperation from the two other major suppliers, the Soviet Union and China. However, fearing that Moscow and Beijing would make unacceptable demands if they were invited to participate in the negotiations—for example, guaranteeing international access to SLV technology, or trying to prohibit U.S. missile defense programs—the United States opted for a strategy of approaching them after the fact and inviting them to adhere unilaterally (Speier int., 1998). This tactic was seen as relatively low risk from a proliferation standpoint, because the Soviets in particular were already practicing unilateral restraint in exporting missile technology (McNamara int., 1998).

Once the MTCR was up and running, Washington made securing Soviet and Chinese cooperation one of its highest nonproliferation priorities. This effort began in earnest following the sale of Chinese CSS-2 IRBMs to Saudi Arabia in 1988 (Holmes tst., 1989c). The United States initiated talks with Beijing and Moscow in May 1988 to request a moratorium on any further sales of MTCR-class missiles to the Middle East (*Washington Post*, 5/26/98). Secretary of State George Shultz followed this up several weeks later by requesting full-scale consultations with China on global missile proliferation (*Washington Post*, 7/15/98). These initiatives led to a series of U.S.–Soviet meetings beginning in September 1988 (Ozga, 1994). Although China declined to participate in a similar process, the United States pressed Beijing on MTCR adherence at nearly all high-level bilateral meetings (Holmes tst., 1989c).

As a result of these bilateral efforts, the United States and Soviets issued a joint ministerial communiqué in February 1990, and then signed a joint summit declaration in June, pledging to adhere unilaterally to the MTCR (which the Russian Federation reaffirmed in January 1991 following the collapse of the USSR). The Chinese, on the other hand, would do no more than provide private assurances that they would refrain from exporting complete long-range missiles to the Middle East (Clarke tst., 1990; Ozga, 1994). Getting a Chinese commitment therefore remained a priority U.S. objective.

Washington also tried to promote MTCR adherence more generally. It had explicitly invited all nations to adhere unilaterally when it first announced the MTCR, pursuant to a provision in the Guidelines to this effect, and in 1990 masterminded an invitation by the Regime partners collectively. In parallel to the central Sino–Soviet effort, the United States launched a bilateral campaign targeting other key nonmembers—both established suppliers (e.g., Switzerland, Sweden) and emerging suppliers (e.g., Argentina, Brazil, Israel)—urging them to adhere to the MTCR as an international export-control norm (Clarke tst., 1989; Verville tst., 1990). In the two years after the MTCR was set up, the United States conducted bilateral missile nonproliferation talks with at least ten nonmember governments (Carus, 1990). These efforts were largely unsuccessful though, with even close allies like Israel firmly rebuffing such overtures (Clarke tst., 1990).

After enacting unilateral missile nonproliferation sanctions in 1990, Washington adopted a de facto strategy of exchanging sanctions waivers in return for formal bilateral agreements committing nonmember governments to adhere to the MTCR.[31] Largely due to this coercive

tactic—in some cases reinforced with the carrot of access to the lucra-
tive U.S. space launch market—Washington was able to negotiate a
series of export-control agreements with key suppliers, including Israel
(1991), Russia (1993), South Africa (1994), and Ukraine (1994) (Bertsch &
Zaborsky, 1997; Bowen, 1997; Ozga, 1994; Pikayev, Spector, Kirichenko,
& Gibson, 1998; State off., 1994; *Washington Post*, 4/10/91).

The Clinton administration expanded the practice of using linkages
to promote unilateral MTCR adherence. For example, the United States
insisted on making such adherence a formal prerequisite for membership in the new Wassenaar Arrangement. Given that many states were
extremely eager to join this successor to COCOM governing conventional arms and technology transfers, this requirement created a powerful incentive for wider MTCR adherence (McNamara tst., 1995;
Tarbell tst., 1995).

These same carrot-and-stick tactics produced only marginal results
with China. In December 1991, in return for relief from recently imposed missile sanctions, Secretary of State James Baker III received a
verbal promise from Foreign Minister Qian Qichen to adhere unilaterally to MTCR export norms. However, in seeking to formalize this
commitment in writing two months later, the Chinese backpedaled,
agreeing only to abide by the original 1987 version of the Guidelines
and explicitly refusing to recognize any version of the Annex (Rennack
off., 1996).[32] Three years of intensive bilateral diplomacy at senior levels, along with a second sanctions waiver, yielded another Chinese
ministerial statement in 1994 (Holum tst., 1998; McNamara int., 1998).
Unfortunately, this new pledge did little more than reaffirm Beijing's
equivocal stance.

In early 1998, Washington sought to resolve this issue by secretly
proposing a grand bargain: It would provide an extensive package of
incentives—including a blanket waiver to Tiananmen Square sanctions
and guaranteed access to the U.S. satellite launch market—in exchange
for an unambiguous commitment to fully and faithfully adhere to
MTCR standards. But when only weeks later allegations surfaced that
this offer had been motivated by improper campaign contributions, it
was quickly dropped (*Arms Control Today*, 3/98; *Washington Times*, 3/
23/98, 4/29/98). Finally, just days after the 2000 presidential election,
the lame duck Clinton administration announced a blanket waiver
for all of the pending missile sanctions cases against China that had
accumulated since the 1994 waiver. In return it obtained for the first
time an unambiguous Chinese pledge to enforce MTCR export-control standards (*Washington Post*, 11/22/00), although China quickly
violated this too (*Washington Post*, 9/1/01, 9/8/01).

In recent years, the United States has also targeted North Korean
adherence. During the 1994 Agreed Framework talks on nuclear pro-

liferation, the chief U.S. negotiator explicitly specified that restraining missile technology exports was a concern that the DPRK needed to address before implementation could move forward (Gallucci int., 1998). Consequently, the United States has held several rounds of inconclusive bilateral talks in which it sought MTCR adherence (U.S. Cong. Senate off., 1998; *Washington Post*, 11/20/98, 9/13/99).[33] However, U.S. intelligence reports apparently indicated that North Korea continued to increase its missile-related exports during this process (*Washington Times*, 10/28/99). Although North Korea eventually agreed to a moratorium on test launches of long-range missiles following a visit by Secretary of State Albright, a broader agreement including export constraints eluded the Clinton administration, despite intensive negotiations in its final weeks. The Bush administration was therefore left to assess whether these efforts were promising enough to continue (*Washington Post*, 3/7/01). After some very public initial hesitation (*New York Times*, 3/9/01), the new administration eventually opted to resume negotiations, albeit at relatively low levels, and only after making it clear that stringent verification would be a firm requirement for any agreement. However, North Korean missile exports apparently are continuing apace, as is its development of the new Taepodong missile (*New York Times*, 7/3/01; *Washington Times*, 7/3/01).

Washington has recently also worked both bilaterally and through the MTCR to induce key transshipment countries (e.g., Singapore, Malta, Cyprus) to adhere unilaterally.

National Enforcement Mechanisms

In the total absence of multilateral compliance mechanisms for missile nonproliferation, the United States has been especially vigorous in its national enforcement efforts in this area. On average Washington sends up to twenty or more interdiction démarches per month on missile-related transfers—plus raising such issues in bilateral meetings—or more than twice the number for CW and BW combined ([State] int.). Indeed, the bureaucracy typically devotes more energy to bilateral enforcement than to multilateral issues (Karika int., 1998; Smoldone int., 1998). Interdiction focuses on MTCR members, adherents, and other supplier or transshipment countries.

The United States sporadically intervened to discourage missile-related transfers to volatile regions like the Middle East even before it had a fully articulated missile nonproliferation policy (Karp, 1989). However, once the Reagan administration instituted a formal missile nonproliferation policy in 1982, Washington routinely began to intervene to block foreign transfers. This required a high degree of delicacy, however, because most such transfers involved firms from the countries with whom Washington was secretly trying to negotiate the MTCR. Consequently, the United States was hesitant to unsettle its negotiating partners by pressing too hard on individual cases (Speier int., 1998).

Once the MTCR was announced, Washington dramatically sharpened, broadened, and institutionalized its interdiction efforts. It established a special interagency process, the Missile Technology Analysis Group (MTAG), to monitor intelligence and coordinate responses (Clarke tst., 1989). In the Regime's first two years, the United States aggressively intervened against transfers by MTCR partners that were inconsistent with its interpretation of the Guidelines. For example, in 1989 the Bush administration sent a succession of increasingly senior delegations to Paris to protest planned sales of rocket engines and technology to the Brazilian and Indian space programs (Clarke tst., 1990; Ozga, 1994). During this period it also sent démarches to block a series SLV-related transfers by German and Italian firms (Bowen, 1997). This immediate post-MTCR period also saw interdiction involving nonadherent countries. For example, almost at once the United States launched an intensive bilateral campaign against transfers by Swiss front companies acting for Third World missile programs (Zimmerman int., 1998). The United States also protested at the highest levels to Israel about its aid to the South African missile program (Sokolski tst., 1989a).

The primary focus of U.S. enforcement efforts since the Gulf War has been to promote Russian and Chinese compliance with their respective MTCR-related commitments. In December 1990, the Bush administration protested forcefully against Soviet plans to sell cryogenic engines and technology to the Indian space program. After the collapse of the USSR, Secretary of State Baker raised this issue in one of his first meetings with the new Russian foreign minister, warning that it was a grave bilateral irritant, while at the same time hinting at greater space cooperation if the deal was terminated. Although the Bush administration subsequently imposed nonproliferation sanctions, and in parallel liberalized Russian access to U.S. satellite launches, the Yeltsin regime refused to back down (Pikayev et al., 1998).

Responding likewise to Chinese plans to sell M-9 and M-11 missiles to Syria and Pakistan respectively, Secretary of State Baker used unusually harsh diplomatic language in a public warning that such transfers would have "profound consequences" for overall Sino–American relations. He then dispatched a senior aide to Beijing to privately deliver this message (*Washington Post*, 6/13/91). In response, China agreed to abandon both deals, ostensibly resolving the issue (Fitzgibbon int., 1998).

The Clinton administration inherited the dispute with Russia over its planned sale to India, giving it considerable attention at senior levels (Gallucci int., 1998; [NSC] int.). Carrying forward the carrot-and-stick approach of his predecessor, Secretary of State Christopher successfully negotiated a settlement in mid-1993. Both Vice President Gore and President Clinton had been directly involved in the negotiations, during which the United States threatened to broaden existing sanctions, cut off wider financial aid, block Russian entry into GATT, and delay COCOM liberalization. Under the final package, the Russian entity, ISRO/Glavkosmos, was permitted to sell a specified number of rocket engines to India. In addition, Russian space launch providers received a higher quota of commercial space launches, and the Russian Space Agency was invited to join the International Space Station project. All told, almost a billion dollars worth of incentives were used. In return, Moscow agreed to cancel plans to transfer production technology along with the engines, as well as to formalize its MTCR adherence in a bilateral agreement that included a compliance mechanism to resolve any future disputes (Pikayev et al., 1998).

Despite these ostensible successes, covert Russian and Chinese transfers have continued to prompt almost constant U.S. enforcement actions in recent years. For example, over the past several years U.S. officials have raised at every opportunity specific cases of ongoing assistance by Chinese entities to the Iranian and Pakistani missile programs (*Washington Post*, 11/13/98; *Washington Times*, 12/7/98). Allegations of massive Russian assistance to missile programs in Iran and elsewhere have also been an increasing source of U.S. concern. Following dozens of formal diplomatic protests over at least two years, Vice President Gore raised the issue during a meeting with Russian Prime Minister Victor Chernomyrdin in February 1997. In the following months, President Clinton, Vice President Gore, and Secretary of State Albright repeatedly pressed their counterparts to take action to cut off these transfers. Finally, in July 1997, Presidents Clinton and Yeltsin agreed to appoint special envoys to resolve the problem. Following two years of regular meetings, Russia agreed to allow U.S. teams to monitor its implementation of export controls (Clinton off., 1998; Commission off., 1998; Einhorn tst., 1997; *New York Times*, 4/27/98, 12/17/98; Reuters, 4/25/98; U.S. Cong. Senate off., 1998; *Washington Post*, 1/18/98, 2/12/98; *Washington Times*, 12/15/98). However, Washington believes that Russian missile transfers have continued (*Washington Post*, 9/8/01).

Although U.S. missile interdiction efforts have relied mainly on bilateral diplomacy, it has also been willing occasionally to use more forceful tactics. In January 1992, Washington provided intelligence that enabled Israel to turn back a North Korean ship thought to be delivering missile-related equipment to Syria by threatening to sink it (*Washington Times*, 1/24/92). A few months later, the United States itself publicly threatened to intercept a North Korean freighter suspected of carrying missile-related equipment to Iran and Syria. However, a U.S. military task force searched for ten days without finding the ship, which managed to deliver its cargo (*Washington Post*, 3/8/92, 3/12/92, 3/14/92; *Washington Times*, 3/10/92, 5/18/92, 7/16/92). Following this public debacle, the United States resorted to acting through transshipment governments, rather than attempting to seize shipments directly. For example, after Moscow refused U.S. requests to block a sale of Russian rocket fuel precursor to Libya in early 1993, the United States induced Kiev to seize the shipment while it was passing through Ukrainian territory (*Washington Post*, 6/24/93). Less than a year later, Saudi authorities acting on a U.S. request boarded the German freighter *Asian Senator*, seizing its Chinese cargo of rocket fuel ingredients (*Washington Post*, 1/23/94; *Washington Times*, 1/26/94). Most recently, after Russia failed to heed a U.S. request, Azerbaijan acted on U.S. information to seize an overland shipment of specialty steel bound for Iran (*New York Times*, 4/25/98).

Beginning in 1990, the United States reinforced its interdiction efforts with nonproliferation sanctions. Congress first considered missile sanctions legislation in 1989. As with CBW sanctions, the Bush administration supported the idea in principle, but opposed automatic triggers. It also vigorously opposed any sanctions that would target MTCR members, arguing that this would impair cooperation within the Regime (Clarke tst., 1989; Executive Office of the President off., 1989a; Sokolski tst., 1989a; Wulf tst., 1989a). The administration worked with Congress to develop legislation that addressed the latter concern by exempting MTCR members. Although still not pleased by its automatic requirements, the White House did not veto the Missile Technology Control Act when it was attached to a major authorization bill in November 1990.

Although strictly unilateral, U.S. missile sanctions are explicitly tied to violations of MTCR standards. The United States tried to get the MTCR to adopt a similar measure multilaterally, but was unsuccessful. Failing this, it urged MTCR governments to institute comparable national measures ([DFAT] int.).

The U.S. missile sanctions law requires severe automatic sanctions for a period of two years against foreign entities (e.g., companies) that knowingly supply or receive MTCR Annex items that contribute to a Category I program in a non-MTCR country.[34] It makes no allowances for economic or political considerations, only allowing the president to waive sanctions if doing so is deemed "essential for U.S. national security."[35] It has been amended on several occasions to broaden its scope and to close perceived loopholes. For example, the so-called Helms Amendment extends sanctions to all missile-related industries in states with nonmarket economies (e.g., China), making sanctions potentially worth billions of dollars in lost trade (CRS off., 1997; OSD off., 1997b). In addition, the George H. W. Bush and Clinton administrations supplemented this law with additional discretionary sanctions through various executive orders. All in all, the missile area has the toughest nonproliferation sanctions on U.S. books.

The first Bush administration set about using this new enforcement tool with marked zeal. Just two years after enactment, it had imposed sanctions on ten separate occasions, including against entities from Russia, China, India, South Africa, Israel, and Pakistan (Ozga, 1994). The Clinton administration likewise pledged, "We are prepared to pursue our nonproliferation goals vigorously even when such efforts involve sanctions and may risk friction in critical bilateral relationships" (Davis tst., 1993, pp. 3–4). In the intervening years, however, it was widely criticized for its reluctance to punish missile-related transfers, legal obligations notwithstanding. For example, in the four years from 1994 to 1997, the U.S. imposed sanctions only twice, and then only against North Korean and Iranian entities, which were already covered by blanket trade embargoes (Jones & McDonough, 1998).

Criticism of the Clinton administration's record on missile sanctions centered on its reluctance to sanction Chinese entities for assisting Pakistan and Iran. Allegations that the bureaucracy was pressured into finding loopholes to avoid sanctioning Chinese entities are borne out by several interviews. A former senior intelligence official—who had antagonized the White House by providing unwelcome proof of Chinese transfers—substantiated such claims in Congressional testimony (*Washington Post*, 10/22/97; *Washington Times*, 6/12/98). In fact, President Clinton inadvertently admitted as much himself, remarking (unknowingly) in front of a reporter that automatic sanctions have created "an enormous amount of pressure in the bowels of the bureaucracy to fudge the finding" (*New York Times*, 4/28/98, p. 1). Nevertheless, Washington continued to use the threat of sanctions to pressure China to cut off transfers. For its part, the Bush administration has moved forcefully to reassert the credibility of automaric sanctions, by punishing Chinese entities for transfers to Pakistan in violation of China's November 2000 commitment (*Washington Post*, 9/1/01).

Alarmed by what it perceived as Moscow's wanton miscreance in permitting Russian entities to assist missile programs in Iran, India, and China, Congress moved to enact a new missile sanctions provision targeting Russia in mid-1998. This in effect would have revoked Russia's immunity as a MTCR member. The measure passed with veto-proof bipartisan support (90 to 4 in the Senate and 392 to 22 in the House), but President Clinton vetoed it. The White House then deftly circumvented a near certain Congressional override of this veto by preempting it by imposing discretionary sanctions on nine Russian entities (*Arms Control Today*, 6–7/98; Associated Press, 7/15/98). Less than six months later, the administration imposed such sanctions on two additional entities, prompting angry protests from Moscow (*Washington Post*, 1/14/99).

Other Capability-Denial Responses

Other than general targeted initiatives like ACME, there have been no apparent cases where the United States has tried to foster such arrangements specifically against missile programs.

It is unclear if the United States has ever used or sanctioned sabotage against missile programs other than in the special case of the Gulf War. There has certainly never been any official confirmation, or even threat, of such activity. That said, a former official notes obliquely that there were a series of "mysterious explosions" at facilities associated with, or providing assistance to, the Condór project in the late 1980s, hinting that this may have involved some type of covert antiproliferation activity by the United States or some other country (Speier int., 1998).

Nonpossession Norm-Building

Global Missile Norm Proposals

The United States has been a long-standing opponent of proposals to try to augment supply-side missile nonproliferation with a global treaty norm. This idea was first proposed by other G-7 governments during the MTCR negotiations. According to the chief U.S. negotiator, however, Washington refused to even consider this proposal. The United States responded that a ban would not address the problem because missile technology posed a greater threat than finished missiles. In addition, Washington argued that the Third World would never agree to an acceptable missile ban, because (1) the United States and other NPT nuclear states insisted on retaining nuclear delivery systems (i.e., necessitating a "have–have-not" arrangement), (2) the United States refused to distinguish between missiles and SLVs (i.e., necessitating a ban on civilian technologies that the Third World would see as perpetuating technological dependency), and (3) missiles were not seen as actual weapons in and of themselves (McNamara int., 1998).

In the late 1980s, as the bilateral INF negotiations were reaching fruition, Assistant ACDA Director Kathleen Bailey was a lone voice in the interagency pushing to multilateralize INF into a nonproliferation norm, even going so far at one point as to have her staff draft an illustrative text. However, the rest of the interagency argued that a global norm would undermine the MTCR while not contributing much in return. Because all agencies staunchly opposed the idea and it was never strongly backed by top echelons within ACDA, the Bailey proposals never received serious consideration (Hinds int., 1998; Smoldone int., 1998).

The first meaningful deliberation on the merits of seeking a global ban occurred in the context of the incoming George H. W. Bush administration's review of arms control and nonproliferation in 1989. However, senior officials from various agencies expressed public skepticism about the concept even before finishing this review (Hinds tst., 1989b; Lehman tst., 1989; Wulf tst., 1989b). Predictably, since the United States was unwilling to give up missiles beyond its bilateral obligations and the review reaffirmed the long-standing technical assessment that SLVs could not be safeguarded against missile applications, the interagency concluded that a discriminatory "have–have-not" treaty, prohibiting SLVs as well as missiles, was not negotiable on acceptable terms (ACDA & State tst., 1990; Speier int., 1998). In the end, Washington satisfied itself with a joint statement with the Soviet Union opining that INF demonstrated to other nations that eliminating missiles could enhance common security (U.S. & USSR off., 1990).

The idea of a global nonpossession norm was resurrected by Canada within the MTCR, taking up an initiative first raised by Australia. At the 1994 MTCR plenary Ottawa called on partners to endorse negotiating a universal legal instrument banning INF-range ballistic missiles. This proposal envisioned a NPT-like "rockets-for-peace" arrangement, with intrusive multilateral verification combined with a codification of the legal right to develop and possess civilian SLVs (Canada off., 1994; Sinclair off., 1995).

The Canadian initiative led to yet another lopsided interagency debate in Washington. The departments of State, Defense, and Commerce reaffirmed their absolute opposition to even exploring the idea. ACDA was divided, with the nuclear arms-control office (whose traditional bilateral business was drying up) expressing interest at the working level, while the nonproliferation bureau sided with the rest of the interagency. Opponents rehashed familiar arguments that negotiations would put pressure on the United States to put its own residual missiles above and below the INF thresholds on the table for a treaty that, if it legitimized SLVs, could do more harm than good by undercutting existing supply-side nonproliferation. Once again, the interagency quickly and decisively reaffirmed its resolute opposition (Smoldone int., 1988; [State] int.).

The United States responded negatively to a follow-up Canadian initiative in early 1995 to convene a special intersessional seminar to consider further its proposal before the next plenary meeting. It circulated a highly critical paper to all of the MTCR members, laying out an array of objections (DFAT off., 1995a). Although the Canadians pressed ahead with a seminar, they withdrew their proposal from consideration in the face of near-consensus opposition led by the United States (Dorling int., 1998; Speier, 1999). Washington was satisfied with this outcome and hoped that it had put to rest the issue of a global missile norm once and for all (Fitzgibbon int., 1998; Smoldone int., 1998; [State] int.).

In 1999 Russia began a concerted effort to revive the idea of a global missile instrument. It pressed not only within the MTCR, but also outside by calling for what it termed a Global Control System. This would involve an approach of trading incentives for responsible missile behavior, defined as anything from greater transparency to an outright ban. Not surprising, Washington was quick to reject key elements of the Russian scheme, but Washington's opposition failed to dissuade Russia from moving ahead on its own, convening widely attended multilateral meetings to try to develop momentum for the idea (Smith, 2001). As a counter to these Russian efforts, Washington at the 1999 MTCR plenary reluctantly agreed to allow the Regime to develop a Code of Conduct Against Missile Proliferation to serve as a voluntary guideline for members and nonmembers. The content of the resulting draft is not yet public, but seems to involve voluntary transparency measures; for example, on space launch programs (Assembly of WEU off., 2000; Smith, 2001; Tigner, 2001). This approach would appear to fall far short of anything like a real global treaty norm.

The new Bush administration has continued to oppose the ambitious Russian Global Control System initiative. It has also resisted moving future norm-building efforts from the current MTCR code discussions (from which it apparently hopes to present a finished document to the rest of the world to take or to leave) to a new Iranian initiated U.N. experts group. (Interestingly, Russia by contrast seems quite content to let this U.N. group take up its GCS proposals.) As for the draft MTCR Code of Conduct itself, the new administration has not reneged on U.S. support. At the same time it has worked to contain the venture, keeping it as a modest, vague framework that would not undermine the supply-side operations of the MTCR. It has therefore resisted efforts by some of its MTCR partners to open the code for wider negotiation with non-MTCR countries, or to portray the code as a first step toward negotiating a more ambitious antimissile instrument. Having been reluctantly convinced by its MTCR partners to develop what it clearly intended as a harmless sop to demands for a global missile norm, it remains to be seen whether Washington will be able to contain a process that may be gathering multilateral steam in what it is likely to consider to be unwelcome directions (McDougall, 2001; Pikayev, 2001; Tigner, 2001).[36]

Other Nonpossession Responses

While it has consistently opposed trying to create a global nonpossession treaty, the United States has fitfully tried to promote nonpossession in ways that would not undermine either supply-side strategies or its own national interests. For instance, in late 1988 the United States offered to sponsor missile-related arms-control talks for the Middle East (*Washington Post*, 12/28/98). In early 1990 the United States and Soviet Union renewed this effort by jointly offering their "good offices" to promote regional missile talks (U.S. & USSR off., 1990). Following the Gulf War, the ACME initiative likewise envisioned Middle East states agreeing to implement a regional missile freeze as a first step to some type of missile-free-zone arrangement (White House off., 1991). The United States subsequently made similar "good offices" efforts to sponsor regional missile talks for South Asia and the Korean Peninsula (U.S. Cong. Senate off., 1998; Wulf tst., 1993). But none of these initiatives so much as got off the ground, because key regional states showed no inclination to renounce their missiles.

In addition to regional initiatives, the United States has opportunistically pressured friendly countries to forgo missile programs. For example, the Bush administration was able to use bilateral leverage to get a formal commitment from South Korea to forgo trying to acquire MTCR-class missiles (Rowen off., 1991). Argentina likewise was pressured into abandoning the Condór II program, including allowing U.S. destruction of its eleven unfinished missiles (Escudé, 1998). South Africa not only was pressured into giving up its missiles, but also its space launch program and associated infrastructure, and to submit to supervised destruction. Washington used incentives as well as coercion, paying for the destruction of missiles and associated infrastructure in several countries (State off., 1999). By 1991, the Bush administration reported that its bilateral efforts had eliminated up to eight missile programs (Clarke tst., 1991).

In 1993 the Clinton administration formalized this policy through its unilateral MTCR membership criteria. This represented a conscious effort to characterize the MTCR itself as a de facto (albeit very limited) nonpossession norm (Davis tst., 1993; [NSC] int.; [State] int.; Wallerstein int., 1998). "That's really a unilateral U.S. norm ... in the nascent stage," a State Department official interviewed observes, "But in effect we're trying to create a possession norm." This same official notes that, by allowing new MTCR members to retain SLVs, this policy poses some of the same risks as a global treaty norm. However, these are greatly reduced because it is narrowly targeted, with the United States having absolute say over who joins, and openly discriminatory, with the United States and other existing members remaining "haves."

Even this modest nonpossession effort proved controversial in Washington, sparking strong bipartisan protests in Congress requiring personal intervention by Vice President Gore. It also was opposed by some within the interagency. These critics asserted that it was a mistake to try to tack on even this limited cooperative nonpossession dimension to the MTCR, because this could detract from its primary supply-side function ([NSC] int.; Sokolski tst., 1996; Wallerstein int., 1998). Moreover, according to a former official, the Clinton administration subsequently backed away from aggressively promoting the MTCR as a global nonpossession norm: "In retrospect . . . they took a wrong turn . . . and then realized that in fact this made no sense and that it could have negative ramifications" (Wallerstein int., 1998).

Consequence-Management

Counterproliferation

Because missiles are not weapons in themselves, deterrence does not apply to them directly, but rather is calibrated to the weapons they deliver. By the same token, missile (and air) defense is one of the main countermeasures against all types of WMD, and virtually the only way to protect against nuclear weapons. Consequently, missile defense programs have been a cornerstone of U.S. counterproliferation efforts, representing a staggering $100 billion investment through 1999 (*New York Times*, 5/24/99).[37]

Like the other elements of counterproliferation, missile defense concepts originated during the Cold War. President Reagan's original Strategic Defense Initiative (SDI) envisioned an impenetrable strategic shield that would eliminate reliance on deterrence to protect the United States against a massive Soviet strike. However, the first Bush administration reoriented SDI to a primarily counterproliferation role with its global protection against limited strikes (GPALS) focus (Clarke tst., 1991; Bush off., 1992). The Clinton administration continued this trend, symbolically recasting SDI as ballistic missile defense (BMD)—a term encompassing both theatre missile defense (TMD) and national missile defense (NMD), the latter representing a truncated version of the original SDI concept—and merging this concept into its overall counterproliferation initiative.

From 1995 to 1997, the United States intensified its emphasis on TMD, expanding and accelerating programs against both ballistic and cruise missiles. These incorporate an array of major weapons systems in various stages of development, including Patriot Advanced Capability-3, Navy Area Defense, Theater High Altitude Area Defense, Navy Theater Wide Defense, Medium Extended Air Defense System, and HAWK

Air Defense System. The Clinton TMD program also included research into advanced concepts such as airborne laser weapons. Many of these programs involved cooperative efforts with allies such as Japan (OSD off., 1996, 1997a). The United States also funded Israel's highly promising Arrow-2 system (*New York Times*, 9/15/98).

The United States likewise continued to pursue NMD, primarily justified by emerging proliferation threats. In the mid-1990s the Clinton administration instituted a plan, dubbed "3-plus-3," that called for developing such a system so that, by the year 2000, it could be fully deployed on three years notice. The 1997 Quadrennial Defense Review called for an additional $2 billion for NMD to ensure that this schedule could be met (*Disarmament Diplomacy* [17], 1997; OSD off., 1997a).

The 3-plus-3 program implicitly reflected the assumption of a 1995 intelligence estimate (NIE-95-19) that emerging missile programs did not pose a short-term homeland threat to the United States. However, as this assumption was increasingly undermined by rapid advances in missile programs in countries like Iran and North Korea, Congress began to press for faster action. In response, the Pentagon's January 1999 budget proposal added $7 billion over six years (*New York Times*, 1/7/99). At the same time, the Senate passed a measure with overwhelming bipartisan support to force the Clinton administration to accelerate significantly scheduled deployment. Following a parallel House bill passed several weeks later with a similar majority, the administration agreed to field NMD systems as soon as technologically feasible (*New York Times*, 3/17/99, 3/18/99, 3/19/99, 5/21/99).

The new Bush administration has repeatedly and insistently identified missile defense, including theater and homeland systems, as one of its top priorities, and has indicated that it plans to pursue a substantially more capable system than that envisioned by the Clinton administration. Administration officials have also indicated that there is no time to lose, expressing open alarm about the pace of proliferation-driven threats. Indeed, Defense Secretary Rumsfeld has chided Russia and other critics of NMD for having made the need for it more urgent by not having done more to assist U.S. nonproliferation efforts in recent years (*Washington Times*, 2/12/01).

In his first major national security speech, President Bush, for all intents, announced that the United States planned to renounce the U.S.–Russian Anti-Ballistic Missile Treaty in order to attain protection against proliferated missiles. He emphasized that U.S. missile defense plans were not designed to undermine Russian or Chinese strategic deterrent forces, but instead are aimed squarely at countering proliferation threats (*Washington Post*, 5/2/01; *Washington Times*, 5/2/01). The Bush administration moved quickly to translate its obvious determination

into concrete, irreversible action. In one of its first major budget decisions, it requested $7.9 billion (a $2.2 billion plus over the Clinton budget it inherited) to speed up deployment (*Washington Times*, 6/27/01).
It followed this by announcing plans to deploy an initial multilayer
shield for both theater and homeland defense by 2005—including
ground and ship launched interceptors and airborne lasers—with work
to begin in 2001 on a new Alaska test site (*New York Times*, 7/12/01;
Washington Post, 7/12/01). This aggressive push for early deployment
of a relatively robust system received a tremendous boost with the
second successful interception of a long-range target missile (*Washington Post*, 7/15/01).

SUMMARY U.S. FINDINGS:
CROSS-CASE PATTERNS

The U.S. approach to antiproliferation has consistently relied on a mutually reinforcing combination of capability-denial and consequence-
management strategies over the nonpossession norm-building approach.
Washington has used the full spectrum of capability-denial instruments, including frequently instituting national export controls beyond multilateral requirements, consistently pushing for the creation
and strengthening of tough suppliers regimes, consistently using a
variety of bilateral and multilateral tools to push for wider export-
control norms beyond the suppliers groups, trying to establish more
stringent targeted denial strategies (e.g., ACME, rogue states), undertaking constant national enforcement actions with a variety of tools
(e.g., interdiction, sanctions) and at all levels, and occasionally even
threatening or using sabotage or destruction against emerging capabilities. This has been the case over time and across the different proliferation areas. In parallel, Washington increasingly has also pursued
every possible avenue of proliferation management to respond to what
it sees as increasing proliferated capabilities.

Although the compromises that have emerged from the adversarial,
frequently chaotic U.S. interagency process, as well as Congressional
versus executive branch interaction, have led to frequent and erratic
policy lurches on minor issues, these have occurred within the parameters of the preferences listed. Moreover, the perspectives of individual
agencies within the interagency system, and to a lesser extent among
a bipartisan majority in Congress, have remained remarkably constant
over almost two decades. Likewise, while major policies have evolved
over time—particularly in response to dramatic events in the international environment such as the Gulf War, as well as the internal policy
reviews accompanying changes in administrations—the unifying pattern has always been to emphasize capability denial tools, augmented

by proliferation management. To the extent that decisions have been made that subverted such tools, these have not been in favor of alternative normative instruments, but rather competing national priorities (e.g., trade, bilateral political relationships).

Washington nonetheless has increasingly come to recognize the importance of nonpossession norms as a secondary approach, not least as a means to bolster capability-denial efforts.[38] As one State Department official observes, "We are legitimized in trying to interdict shipments and sanctioning people and controlling exports and all of that because there is this global norm . . . and so that fact helps us do all these other things that really carry the bulk of the nonproliferation effort" (int.). However, it has displayed varying inclinations to institutionalize normative instruments across the different proliferation areas, depending on different technical assessments regarding the susceptibility of relevant technologies to cheating and break-out, as well as the costs involved.

This consistency in applying a capability-denial strategy of nonproliferation across the different areas, while differentiating its support for cooperative nonpossession norms, reinforces the conclusion that the latter represents a subsidiary antiproliferation strategy. The proof of this is that whereas Washington has repeatedly been willing to undermine normative instruments to bolster capability-denial and consequence-management tools, it has in virtually every instance resisted damaging the latter for the sake of the former.

Washington has also consistently been unwilling to pay high costs (e.g., exposing commercial or national security secrets) in order to secure or strengthen nonpossession instruments. For example, in part because of such costs, the United States resisted highly intrusive verification arrangements for the CWC, and rejected a verification regime to strengthen the BWC. By contrast, the United States has been willing to expend vast political and economic capital on developing and enforcing capability-denial instruments and building counterproliferation and deterrent capabilities.

Even the conditional support that Washington has given to applicable normative treaty instruments would have been far less than was the case had it not been for highly idiosyncratic factors. It is unlikely that the United States would ever have gone along with complex CWC arrangements to combat proliferation if it had not been saddled with such a template from its own bilaterally oriented disarmament proposals from the Cold War period. Even so, it is clear that the United States would never have agreed to the CWC had it not been for the entirely idiosyncratic determination of the first President Bush. Likewise, the interlude of U.S. willingness to consider upgrading the BWC with intrusive features, tepid as it was, only occurred because a single

NSC staffer was willing and able for a time partially to override inter-agency consensus.

In summary, the United States has always strongly favored the capability-denial approach across the board, increasingly reinforced by robust consequence-management strategies, with sometimes reluctant support for norm-building as a supplementary approach.

NOTES

This chapter was subject to security review by the U.S. Department of Defense. No significant changes resulted from this process.

1. Unlike nuclear controls, CB/M controls were never embodied as such in identifiable lists. Rather, they were grafted onto the existing strategic trade controls by adding relevant items to the State Department's munitions list and the Commerce Department's dual-use commodities list (Bryen tst., 1989). This remains the case today.

2. Regional arms control was sporadically identified during this period, and to a lesser extent subsequently, as a "demand reduction" component of proliferation response. However, evidence suggests that this may have been a case of inventing a nonproliferation function for something that was, and would continue to be, pursued for other reasons (e.g., regional stability).

3. In the end no significant progress was made on the conventional arms-transfers issue either. The United States aggressively pursued a prenotification agreement. However, China pulled out of the talks following the Bush administration's decision in mid-1992 to approve the sale of advanced military aircraft to Taiwan.

4. For some reason counterproliferation was not explicitly addressed in PDD-13 as a pending initiative.

5. Needless to say, this initiative applied only to U.S. national export controls that went beyond the requirements of the nonproliferation regimes, and so did not impact the various multilateral lists.

6. The act was not renewed. However, its provisions have been carried forward by executive order.

7. Cambodia, Cuba, Iran, Iraq, Libya, North Korea, Syria, Vietnam, and all COCOM proscribed destinations.

8. Rumors persist that the White House may have known about Ledogar's gambit in advance.

9. Congressional critics charge that the government of China also should have been sanctioned in this case, and that the administration's actions only "met the bare requirements of U.S. law" (U.S. Cong. Senate off., 1998. p. 13).

10. Press reports and some members of Congress speculated that this attack was motivated by an embattled president's desire to distract public opinion from the mounting sex and perjury scandal that eventually led to his impeachment.

11. This was identical to the strategy that was then being pursued in nuclear arms control, where the deployment of INF missiles (Pershing II) in Europe was approved contingent on, and parallel to, negotiations to eliminate this class of weapons.

12. This would have occurred in the context of the then ongoing formal review of overall disarmament and nonproliferation policies that had been initiated a few months earlier.

13. At this point it was assumed that verification of U.S.–Soviet reductions would be carried out bilaterally under separate bilateral inspection procedures.

14. Because the WEOG could not agree on a unified Western position, the debate on challenge inspections at this point had not yet reached the main negotiations.

15. Under a unilateral reservation to the 1925 Geneva Protocol, the United States had maintained the right to use RCAs under four specified circumstances. During the CWC negotiations, the U.S. had insisted on being allowed to retain this reservation, refusing to back down under any circumstances. The issue was only resolved on the final day of negotiations by adopting intentionally ambiguous language, prescribing the use of RCAs as a "method of warfare" without defining this term (Donadio int., 1998). The Bush administration had made a legal determination that this allowed for all U.S. conditions of use to be retained (Donadio int., 1998; Shalikashvili tst., 1994; Slocombe tst., 1994). However, even as the Senate was holding its first round of hearings on the CWC, a low-level official on the Clinton NSC staff pushed through a new legal interpretation, eliminating two of the four conditions of use (int.). This, in turn, led to a unanimous protest by the military's theatre commanders-in-chief, word of which eventually was leaked to Senator Sam Nunn (Deutch tst., 1994). According to a very senior OPCW official, there was no multilateral pressure on the United States to revise its position (int.). Indeed, the only external pressure for this change, and the disastrous delay and recriminations that it engendered, seems to have come from a single Western ally ([OSD] int.).

16. As a compromise between having no provision for universality on the one hand and setting an impossibly high bar on the other, the treaty specifies entry into force after a specified number of countries had deposited their ratification instruments.

17. The implementing legislation was more problematic than ratification because (1) it needed to be passed by the House as well as the Senate, (2) it highlighted many of the most controversial elements of the treaty (e.g., intrusive inspection procedures), and (3) the external deadline for becoming an original States Party did not apply.

18. The term "conditions" was used instead of the usual term "reservations" because the latter are expressly prohibited under the terms of the treaty itself. Interestingly, one of the conditions is that the executive branch will never impinge on the Senate's constitutional prerogatives by accepting such a restriction on reservations in any future negotiations.

19. Many CWC States Parties believe that some of these U.S. conditions constitute de facto reservations in the formal sense. Moreover, the Senate considered, but in the end declined to pass, a number of even more onerous conditions that the president said he could not accept. These included requiring ratification by China, Iran, Iraq, Libya, North Korea, Syria, and Sudan; withholding deposit of the instrument of ratification until Russia had ratified and the president had certified that Russia was in full compliance with the BDA; presidential certification that the United States could detect militarily signifi-

cant violations with high confidence; requiring the president to bar OPCW inspectors of nationalities of states that violated U.S. nonproliferation laws; and amending the treaty to eliminate Articles X and XI (*Arms Control Today*, 4/97).

20. Moscow did not acknowledge ever having had a BW program. Therefore, unlike the United States, it did not indicate that it had destroyed or converted its stockpiles and production facilities after acceding to the BWC.

21. These transparency measures were aimed squarely at the USSR, since the information involved was readily available for Western countries from public sources.

22. One of the arguments against BWC verification is that the vague nature of its prohibitions make it difficult to ascertain what would constitute a violation. However, the United States has consistently taken the position that further defining Article I would limit the scope of the treaty. This was an issue of tension in the Protocol negotiations.

23. After a promising start, the Trilateral Process, like the BDA in the CW realm, ultimately failed. Despite years of talks, Moscow stonewalled on allowing any inspections at military facilities ([State] int.; Goodby int., 1998). Washington continues to allege that the Russian Federation, along with several other parties, including China, is violating the BWC (ACDA off., 1997a; Einhorn tst., 1997; OSD off., 1997a; *Washington Post*, 7/15/95, 2/26/98; *Washington Times*, 8/8/96, 8/16/97).

24. WHO had reached a consensus recommendation to destroy these stocks in order to declare that this disease had been eradicated as a threat to humanity.

25. That said, observers such as Ozga (1994) and Khromov (1998) note that Washington has been willing to violate its own export-control policies and stretch the MTCR rules in cases involving Israel.

26. This "no offshore procurement" policy is implemented by requiring (and denying) export licenses for U.S. firms to provide the technical specifications that a foreign firm needs to bid on supplying components. In cases where this proves impractical, the policy is enforced through Treasury Department import licenses for Defense-related items (Smoldone int., 1998).

27. However, ambiguous language was inserted into the Guidelines specifying that they were not intended to impede national space launch programs as long as such programs could not contribute to systems for the delivery of WMD. Given that the United States had always insisted that SLVs inherently pose a proliferation risk, and more important that the Annex explicitly treats SLVs as being identical to ballistic missiles, Washington viewed (and continues to view) this clause as having no practical effect. To the extent that the United States has ascribed any meaning to this clause, it is along the lines that its intent can be met through the availability of launch services rather than SLVs as such.

28. France refused to acknowledge that MTCR rules prohibit support to Category I SLV programs until July 1992 (Ozga, 1994).

29. The Guidelines were revised accordingly in January 1993, based on the recommendations of a technical working group on how to implement this decision (Ozga, 1994).

30. In 1995 Brazil became the first new member under this policy to join the MTCR while retaining its space launch program. Critics assert that, although

designed to strengthen the effectiveness of the MTCR as a cartel by luring in as many suppliers as possible, this membership expansion policy facilitates intraregime proliferation of relevant technology to countries who are both suppliers and receivers, particularly given the subsequent U.S. failure to secure tougher controls on interpartner trade.

31. Immunity against future sanctions was provided by conferring on such countries the status of MTCR adherent for the purpose of U.S. law, thus invoking the exception that the law provided for MTCR members (CRS off., 1997). Only countries that sign a formal bilateral MOU (i.e., not unilateral adherence) qualify for this status (Lumpe, 1994). However, this immunity was conditional, in that the United States reserved the right to revoke these agreements in the event of noncompliance.

32. This odd formulation in essence nullifies any commitment. The 1987 Guidelines do not include CBW-capable missiles, nor the key concept of range or payload tradeoff. Moreover, the Annex represents an essential implementing requirement for any version of the Guidelines.

33. The United States has also sought a freeze on North Korea's domestic missile programs as an interim step to some type of peninsularwide disarmament arrangement.

34. For transfers of Category II items, the sanctioned entity is restricted from receiving any MTCR Annex items from the United States. In the case of Category I transfers, the entity is banned from receiving virtually any weapons-related items. If the transfer is deemed to have made a substantial contribution to the Category I program, the entity is also banned from exporting to the United States.

35. This extremely high waiver threshold is much stricter than for CBW sanctions, which merely require a waiver to be in U.S. national interests. Moreover, the president is required to formally justify all such waivers to Congress.

36. In addition to the published sources cited, some additional information on the rapidly evolving state of play of the Code of Conduct, Global Control System, and U.N. missile group initiatives is derived from discussions at a 2001 conference of academics and officials (from Western and other countries) on missile proliferation and defense issues that was sponsored by the Southampton University (United Kingdom) Mountbatten Centre and conducted on a nonattribution basis.

37. Including SDI expenditures during the Cold War.

38. It is arguable, however, that this recognition is relatively recent. Given that prior to the Gulf War the United States saw the BWC and CWC almost exclusively in terms of bilateral disarmament, capability-denial may be seen as the only U.S. proliferation response during the Reagan and early Bush periods.

Chapter 4

Australian Proliferation Response

The purpose of this chapter is to provide a comprehensive account of Australian responses to proliferation. Its structure parallels that of Chapter 3 as closely as possible in order to facilitate structured comparison between the United States and a close ally. This comparative analysis occurs in Chapter 5.

OVERVIEW

General Priority

Nonnuclear proliferation response priorities have been set by the foreign affairs establishment in successive Australian governments with almost no outside pressure or even attention. No Parliamentary committee has ever held a relevant oversight inquiry. Likewise, few pertinent questions have been posed during Parliamentary debate. As for the press, other than post–Gulf War stories about Iraq, there has been relatively little coverage of either relevant proliferation threats or policy responses by Australia, its antiproliferation partners, or the international community generally. For example, between 1992 and 1999 the *Sydney Morning Herald* carried only sixteen stories mentioning any aspect of CB/M proliferation threats. During the same period, there were just over twenty stories reporting on responses to prolif- eration—the majority about U.S. nonproliferation sanctions against China—only one of which involved action taken by the Australian government. Australian antiproliferation priorities therefore have been internally rather than externally driven.

Unlike most of its Western counterparts, Australia displayed rela- tively little interest in disarmament and nonproliferation during the 1960s and 1970s (Siracusa & Cheong, 1997; Walsh, 1997). This changed at the bureaucratic level once the Department of Foreign Affairs (DFA) began to participate directly in multilateral disarmament negotiations when Australia joined the CD in 1979 (Findlay int., 1998).

Nuclear disarmament became a national priority following the elec- tion of the Labor government of Bob Hawke in 1983. This emphasis was generated at the highest political levels and handed down to the bureaucracy to implement. However, such political attention was nar- rowly focused on nuclear issues: primarily superpower disarmament, and secondarily nuclear nonproliferation (Butler, 1990, int., 1998; Har- ris int., 1999; [DFAT] int.; Walker int., 1998). For example, a major 1986 Parliamentary report (Parliament off., 1986) on national disarmament priorities only mentions nonnuclear issues in passing.

The reasons for the Hawke government's keen interest in nuclear disarmament were largely rooted in internal Labor Party politics. Prime Minister Hawke was determined to shed Labor's anti-American im- age by promoting a strong bilateral security relationship. However, the party's left wing fiercely opposed the ANZUS alliance generally, and the Joint Facilities in particular, as well as Australia's role as a major exporter of nuclear material.[1] Hawke and his foreign minister, former Labor leader Bill Hayden, therefore explicitly regarded anti- nuclear activism as a means to placate this core political constituency on these issues (Butler int., 1990; [intelligence] int.; Harris int., 1999; Mediansky, 1992; Miller, 1988; Walker int., 1998; White int., 1999). Ac- cordingly, Hayden created a high-profile position of roving disarma- ment ambassador, making it clear to the first incumbent that the job had a critical domestic component. Indeed, although based in Geneva, Ambassador Richard Butler spent a significant portion of his time back home on speaking tours (Butler int., 1998).

The domestic disarmament imperative largely dissipated with the initial thawing of the Cold War beginning in the mid to late 1980s. But as one long-time senior official observes, by then it had become a habit within the bureaucracy (White int., 1999).[2] Although nuclear disarma- ment had been the priority in all of this, the growth of disarmament assets and expertise at DFA had a spill-down effect. Because activism in other nonnuclear areas bolstered Australia's exposure in disarma-

ment fora, such efforts were seen to complement its nuclear disarmament agenda. For this reason, soon after taking office Foreign Minister Hayden instructed the disarmament bureaucracy to boost
Australia's international profile on any and all disarmament issues
(Gee int., 1998). Consequently, nonnuclear issues, particularly CW disarmament, became supplementary priorities at the senior bureaucratic
level as early as the mid-1980s.[3]

The focus on nonnuclear issues was reinforced in the late 1980s by
the ascension of the follow-on Labor government of Paul Keating,
whose new foreign minister, Gareth Evans, was eager to make his own
mark, and therefore less invested in his predecessor's nuclear priorities. By the early 1990s, the nonnuclear proliferation areas had offi-
cially been accorded equal priority (Jones int., 1998), with CW in reality
receiving the most attention (Evans int., 1998; [DFAT] ints.).

Unlike in the nuclear area, where an East–West nuclear strike could
have targeted Australia directly, the focus in the other areas as early as
the late 1970s was on horizontal proliferation rather than the Soviet
threat and associated East–West disarmament. This focus was derived
from a perceived security imperative to keep WMD, particularly CW,
out of Australia's strategic region (Butler int., 1998; Findlay int., 1998;
Harris int., 1999; Reese int., 1998; Walker int., 1998; White int., 1999).
At the same time, regional proliferation was not seen to pose any immediate threat in the 1980s. Canberra therefore perceived proliferation as a latent problem that needed to be preempted, rather than as
the kind of clear and present danger that forward-deployed American
forces faced (White int., 1999).

Even after global proliferation rose to the fore of the international
agenda in the early 1990s, Australia's main concern remained regional
and prophylactic. A succession of Defence white papers identified preventing WMD proliferation in Australia's immediate region (Southeast Asia and the South Pacific) as a key strategic interest, while noting
the complete absence of any such threat (Defence off., 1987, 1994, 1997).
Thus, while proliferation response has unquestionably been an important priority, it has not been at the top of the Australian national
security agenda. For example, throughout the 1990s antiproliferation
was a lower priority for senior DFAT officials than efforts to strengthen
regional security architecture ([DFAT] int.).

The general level of interest in proliferation response—measured in
terms of both declared policy and resource allocation—has been maintained since the conservative Liberal–National Coalition government
of John Howard came to power in 1996 (ints.). Although the Howard
government's new foreign policy promised to realign priorities to stress
national interests rather than altruistic concepts such as good international citizenship, it has explicitly identified preventing proliferation

regionally, and implicitly by extension globally, as representing just such a pragmatic national interest (DFAT off., 1997a).

General Doctrine and Policy Initiatives

Canberra has never promulgated a formal antiproliferation strategy as such. However, there has been a cohesive, long-standing national consensus on the means by which to pursue Australia's interests in preventing proliferation in Southeast Asia. The linchpin of this strategy has been that the best way to prevent regional proliferation is to conduct a preemptive forward defense by promoting global nonproliferation measures. From the very start this effort has centered on building and strengthening cooperative norms against possession. Australia provided a cogent summary of this strategy in a 1990 classified presentation to Washington:

Australia's preferred approach to non-proliferation is multilateral, seeking to achieve conventions which would contain the spread of weapons of mass destruction, and lock in to specific agreements the maximum number of countries. We would wish to avoid alienating Third World countries in the process of checking weapons proliferation, if only because Third World countries are themselves becoming proliferators, and south–south trade in armaments is an increasing phenomenon. (DFAT off., 1990g)

Foreign Minister Evans made essentially the same point publicly the next year, stating that although supply-side nonproliferation regimes were useful as interim arrangements, a web of universal treaties banning possession represented the only permanent solution (Evans off., 1991b). A later internal policy document likewise pointed to the importance that Australia attached to "the treaty network needed to underpin global norms against the spread of weapons of mass destruction," noting, "The maintenance of strong global norms against the acquisition of such weapons is central to our interest in preventing proliferation in our region" (Bird off., 1994b).

The consensus underpinning Australian antiproliferation policy has been so strong that it has precluded interagency discord on major policy questions. Only one relevant dispute (on CW-related export controls) has ever needed to be taken to the cabinet for decision (Evans int., 1998; Gee int., 1998; White int., 1999). For its part, DOD has always been content to cede policy management to DFAT, while providing technical support as needed.[4] The only limited exceptions have been in the missile realm (see later discussion), but these have usually been quickly and amicably resolved at relatively low bureaucratic levels ([DOD] ints.). As a senior Defence official commented, "We've left it to DFAT because they've been very good at it, and they haven't been trying to achieve anything that we haven't been trying to achieve" (White int., 1999). Nor has there been any notable internal strife within DFAT, with the regional and trade components of the foreign affairs bureaucracy generally deferring to the disarmament branch (Evans int., 1998; Harris int., 1999; [DFAT] int.).

The ascension of the center–right Howard government in 1996 did not lead to any meaningful change in Canberra's antiproliferation strategy ([DFAT] ints.). This is somewhat surprising, since Foreign Minister Downer consciously shifted Australian foreign policy away from global and multilateral activism toward a more bilateral and regional emphasis, as well as cleaving closer to U.S. leadership (DFAT off., 1997a; [DFAT] ints.). However, proliferation-response policies appear to have been exempted from these trends, reflecting both continuity of senior career officials—and a solid bipartisan political consensus ([DFAT] ints.).

This assessment of continuity seems ubiquitous, including among knowledgeable members of the political opposition. According to the chief foreign policy advisor for the Labor Party, the Howard government supports virtually every nonproliferation position in Labor's foreign policy platform (Dorling int., 1998). Even disarmament stalwarts from prior Labor governments, like former Foreign Minister Gareth Evans (int., 1998) and former Disarmament Ambassador Richard Butler (int., 1998) share this assessment. The latter observes, "Speaking objectively, I think there's been almost no fundamental or substantive difference in the shift from 13–14 years of Labor to this rather stridently conservative government of John Howard on these issues. . . . At the fundament of policy I would perceive virtually no difference."

Canberra has instituted few policy initiatives in the past two decades spanning proliferation areas. The only notable exception was the introduction of sweeping catch-all controls through the *Weapons of Mass Destruction (Prevention of Proliferation) Act 1995* (Defence off., 1998c). Although Australia had initially rejected U.S. calls starting in 1990 for other Western countries to institute catch-all controls, a series of potentially embarrassing exports over the next few years convinced the Keating government that such measures were in fact necessary to preserve Australia's reputation as a steadfast opponent of proliferation ([DFAT] int.).

While Australia has tended to avoid sweeping initiatives, it has had to react to such initiatives by others. For example, it worked behind the scenes over several years to derail post–Gulf War efforts by the United States and other Western states to strengthen institutional cooperation between the nonproliferation supplier regimes. This opposition was based largely on concerns that such institutionalization might harm global treaty norms by antagonizing Third World countries (DFAT off., 1993a; Jones off., 1991).

Australia also firmly rebuffed U.S. overtures beginning in 1994 to cooperate on counterproliferation. Despite determined American wooing, culminating in a detailed U.S. proposal offered during a visit by Deputy Assistant Secretary of Defense Mitchel Wallerstein, Canberra showed no interest. U.S. participants recall it becoming obvious during the Wallerstein visit that Canberra had no intention of even considering the proposal, with senior Australian Defence officials expressing polite lack of interest while DFAT officials voiced open hostility ([OSD] int.; Wallerstein int., 1998).

Australian officials acknowledge that both DFAT and DOD had agreed beforehand to reject the idea. "We conveyed more or less politely that we share your objectives," recalls a senior Defence official, "but we don't think this is a particularly smart way to do it" (White int., 1999). DFAT, for its part, was concerned that Western cooperation on counterproliferation would hurt multilateral treaty norms by undermining the perception of shared interests with developing countries ([DFAT] int.). Defence shared this concern, and in addition was skeptical about the military effectiveness of such programs, as well as whether the costs involved would be justified in the absence of any regional WMD threats ([DOD] int.; White int., 1999). This judgment was manifest in its most recent white paper (Defence off., 1997), which does not mention even in passing needing to be prepared to operate in a WMD environment nor defending against ballistic or cruise missiles.

CASE STUDY: CHEMICAL WEAPONS

Capability-Denial

National Export Controls

Australia instituted restrictions on the export of eight CW-related chemicals to Iraq and Iran in the latter part of 1984. This was a reaction to the U.N. secretary general's findings that Iraq had used CW against Iran. The specific action was taken in direct response to bilateral pressure from the United States, which after implementing such controls in March had pressed allies such as Australia to do the same ([DOD] int.; Olmer tst., 1984). Beginning in August 1985 (i.e., following the first AG meeting) these licensing requirements were changed to apply universally to any destination. This nonspecific approach was designed to minimize the discriminatory appearance of export-control measures ([DOD] int.; Dunn, 1989).

Like the United States, Australia's initial controls covered a few more precursor chemicals than the five that were eventually adopted in the initial AG process. When the AG finalized both its Core and Warning

Lists at its fourth meeting in May 1986, Australia and other delegations announced that they also planned to institute national controls
on most items on the voluntary Warning List. This was designed to
show leadership in the effort (see later discussion) to expand the Core
List beyond just five chemicals by setting a good example. The forward-
leaning strategy prompted a rare interagency rift, however, with the
Department of Industry, Technology, and Commerce, the Business
Regulation Review Unit, and the Defence Support organization (responsible for defense industries) raising vigorous objections. This dispute remained unresolved for almost a year, despite being fought all
the way up to the ministerial level. In the end the decision needed to
be taken to the cabinet, where the ministers for Foreign Affairs and
Defence (the latter of whom had previously overruled the subordinate Defence Support organization on the recommendation of his
policy and technologies staffs) prevailed ([DFAT] int.). On 29 May 1987,
Australia therefore added controls on twenty-two additional chemicals (Dunn, 1989; Hayden tst., 1989). Australia never again instituted
national measures beyond those agreed multilaterally among AG partners (other than in the case of general catch-all controls).[5]

Canberra has tended not to exceed standard AG practices in implementing its export controls. For example, it has consistently eschewed
applying tougher rules for sensitive destinations, with no presumed
embargo on certain countries. At the same time, it has been scrupu-
lous in its national implementation of AG standards. For example, in
practice Australia rarely if ever approves licenses for CW-relevant exports to countries that are suspected proliferators ([DOD] ints.).

Multilateral Export-Control Regime: Australia Group

Australia has always had a complicated and ambivalent relationship with the multilateral suppliers regime that bears its name. It is
important to note that Australian attitudes regarding the AG have always to some extent been influenced by its position as the regime's
chairman and namesake. Most officials readily admit that Australia's
unique role inevitably has had an impact on its national perspective.
In addition to always having had the responsibility to seek and represent consensus positions, Australia has derived considerable prestige
and influence from the AG in other disarmament areas. For example,
it was largely because of its association with the AG that Washington
asked Canberra to host the 1989 Government–Industry Conference on
CW, the event that cemented Australia's leading role in CWC negotiations. Such wider benefits have not been lost on Canberra. A 1991 internal Australian reporting cable from an AG meeting notes, "The
benefit for Australia's standing in the field of arms control . . . is sub-

stantial, considerable influence with the Western Group flowing from our role in the Australia Group" (DFAT off., 1991k, p. 3). Another lauds "the reputational impact for Australia" (DFAT off., 1992c, p. 3). Indeed, one pivotal official remarks that Australia would likely have been much less interested in the regime had it not been for its having such leadership responsibilities and privileges ([DFAT] int.).

Australia has played an equivocal role in multilateral CW export controls from its earliest involvement. In 1985 Canberra initiated the process that over time became the AG, but there have been credible suggestions that the idea may actually have originated in Washington. Whether or not Australia was acting independently or at Washington's behest, it had complex political motivations for undertaking the initiative. For example, Foreign Minister Hayden had previously incurred the ire of Prime Minister Hawke for creating strain in the bilateral relationship with Washington by being too aggressive in promoting nuclear disarmament proposals that were patently unacceptable to the Reagan administration. Consequently, DFA officials who came up with the proposal for a multilateral meeting on CW export controls knew that Hayden was eager to offer a proposal at high-level U.S.–Australian disarmament consultations in early 1985 that the United States would welcome and on which Canberra and Washington could work together cooperatively ([DFA] ints.).

Australia certainly did not foresee what it was getting into when it volunteered to host an inconspicuous meeting at its Brussels embassy so that export-control officials from various Western countries could compare notes on the recent measures that they individually had taken to cut off transfers of CW precursors to Iraq and Iran. This was envisioned as nothing more than an informal consultation to discuss an immediate, narrow problem. Officials anticipated that there would be just the one meeting, with some suspecting privately that perhaps a follow-up meeting might prove necessary ([DFA] int.; Walker int., 1998). In line with these modest expectations, Australia sent less than a handful of delegates to run the meeting, who arrived with no definite ideas to propose (Gee int., 1998).

Those who organized the initiative never imagined that it would lead to the creation of a new multilateral suppliers regime, or even to the adoption of additional national controls, or even necessarily to informal harmonization of existing measures (Walker int., 1998). As one official involved directly in the original planning recalls, "Initially there was no commitment that this was something we were going to be doing for a decade or more. It was just really . . . 'here's a problem, let's everyone sit down around a table,' and once they got around a table they decided it would be useful to get around a table again in a few months time, and so it went" ([DFA] int.).

For the next two years this dynamic led Australia to host a series of meetings, in each case without knowing if it would be the last ([DOD] int.). The main Australian goal in this process was to expand the "least common denominator" Core List to include all of the chemicals that Iraq was actually trying to acquire for its CW program. This was seen as a minimal necessity to rationalize controls, which as things stood, for example, controlled potassium fluoride but did nothing about functionally equivalent sodium fluoride (Gee int., 1998).

Although these meetings were vigorously supported by their Australian chairman, Assistant Secretary Ronald Walker, others within DFA were uneasy. "Some people thought we were sticking our necks out too much," a former official recounts, concerned that "this would be seen in the same way as the Nuclear Suppliers Group was seen, as rich countries depriving developing countries of . . . technology" (Findlay int., 1998).

As the process evolved, Australia found itself in the ambiguous position of supporting further progress in instituting additional controls, while at the same time trying to avoid fostering a discriminatory mechanism that could undermine or compete with a future multilateral CW ban. This was an explicit Australian concern from the onset, shared in many European capitals. Australia tried to counter this possibility by pressing as early as before the second meeting to invite non-Western participants, so that the nascent process would not be perceived by outsiders as a discriminatory "rich man's club," although this proposal was blocked by the United States (Gee int., 1998; Walker int., 1998). Australia, in turn, rejected U.S. suggestions to institute a list of target countries that would be subject to more stringent controls, again to avoid discriminatory appearances (Gee int., 1998). Most important, it forcefully stressed at the very first meeting that it regarded export-control arrangements as interim measures pending completion of the CWC negotiations. Australian officials reiterated this point repeatedly as the process moved forward (Butler int., 1998; Gee int., 1998; [DOD] int.; O'Sullivan int., 1998; Walker int., 1998). Indeed, when Foreign Minister Hayden in 1987 finally authorized recognizing the meetings as an ongoing process, he conditioned his approval on Australia formally recapitulating its understanding that this was a strictly transitional arrangement that would be replaced by the CWC ([DOD] int.).

Because it saw the AG only as an interim mechanism and believed that such a stopgap measure was urgently needed to address short-term problems such as Iraq's blatant efforts to acquire CW-related assistance from Western companies, Australia was happy to continue to use its authority as chairman of the newly institutionalized process in order to promote wider controls. It acted in close cooperation with a small cluster of governments that shared this agenda, including the

United States, Britain, and The Netherlands, arrayed against a majority of fence-sitters and a core group that staunchly resisted any additional controls, including Germany, France, and Japan (int.). Australia's activist posture during this period was based not only on the perception that the CWC was still a long way off, but that even a strengthened AG would remain an extremely modest endeavor. A DFAT official explains the reasoning at the time: "The Australia Group after all was only an informal meeting to compare policies. . . . It was never designed to be a multilateral . . . enforcement mechanism. And since there are billions of meetings run by billions of people every day in the world, why shouldn't these particular people turn up at some place in Paris and have a meeting to talk about what they do on a national basis" (O'Sullivan int., 1998).

Any potential tension between strengthening the AG and concluding and implementing the CWC therefore was abstract enough in the period up to 1990 that senior officials in Canberra did not see any reason for immediate concern (Jones int., 1998; O'Sullivan int., 1998; Reese int., 1998). At the same time, Australia was not concerned about opposing CWC provisions that could undermine AG operations (since it assumed the CWC would replace the AG if and when it was completed). For example, far from joining U.S.–led negotiating efforts in Geneva to dilute Articles X and XI (on technical cooperation and assistance), Australia supported providing States Parties with enhanced access to technology as an incentive for Third World participation. In fact, Australia played a key behind-the-scenes role in pressuring Washington to accept at a minimum the ambiguous language that eventually was included in the final treaty (and which was the focus of so much ire in the U.S. Senate) (Gee int., 1998).

The 1990–1991 Gulf Crisis complicated Canberra's thinking about the AG and its relationship to the CWC, but at first did not alter the fundamental Australian equation. Although the crisis, together with the commitment of President George H. W. Bush, raised the prospect of real progress in Geneva, the end of the CWC negotiations was still nowhere in sight. Meanwhile, the menace of Iraq's WMD programs, and revelations of continuing Western assistance, created an urgent short-term imperative to strengthen the AG. Australia therefore went along with U.S.–led efforts during and immediately following the crisis to strengthen the regime, without worrying or changing its basic assumptions about its future if and when the CWC was finalized ([DFAT] ints.; Jones int., 1998). However, it did not play an active role in forcing these developments, instead allowing external events to shape a consensus ([DFAT] int.).

This delicate balance in the Australian position regarding the AG shifted sometime in the middle of 1991. The reasons were twofold, both relating to the CWC. First, it became apparent that an agreement in Geneva was seriously in the offing. Second, Washington, having never ascribed to the Australian position that the AG represented an interim arrangement, began explicitly to challenge the notion that it should be eliminated, or even substantially modified, after the CWC entered into force.

Australia became increasingly wary of U.S. plans to continue to strengthen the AG. As a pivotal middle-level official recalls, "If there was one problem . . . that caused ruptures . . . it was the intense interest of the U.S. Administration in using the Australia Group suddenly to launch export controls on the world following the Iraq crisis. Our view was that they were simply reaching far too far, far too fast, and in ways which were simply not sensitive to making progress in this field" [DFAT] int.).

Consequently, Canberra consciously sought to obstruct any further strengthening of the regime. For example, it opposed U.S. efforts to have the Group adopt a spate of national measures, such as catch-all controls that Washington had instituted in late 1990 ([DFAT] int.).

These developments prompted an internal policy review in Canberra on the future of the Group. The prevailing view that emerged reaffirmed the long-standing position that as a matter of principle the AG in any shape or form should be eliminated once the CWC was finished. A few officials had argued that there might be useful scope for some type of modified suppliers arrangement to augment CWC, analogous to the relationship between the NPT and NSG ([DFAT ints.). Even this bureaucratic minority agreed, however, that the AG was expendable. As one key official recalls, the unchallenged consensus was, "We should not let the Australia Group get in the way of the conclusion of the negotiation of the Convention, and if ditching the Australia Group is the price that we have to pay for getting the Convention, then let's look seriously at getting rid of the Australia Group" (Gee int., 1998).

By early 1992 it was clear that the AG issue was threatening to derail the Geneva talks at a sensitive stage, perhaps irredeemably. Australia was determined to use its influence as chairman to force the AG partners to confront this question directly. This put Canberra on a collision course with Washington. The Bush administration let Canberra know that not only would it block consensus within the Group on any suggestion to even consider eliminating the AG, but that it would be profoundly irked if Australia supported such a proposal either as chairman or even in a national capacity.

Based in large part on this bilateral pressure from the United States, as well as on Australia's consensus-building role as chairman, Foreign Minister Evans opted to steer a middle course. He directed his staff to push for concessions in terms of significantly curtailing the scope of the Group's activities, while avoiding any direct call for its automatic dissolution (DFAT off., 1998; Gee int., 1998; [DFAT] int.). This represented a retreat from the long-standing Australian stance, but nonetheless showed considerable flexibility in addressing Third World concerns.

Canberra circulated a confidential paper to its AG partners on 18 May, laying out its new national position on the Group's future. After recalling that Australia had always described the Group as an interim arrangement, including in bilateral exchanges with Third World countries, the paper stated,

We have been conscious that if the Geneva negotiations continue to fail to produce a Convention soon, the Australia Group activities would then face an indefinite and probably expanded future as the only, albeit inherently unsatisfactory and limited, international line against CW proliferation. On the other hand, if a CWC along the lines we have been proposing is achieved in the near future *some significant modification to the Australia Group's activities is inevitable over the next few years.* (DFAT off., 1992b, pp. 1–2, emphasis added)

It concluded that if the AG were to continue after CWC entry into force—a question that was left pointedly open—then its basic functions, procedures, and even name would need to change significantly. Specifically, the paper asserted that any vestigial suppliers arrangement outside the CWC framework should limit itself to items not covered by the CWC (e.g., non-CWC chemicals, equipment, and technology, and BW-related items).

Tensions erupted with the United States when this position was debated at the AG plenary meeting a few weeks later. Far from being willing to consider reigning in the Group, the United States was still pressing to strengthen it further. A classified diplomatic cable that the Australian Delegation sent to Canberra reported,

Some in the Group are deeply committed to export controls and value the Australia Group as the prime mechanism for working against CBW proliferation. [Sentence deleted]. It required some effort on the part of those, including pre-eminently ourselves, who attach primacy to the successful conclusion of a CWC this year, to reign in those who wanted to take measures . . . to strengthen the Regime irrespective of the presentational impact such a development would have . . . in Geneva. (DFAT off., 1992c, p. 3)

A U.S. official recounts the same dispute from the opposite perspective: "At that point the Australians . . . were pretty much willing to do anything to close the Convention" (Inglee int., 1998). The meeting ended with no agreement on what specific action, if any, AG members would take.

Into this impasse stepped the U.S. and Australian CD ambassadors, who, with the collusion of their counterparts from the other AG states, hatched an audacious cabal to negotiate a compromise between themselves without the authorization or knowledge of their respective governments. These walk-in-the-woods talks produced what became known as the O'Sullivan Statement, which said on the one hand that AG governments would review their export-control procedures in light of the CWC, but on the other promised no definite action as a result. This formulation was accepted by the WEOG in Geneva in mid-July 1992, and only then sent to capitals for approval on a take-it-or-leave-it basis.

Although the unexpected arrival of the O'Sullivan text did not generate the kind of indignation in Canberra that it did in Washington, DFAT was not happy with the flimsiness of this pledge. Its concern was that this intentionally ambiguous language did not go far enough and was not explicit enough to address the concerns of Australia Group critics. However, Ambassador O'Sullivan personally weighed in to defend the text. He argued that he was convinced beyond any doubt that this noncommittal formulation was the most that Washington would consider, that any attempt to modify it would lead to the fragile compromise unraveling, and that even this was going to be a hard sell in Washington for his American counterpart (and Geneva co-conspirator). Based on this judgment by its senior disarmament diplomat, Canberra concluded that it had no choice but to embrace the O'Sullivan Statement ([DFAT] ints.).

DFAT aggressively sought to sell the compromise, sending a "flying team" of senior officials to Washington and other capitals. According to participants, the Australians employed a brazen strategy of playing both sides against the middle. In Washington they emphasized the lack of commitment involved. They then turned around and made the very opposite case by stressing the extent of the commitment involved to partners such as Canada and Sweden that, like itself, wanted to go further, and to the chairman of the CWC negotiations, who passed this rendering on in explaining the O'Sullivan text to nonaligned delegations. Australia thus consciously sought to mask the unresolved rift among AG partners by encouraging them, as well as the NAM, to interpret the ambiguous text in different ways ([DFAT] int.; Mahley int., 1998). In diplomatic terms, it did what is known as "papering over" the issue.

The O'Sullivan Statement fulfilled its immediate purpose, satisfying the NAM at a crucial juncture and allowing the CWC negotiations to proceed rapidly to a successful conclusion. However, the circumstances by which the statement had been agreed upon within the AG and accepted by others rendered conflicting interpretations inevitable. Such different understandings of what had been agreed to existed not only between AG and NAM governments, but among AG governments themselves. The CWC now in hand, the AG partners needed to decide the Group's future in earnest.

Not surprising, Canberra's interpretation of the O'Sullivan Statement leaned toward its long-standing preferences. An internal memorandum to Foreign Minister Evans prior to the December 1992 AG meeting, the first after the completion of the CWC negotiations, warns, "Achievement of a common position in the Group on its future direction, particularly with respect to the relationship with the CWC, will not be an easy task [remainder of sentence deleted] . . . We will have our work cut out to ensure that an export controllers' frolic does not frighten the CWC horses!" (Dauth off., 1992c). The memo proposes a strategy to meet this goal while avoiding open intra-AG conflict, wherein Australia would seek to reaffirm the O'Sullivan Statement (presumably without further clarification) while dampening any efforts to expand or strengthen the Group.

While Washington adamantly adhered to its minimalist reading of the O'Sullivan Statement, Australia continued publicly to articulate a more forward-leaning interpretation. For example, in his speech at the CWC signing ceremony on 13 January 1993, Foreign Minister Evans emphasized that one of the Convention's chief benefits would be to enhance peaceful trade in dual-use chemicals. He then observed, "It was in this context that my country and other members of the Australia Group announced on 6 August last year in the Conference on Disarmament their commitment to review their policies on harmonization of export controls, *with the aim of removing restrictions* so as to benefit states parties acting in full compliance with the convention" (Evans off., 1993b, p. 1, emphasis added). Clearly, this was pushing the boundaries of the commitment that some other AG states perceived in the O'Sullivan Statement.

But over the next few years, Canberra adapted to living with the status quo, abandoning active attempts to scale back the Group's activities. Instead, Australia adopted a defensive strategy, concentrating its energies on heading off any initiatives that could been seen as further entrenching the AG institutionally. It also called on other members to shoulder a larger share of the burden of responding to continuing attacks on the Group's legitimacy by radical NAM states such as Iran. Meanwhile, as the chair, it continued to perform its duties managing the Group's smooth operation. Finally, in a tacit acknowledgment that the Group would continue to exist for the foreseeable future, Australia dropped its opposition to allowing new members to join (this policy had been adopted as part of its antientrenchment strategy), returning to its earlier support of geographic diversification as a means to offset perceptions that the Group was a discriminatory North–

South arrangement (Bird off., 1994a, 1994c; DFAT off., 1993g, 1994a, 1994b, 1994c, 1995b; Steele off., 1993).

By the time CWC entry into force became assured in 1996, Australia had quietly stopped referring to the interim nature of the AG ([DFAT] int.). This change was explicitly acknowledged in an internal paper for new Foreign Minister Alexander Downer following the change in government. It explained that although the AG had previously been regarded as an interim arrangement pending the CWC, Australia now believed that it continued to play a useful, complementary role. However, the same paper comments, "In our view supply-side measures, such as export controls, cannot equate with the effectiveness of . . . a legally-binding global norm against these weapons" (Steele off., 1996, p. 1). Moreover, at a subsequent AG meeting Australia continued to pursue all of the same priorities, including resisting further entrenchment (DFAT off., 1996b).

Although Australia by the late 1990s had reconciled itself to retaining the AG for the time being, it still did not necessarily see this as an indefinite state of affairs. Canberra was therefore quite alarmed by the U.S. CWC ratification condition requiring the AG to retain controls on exports to non-AG states that are at least as effective as those in place at the time of U.S. ratification. The Australian view was that a final decision on the long-term status of the AG was still pending, although this should be deferred until the effectiveness of the CWC could be assessed. As a classified reaction to the U.S. CWC ratification condition stated, "It would be premature for the Group to seek to make adjustments to AG controls pursuant to the O'Sullivan Statement or otherwise. However, we do not think that the door should be completely shut on the possibility of adjustments to AG controls at some future time" (DFAT off., 1997c, p. 3). According to a middle-ranking official closely involved in these issues, the prevailing view within DFAT is that the question of whether the AG should continue to exist, and if so in what form, will need to be reconsidered after the CWC has had a better chance to establish itself ([DFAT] int.).

Wider Export-Control Norms

Although Australia has ceaselessly pressed for the AG to be as transparent as possible about its operations and has often taken it upon itself bilaterally to explain the Group's activities to nonmembers, it has tended not to favor bilateral or multilateral efforts to induce nonmembers to adhere unilaterally to AG export-control standards. This was less true in the formative two years of the AG, when Canberra encouraged a few other potential suppliers such as South Korea and Turkey to adopt national measures so that they would be qualified to join the consultations in a bid to widen geographic participation (Gee int., 1998). At one point Australia on its own initiative even prodded East Germany to try to start a parallel process among Warsaw Pact members (Walker int., 1998).

By the time the AG had solidified into a more or less standing institution, however, Australia was shying away from any effort to hold it up as a model for others to emulate. This inclination against pushing export controls beyond the Group has been a consistent feature of Australian policy since at least the late 1980s. The main reason for this has been concern that aggressively promoting wide adherence to export controls would undermine cooperation on the CWC, first in its negotiation and later in its implementation ([DOD] int.).

Canberra has not merely declined to promote wider adherence. On at least one notable occasion it actively "hijacked" a high-level multilateral initiative by the United States. After failing to get restrictions on CW-related transfers endorsed at a high-level, global conference that it sponsored in Paris in January 1989, the United States set out to try again in a more conducive multilateral fora. As discussed in Chapter 3, Washington hit upon the idea of involving representatives of governments and their national chemical industries in a major conference to promote national export controls. Eager to announce this initiative at a meeting to which he was traveling, Secretary of State James Baker placed an impromptu telephone call from his plane to Australian Foreign Minister Gareth Evans, explaining the idea and asking if Canberra would be willing to play host to such a meeting. Evans (int., 1998), who received this call at home in the middle of the night without any advanced warning, recalls, "So I said on the spot OK."

According to a participant in the planning for this conference, the bureaucracy was dismayed when it learned that the foreign minister had spontaneously agreed to have Australia play a prominent role in promoting wider application of export controls. "We recognized that that was a very divisive issue, and we decided for ourselves that rather than making it something getting support to the Australia Group [rules], what we should be doing is getting industry to support the CWC." This same official notes that consequently, in taking the initiative forward, "It was twisted around from being a nonproliferation conference to a CWC support conference" (int.). Evans (int., 1998) himself readily acknowledges that in picking up the ball and running with it, Australia reconceptualized the original purpose of Baker's initiative.

This reorientation was codified in Parliamentary debate on 2 May 1989, when Prime Minister Hawke was challenged with the question, "Does Australia continue to seek a total ban on chemical weapons, or will the international conference on chemical weapons, to be held in Australia later this year, divert the negotiations to the much weaker goal of nonproliferation?" The prime minister responded, "The conference will not be in any way an attempt to establish what could be called a second track alternative to the Chemical Weapons Convention" (Hawke tst., 1989, pp. 1689–1690). A few weeks later, Foreign Minister Evans likewise informed delegates at the CD in Geneva that the purpose of the conference was to contribute to progress in the CWC negotiations (*CWC Bulletin* [5], 1989). These public statements focusing on CWC were reinforced with private bilateral pledges to several NAM governments that the subject of export controls would not be discussed at all (int.). True to this intent, Australia not only kept export controls off the formal agenda, but at the conference itself Australia used its position as host to deflect repeated U.S. attempts to raise the issue of restricting transfers (Burck & Flowerree, 1991; Findlay, 1989).

Since the entry into force of the CWC, Australia has been somewhat more supportive of encouraging non-AG governments to implement national export controls pursuant to the Convention's nonassistance obligations ([DFAT] int.). That said, it has never been a prominent supporter of the CWC's nonassistance element, instead focusing on the provisions for verifying nonpossession (see later discussion). Moreover, as noted, at the same time it has supported Articles X and XI (on technical cooperation and assistance). These clauses in effect counterbalance the CWC's nonassistance obligations. In addition to supporting relatively robust language for these articles during the negotiations (Gee int., 1998), Australia has subsequently led efforts within the OPCW to promote technical cooperation. For example, it was an active participant in the OPWC PrepCom's working group on technical assistance and cooperation, in which it led the fight to provide a separate budget item for this purpose, and has subsequently fought to increase this budget item ([DFAT] int.; George int., 1998; Taubman off., 1994).

National Enforcement Mechanisms

Australia has a great deal of clout in the Asia–Pacific region, and holds regular high-level bilateral contacts with important regional players, including China. It often takes bilateral actions that reinforce those of the United States and others (Evans int., 1998). For example, as one official notes, "We do a lot of [bilateral] activities to get people to sign up to the [nonproliferation] treaties" ([DFAT] int.), such as strenuous high-level bilateral efforts to get governments globally and regionally to sign and ratify the CWC (see later discussion). It has certainly therefore been within Australia's scope to contribute to enforcing restraint on CW-related transfers. However, as a general rule, Australia has deliberately refrained from undertaking national interdiction actions against CW-related transfers by third parties.

Although it has often had intelligence on transfers of proliferation concern, Canberra has preferred not to intervene with the governments involved beyond urging restraint in general terms.[6] On a number of occasions Washington has approached Canberra with specific intelligence on a pending transfer and asked it to intervene with relevant governments—whether AG members or not—but, as a rule, these requests have been rebuffed.[7] In declining to take action in such cases, Australia has reminded Washington that AG implementation is left to national discretion, and that external enforcement is therefore inappropriate, all the more so for nonadherents like China who are not bound by AG rules ([DFAT] ints.; [DOD] int.; Gee int., 1998).

Australia has no nonproliferation sanctions whatsoever other than those required under international law (e.g., UNSC sanctions on Iraq) ([DFAT] int.). Whereas Canberra has not necessarily been distressed that Washington has reinforced the AG through its interdiction activities despite its own disinclination to do so ([DFAT] int.), it has worried that unilateral U.S. sanctions might be associated somehow with the AG. Australia has taken the firm position that sanctions of any kind are inappropriate as a means to enforce export-control regimes ([DFAT] int.).

Other Capability-Denial Responses

There have been no apparent cases where Australia has used other denial measures against CW programs, such as targeted denial or sabotage or destruction.

Nonpossession Norm-Building

Global Nonpossession Norm: Chemical Weapons Convention

Australia gained membership in the CD in 1979, just before the issue of CW disarmament was remanded to Geneva following the collapse of bilateral talks between the superpowers. Because Australia was eager to find a niche in which to make its mark in the CD, and consistent with its acute historical aversion to gas warfare, it decided to concentrate on this fledgling agenda item ([DFAT] int.).

From the beginning, the main Australian priority was to ensure that a global CW ban included stringent verification provisions. A former Australian negotiator recounts, "We were very keen to get proper verification in there, and I think we were pretty much at the cutting edge in terms of pushing for really intrusive verification" (Findlay int., 1998). Therefore, like most other Western countries, Australia never considered the Soviet preference to get a quick, lean treaty by applying the BWC model (i.e., a legal prohibition without complex verification and compliance mechanisms). Unlike most of the WEOG, however, the Australian focus was not on verifying Soviet disarmament, but rather on verifying Third World (and especially Asia–Pacific) nonproliferation (Findlay int., 1998; Walker int., 1998).

Prior to the United States tabling its 1984 draft text, the Australian delegation focused its energies on chipping away at resistance, primarily from the United States, to even establishing an actual negotiating mandate (Findlay int., 1998). One of the few substantive CW issues debated by the CD during this period was Australia's proposal to include a reaffirmation of the 1925 Geneva Protocol prohibition against use in a new treaty. This initiative had the novel distinction of being opposed by all NATO and Warsaw Pact members. Unfazed by nearly universal opposition, the Australian delegation exerted a great deal of effort assembling a "coalition of the willing," comprising a handful of small neutral and nonaligned states, which eventually won over the opposition. While Australia did sincerely want to see this addressed, it also had an ulterior motive for pressing the issue: to perpetuate debate on *something* in order to keep the CW negotiations alive (Walker int., 1998).

Australia enthusiastically welcomed the U.S. draft text, tabled at the CD by Vice President Bush in April 1984, both for opening the door to real negotiations and, more important, because its "anytime, anywhere" approach to verification was very similar to Canberra's own position. Australia was the only country in the CD immediately to respond positively to the initiative, and subsequently worked actively behind the scenes to persuade other delegations to support the "anytime, anywhere" concept (Butler, 1990; Findlay int., 1998; Walker int., 1998). A month after the U.S. draft was tabled, in a public speech during a state visit to Moscow, Foreign Minister Hayden expressed strong support for the proposal generally, and in particular for the verification provisions that his Soviet hosts had angrily scorned as an insincere propaganda ploy by the Reagan administration (Hayden off., 1984).

For the next several years, Australia intrepidly worked to generate momentum in the negotiations. Its major contribution was to spearhead development of the technical schedules (i.e., lists) of CW-relevant chemicals. It volunteered a succession of talented diplomats to chair the relevant multilateral working group (one of only three in the CWC negotiations at the time), and contributed significant technical resources to this effort (Butler int., 1998; Findlay int., 1998; Hayden tst., 1986). It also took on the role of WEOG coordinator beginning in 1985 (Parliament off., 1986). Based on this prominent involvement, Australia's foreign minister was able to proclaim, "The Government has greatly expanded Australia's involvement in efforts . . . to conclude the Convention, to the point where foreign commentators have spoken of 'Australia's Leadership' in this area" (Hayden tst., 1986). Prime Minister Hawke echoed this sentiment, noting that Australia was playing a "prominent and almost pre-eminent role" in the CWC negotiations (Hawke tst., 1989).

In addition to this active multilateral involvement, almost as soon as the United States proposed the idea of "anytime, anywhere" challenge inspections, Australia began unilaterally to examine how this hazy principle could be made to work effectively in practice. Defence officials noted that procedures would need to be developed to guard against frivolous or malicious targeting of non-CW related facilities, especially sensitive sites such as the Joint Facilities. DOD and DFAT cooperatively developed a national position that addressed these concerns while preserving the principle of unrestricted "anytime, anywhere" inspections (Walker int., 1998; White int., 1999).

DFAT also early on solicited suggestions from the Australian chemical industry in order to ensure that any inspection procedures being developed would work in the real world. As part of this effort, Australia in January 1986 staged an unprecedented national trial inspection at a commercial facility in Melbourne, reporting positive results to the CD in a formal paper a few months later (Findlay int., 1998; Freeman & Mathews, 1988; O'Sullivan int., 1998). Australia also pushed CWC negotiators to look ahead to structural and organizational questions. Specifically, it advocated diverse regional representation in the decision-making body of the future implementing organization, so that the Third World would not see the CWC as a tool of the Western industrialized states (Butler int., 1998).

Australia's multifaceted activism throughout the mid to late 1980s is quite surprising when one considers that its context was a moribund negotiating environment in which most key players—the United States, the Soviet Union, and the NAM collectively—showed no desire to make meaningful progress. What is not surprising, however, is that Australian activism increased dramatically when the multilateral climate rapidly began to improve in 1989.

In retrospect, the September 1989 Canberra Government–Industry Conference marked the onset of the CWC endgame, broadly defined. It was also a watershed for Australia's engagement. His personal involvement through chairing this meeting led Foreign Minister Evans to escalate the CWC negotiations to among DFAT's highest priorities (Evans int., 1998). Henceforth, the issue was managed at very senior levels, characterized by the routine involvement of Deputy Secretary Michael Costello (Mahley int., 1998; *Sydney Morning Herald*, 5/27/93). Perhaps partly due to this high-level oversight, virtually no serious internal fissures would arise on CWC negotiating positions during the intense and often volatile endgame years; not between the Geneva delegation and Canberra, nor between agencies, nor within agencies, nor between the government and the political opposition, nor between government and industry ([DFAT] int.; Reese int., 1998).

Immediately after the Government–Industry Conference, Foreign Minister Evans instructed Disarmament Ambassador David Reese to sound out his counterparts in Geneva about convening a CD meeting at the ministerial level in order to give a political boost to the CWC negotiations. However, this proposal was firmly rebuffed by the United States, which asserted that there were still far too many unresolved negotiating issues to even contemplate such an initiative (Reese int., 1998).

Australia was dismayed when a few months later the United States changed key, long-standing elements of its negotiating position. The first blow came in June 1990, when the United States insisted on producing and retaining a residual "security stockpile" of binary weapons pending universal adherence to the CWC by all CW-capable states. Although its public reaction was muted, Canberra privately beseeched the Bush administration to rescind this proposal, arguing that it would make the Convention unsaleable to Third World countries (Gee int., 1998; Walker int., 1998).

A second, arguably more serious blow to Australian aspirations for a robust CW ban came in August. Without warning or discussion, the United States withdrew its support within the WEOG for "anytime, anywhere" challenge inspections, insisting that States Parties should retain an ultimate right of refusal (Cousins off., 1991a). Knowing that some in Washington were unhappy about this new stance, Canberra launched an orchestrated, high-level bilateral campaign to persuade Washington to reverse its reversal.[8] According to numerous Australian officials, this represented a conscious effort to bolster the leverage of agencies (e.g., ACDA) that were arguing for more rather than less intrusive verification.

Parallel to these behind-the-scene efforts to respond to developments in the WEOG, Australia worked to sustain political momentum in the broader CWC negotiations. In March 1991, Foreign Minister Evans wrote to each of his counterparts in CD member states to revive the idea of convening a CD ministerial meeting as soon as possible before the end of the year. He explained that such a meeting was needed to address the many thorny outstanding issues at a political level, including verification, universality, technical assistance and cooperation, and organizational structures (Evans off., 1991a). He reiterated this call publicly in May at a U.N. conference, and then promoted the initiative in bilateral meetings with various counterparts (DFAT off., 1991a, 1991b; 1991c; Evans off., 1991b).

Meanwhile, the tempo of behind-the-scenes developments quickened. Washington sent a delegation to Canberra on 2 May 1991 to preview a new proposal on challenge inspections. According to the lead Australian official at this meeting, the United States stressed that its proposal was loosely based on the British concept of "managed access," albeit a more restrictive version, and therefore was more forward leaning than its August position. U.S. officials also made it clear that this position was the product of a bitter and protracted interagency struggle, and that as such it represented the full measure of U.S. flexibility (Cousins off., 1991a). Secretary of State Baker reiterated this latter point personally to Foreign Minister Evans a short time later (O'Sullivan int., 1998).

Canberra's initial assessment was that "the new U.S. position . . . is a substantial advance on their previous position" on challenge inspections, given that it not longer embraced an absolute right of refusal (Cousins off., 1991a, p. 2). Even so, while Australia welcomed this as a step in the right direction, it still saw the specific proposal as unacceptable. For example, Australia told the United States that a number of glaring loopholes would need to be tightened, including procedures for defining site perimeters and for securing the site during delays in access, the precise degree of access when managed access was evoked, and reasons for which it could be evoked for (Cousins off., 1991a).

Canberra's perceptions of the new U.S. position on challenge inspections were doubtless enhanced by President Bush's surprise announcement less than two weeks later on 13 May that the United States would abandon its insistence on retaining a security stockpile and would immediately renounce in-kind retaliation. Australia publicly welcomed this step as a major U.S. concession (Evans off., 1991b). In the face of the positive atmosphere created by this development, and having been convinced that the U.S. interagency had been pushed as far as it would go, senior officials decided not to oppose the new U.S. position as a basis for further negotiations within the WEOG, while instructing the Geneva delegation to rally support for the changes that Canberra felt were needed to make it minimally acceptable (Cousins off., 1991a).

Washington then approached Australia (along with Britain and Japan), asking it not only to accept the new U.S. proposal as a basis for further negotiations, but actually to cosponsor it in order to forestall other WEOG members' rejecting it out of hand. This request presented Canberra with an unpalatable choice. The bureaucracy vehemently argued against associating with a position that grossly violated Australia's fundamental tenets on verification ([DFAT] int.; [DOD] int.). After an agonized internal debate, however, senior officials sided with Disarmament Ambassador Paul O'Sullivan, who asserted that, tactically, it was better to go along with the United States now and then try to improve the proposal in negotiations within the WEOG. Otherwise,

O'Sullivan warned, there was a strong possibility that WEOG negotiations would stall indefinitely, or even worse, that the United States
would be driven to circumvent the WEOG altogether by tabling its
proposal in the broader negotiations, where it would likely find considerable support from key nonaligned members (Cousins off., 1991b;
O'Sullivan int., 1998). A memorandum explaining the rationale for this
decision to the foreign minister stated,

We are more concerned to put a workable CWC in place as soon as possible in
order to establish norms which can help to constrain CW proliferation pressures which are already evident in our region and elsewhere. In this respect
we are more concerned to promote a reasonably satisfactory regime which is
adopted by the CD and achieves wide and early adherence rather than allow
a search for an elusive optimal formulation to remain locked up in intermi-
nable negotiations in Geneva. (Cousins off., 1991b, pp. 3–4)

Events unfolded rapidly once the U.S. proposal was tabled in the
WEOG in early July as a joint U.S., Australian, British, and Japanese
paper. The Australian delegation immediately began to lobby other
WEOG delegations bilaterally, on the one hand to convince those opposing *any* restrictions on access to accept the U.S. proposal as the basis
for negotiations rather than rejecting it outright, while on the other hand
to garner the broadest possible support for specific improvements that
Australia believed were essential to make it minimally acceptable
(Cousins off., 1991b). According to an internal account,

We utilised our position to play a bridging role with some success. A separate
tactical question is whether we moved too soon in accepting the U.S. proposal
as a basis for further negotiations. We deliberately took this position in the
knowledge that others [deleted] had adopted a more outspokenly critical approach at the beginning. One factor was our desire to keep the U.S. engaged in
negotiations with other Western Group members, with a view to improving their
proposals, rather than run the risk of the U.S. deciding to push its proposals
unilaterally amongst the full CD membership. (Cousins off., 1991b, p. 2)

The same document went on to aver that cosponsoring the U.S. proposal "will not constrain our ability to work for further improvements
during the next stage of negotiations" (p. 5). Sure enough, as soon as
the proposal was accepted by the WEOG as a basis for negotiations,
Australia began pressing the United States bilaterally to tighten its
many loopholes ([DFAT] int.).

Having cosponsored the U.S. position, Australia's avowed goal was
to inch it as far as possible toward the original, less-restrictive British
conception of managed access. For example, by late September, thanks
to intense external pressure from the allies and internal White House

intervention, the verification proponents in the U.S. interagency had garnered shaky support for a new compromise position that moved the United States closer to British-style managed access (see Chapter 3). This occurred just as Australia sent yet another delegation to Washington to lobby for just such flexibility, led by DFAT Deputy Secretary Costello and Assistant Secretary Richard Starr. In a meeting on 21 September, ACDA Director Ronald Lehman spelled out this new stance as a position that Washington tentatively was considering. He asked the Australians to front for the United States by tabling it as an Australian compromise that the United States could then negotiate on whether to accept depending on the reaction of other WEOG members (Mahley int., 1998). Australia promptly agreed to this ruse in order to foster negotiating momentum. This episode typifies the pragmatic, opportunistic role that Australia played behind the scenes during this period as the WEOG haggled over the details of managed access.

At some point during these behind-the-scenes bilateral dealings with Washington in the autumn of 1991, Australian officials came up with an audacious plan to bilaterally negotiate a comprehensive compromise with Washington that would address all of the outstanding disputes in Geneva, great and small, as reflected in bracketed language in the rolling negotiating text. The goal was to come up with a package that would address the many concerns of many governments, but in a way that Washington could accept. This bold idea was triggered by an offhand remark by ACDA Director Lehman, who mused to a senior Australian official that, when he had been chief START negotiator, he had always liked to have a complete treaty in his breast pocket that he knew he could sign on the spot, in order to help himself focus on the big picture during intricate technical negotiations. To Lehman's Australian listener, this passing remark suggested a way for Canberra to contribute decisively to the progress of the CWC negotiations (Mahley int., 1998; O'Sullivan int., 1998).

In effect, Australia proposed to take upon itself the task of negotiating with the United States bilaterally on behalf (unbeknownst to them) of the interests of all of the other CD delegations. As one observer notes, this represented a "crash through or crash" approach (Findlay, 1993, p. 19).

The process itself involved an intense series of highly secret bilateral negotiating rounds in Washington, with Australia trying to press the envelope of U.S. flexibility. The lead U.S. negotiator in these talks recalls, "When [Australian Foreign Minister] Gareth Evans put that text down, he knew that the U.S. could sign it because of six months of work that we had had very quietly. . . . There were a lot of fights bilaterally in that process" (Moodie int., 1998). Another U.S. participant ruefully recalls that the bilateral process was so intensive that talks were not even suspended for Thanksgiving, perhaps the most sacro-sanct American family holiday ([OSD] int.).

At the end of the day, Australia would have preferred a much more rigorous treaty than the one that emerged from this process, particu-larly in terms of stringent verification. But it had obtained major U.S. concessions on a number of key issues. Based on its protracted talks in Washington, it concluded that the resulting draft text embodied the maximum flexibility that could be obtained from Washington, and that in the final analysis it was better to have a less-rigorous treaty than no treaty ([DFAT] ints.).[9]

Bilaterally agreed text in hand, Australia moved on to the next chal-lenge: selling it to the rest of the CD as a "model compromise" that would allow the CWC negotiations to proceed to a quick and success-ful conclusion. Even as Foreign Minister Evans tabled the Australian draft text in Geneva on 19 March 1992, Australian officials were trav-eling to some thirty-three capitals to explain and promote it in face-to-face meetings (*CWC Bulletin* [16], 1992; Findlay, 1992a). This marked the beginning of intensive Australian involvement at the highest lev-els to push the negotiations to closure.

The Australian text succeeded in changing the fundamental dynamic of the negotiations. As one of its primary authors notes, "The Austra-lian initiative was instrumental in shifting the negotiating climate in the CD from a circular, unproductive issue-by-issue negotiation, to a comprehensive, package approach for completion of the treaty text" (Letts, 1992, p. 6). For the remaining months of the negotiations, Aus-tralia would play a central role in facilitating compromises. Foreign Minister Evans returned to Geneva repeatedly, often remaining for unprecedented, extended periods, in order to resolve specific prob-lems in bilateral meetings on the margins of the negotiations. He re-calls, "You had me as the Minister fighting it out on an equal basis with these lowly disarmament ambassadors, who didn't think of them-selves as lowly and who were quite sort of chuffed by the attention they were given" (Evans int., 1998).

For the most part, Australia focused on finding common ground, rather than promoting its own national agenda. However, it contin-ued to press certain national priorities—for example, holding the line on tough verification and urging that early attention be given to struc-tural and organizational issues—so that the treaty could be effectively implemented as soon as it entered into force (O'Sullivan int., 1998).

Australian activism in the CWC negotiations culminated in a sus-tained campaign on behalf of the final text to emerge from Geneva. It was among a handful of governments, along with Germany, The Neth-erlands, and the United States, to engage in intensive bilaterally lob-bying once this text had been remanded to CD capitals for final approval (Findlay, 1993). Subsequently, Canberra lobbied for a favorable vote in the UNGA to endorse the treaty, and then for the widest possible number of signatures. It was especially active in urging China to become an original signatory. Later it worked bilaterally to secure the post-signature ratifications needed to allow the treaty to enter into force. It was particularly successful at delivering the support of the countries in its immediate region, with which it had been laying the groundwork for several years (see later discussion) (DFAT off., 1992d, 1994f; [DFAT] ints.; Findlay, 1993).

As the prospects for U.S. ratification stalled in the Senate over the next several years, Australia likewise worked publicly and privately to encourage progress (O'Sullivan int., 1998). Once Hungarian ratification in late 1996 triggered the countdown to entry into force, Canberra stepped up its public calls for both the United States and Russia (as the only declared possessor states) to ratify in time to become original States Parties.

Australia itself was the sixth signatory (and one of the first Western governments) to accede to the treaty on 6 May 1994. Both houses of Parliament unanimously had passed the ratification legislation unamended on 25 February with the support of all political parties, including the main conservative opposition, fringe parties, and independents. This bill included several hundred pages of detailed procedures to govern national implementation. Parliamentary debate was limited to speeches on behalf of the major and minor parties to express unconditional support for CWC ratification, and to commend Foreign Minister Evans and DFAT for their decisive roles in shepherding the negotiations to a successful conclusion (Attorney's General Department off., 1998; Evans off., 1994b; Parliament House off., 1994; Parliament Senate off., 1994a, 1994b, 1994c).

Canberra remained engaged on CWC issues at very senior levels throughout the extended work of the PrepCom in The Hague. This keen political interest in what was ostensibly a technical process was based on the perceived need to insure that, under the guise of developing implementation procedures, other governments were not permitted to dilute the terms of the treaty, particularly in terms of verification. "That was our main focus in the PrepCom process," a middle-ranking official recollects, "to make sure there wasn't any watering down of those provisions" ([DFAT] int.). A particular concern at very senior levels was that the United States was not doing anything to counter attempts by both Israel and France within the WEOG, and some NAM countries in the wider forum, to "walk back" intrusive on-site inspections. This was all the more irritating to Canberra because it had been Washington that had insisted that Israel be allowed to join the WEOG. Indeed, some Australian officials suspected that Washington (or at least certain U.S. agencies) was intentionally using Israel as a stalking horse in the WEOG to undermine verification. Australia consequently was forced to fight a rearguard action. It complained bilaterally to Washington, saying that it expected U.S. support in maintaining the hard-fought compromises that had been negotiated in Geneva ([DFAT] ints.).

Prior to entry into force, Foreign Minister Downer of the new Howard government made a special trip to the PrepCom in order to send an unmistakable signal that Canberra remained committed at the highest levels to full and effective implementation (*CWC Bulletin* [35], 1997).

Although Australia remains concerned about the unilateral conditions that the United States applied pursuant to the terms of its ratification, it has been generally satisfied with the operation to date of the CWC since entry into force ([DFAT] ints.). Its main interest looking to the future will be to ensure that the OPCW remains healthy and vigorous, particularly in light of recent budget problems.

Other Nonpossession Responses

Australia is perhaps the only Western government that actively tried to promote regional nonpossession structures as well as a global ban. The preeminent example of this is the Chemical Weapons Regional Initiative (CWRI), launched with considerable fanfare by Prime Minister Hawke in June 1988 (*CWC Bulletin* [2], 1988). The process involved twenty-two governments, representing most of the countries of Southeast Asia and the South Pacific, participating in a series of annual political seminars plus additional technical workshops (DFAT off., 1994f; McCormack, 1993). As noted, this initiative ultimately facilitated CWC entry into force by laying the groundwork for early regional ratifications. Its primary purpose, however, was to ensure strong regional implementation within the global treaty structure. This strategy reflected the fact that the main Australian interest in the global CWC was to prevent proliferation locally ([DFAT] int.).

Australia earlier had flirted with bone fide CW-free zones. In the internal deliberations that eventually led to the CWRI, DFAT gave serious consideration to proposing a regional CW-free zone as an immediate step while CWC negotiations continued. However, because such instruments had previously been proposed by Warsaw Pact states as alternatives to a universal instrument, the concept ultimately was rejected for fear of undermining the CWC negotiations (Findlay int., 1998; Walker int., 1998). Nonetheless, according to an official directly involved in the process, CWRI was always seen as laying the groundwork for a regional CW-free zone as a hedge against not achieving a global ban if it came to that. He states, "Of course, while the CWC negotiations process was alive, we used the regional initiative as a means to drive countries in the region to a level of awareness of the potential problem, hoping to get them on board the CWC. [But] if the CWC hadn't worked out, we would have tried to turn the regional initiative into some kind of regional chemical weapons free zone" ([DFAT] int.).

Further, during the Gulf War, Australia privately urged Washington to consider sponsoring a CW-free or WMD-free zone in the Middle East as an interim measure pending completion of the CWC (DFAT off., 1990g). In addition, the primary Australian motive for participating actively in the post–Gulf War multilateral security talks associated with the Middle East peace process, which did not specifically address proliferation, was as a means to address the underlying conditions that were creating demand for WMD. This was explicitly seen as a way to foster eventual participation in global nonpossession norms, and in particular the CWC, in a region that represented a cauldron of proliferation ([DFAT] int.).

Australia has thus actively promoted regional nonpossession arrangements and associated initiatives for a variety of purposes: as interim measures pending a global ban, as fallback measures in case an acceptable global instrument failed to materialize, and as supplemental measures to reinforce participation in, and implementation of, the global instrument.

Consequence–Management

Counterproliferation

The Defence Science and Technology Organization (DSTO) has engaged in research on CW defense for several decades. This effort has always been exceedingly limited though, and has focused on disarmament verification issues in addition to military applications. DSTO has concentrated primarily on niche research, rather than trying to pursue a comprehensive program with extremely finite budgetary resources (Brabin-Smith tst., 1997; Punch tst., 1995).

In addition, the Australian Defence Force has maintained an inventory of basic protective equipment (i.e., gas masks), as well as limited personnel training in its use. However, these programs have been modest in the extreme. For example, when Australia deployed a very small contingent of mostly naval forces as part of the 1990–1991 Gulf War coalition, the ADF was hard pressed to find enough gas masks to equip it, since most in its inventory were reaching the end of their useful lives (Ray tst., 1990).

The limited extent of Australia's defensive capabilities has not been the inadvertent result of dereliction or oversight. Instead it has reflected quite conscious policy decisions to forgo counterproliferation. The 1987 *Defence White Paper* (Defence off., 1987) specifies that the ADF would only maintain very basic CBW protective capabilities, representing a low priority. U.S. overtures in the mid-1990s for enhanced counter-proliferation cooperation, which Australia rebuffed, had focused primarily on the CW area ([OSD] int.). Subsequently, the Howard government released a formal policy foreign policy white paper stating, "The global treaty banning chemical weapons . . . advances Australia's national security by . . . removing from the Australian Defence Force the onerous requirement to be equipped to operate in an environment where chemical weapons are being used" (DFAT off., 1997a, p. 47).

In recent testimony, the head of DSTO noted that although U.S. Defense Department assessments had argued for developing new CBW counterproliferation capabilities, there had been no consideration given at the ministerial level to augmenting Australian activities in this area (Brabin-Smith tst., 1997). Interviews with current officials confirm that Canberra's disinterest in CBW countermeasures remains firmly intact.

Deterrence

To the extent that Australia has any deterrent capability against CBW attack, it is derived largely from the extended deterrence that it receives as a close ally of the United States. In this sense, Australia's policies on CBW deterrence boil down to its measure of support for U.S. deterrent postures.

It has already been noted that Australia was actively hostile to U.S. attempts to preserve its in-kind deterrent capabilities during the CWC negotiations, most notably by opposing the Bush administration's security stockpile proposal. As for nuclear deterrence, Canberra has not taken a formal position on recent U.S. decisions to expand the umbrella of nuclear deterrence to cover CBW attacks, including against U.S. allies (White int., 1999). However, it has taken actions that implicitly undercut the U.S. position. In 1995 the Australian government argued before the World Court that if the court were to render an opinion on the legality of nuclear weapons, then it should find the use or threat of use of nuclear weapons illegal under all circumstances (DFAT off., 1996a).[10] The next year, the government-sponsored Canberra Commission for the Elimination of Nuclear Weapons explicitly rejected the notion that nuclear weapons could have value or legitimacy in deterring CBW attacks. In its lengthy analysis of this issue, the Commission's official report, as presented to the international community by Foreign Minister Downer, asserts that, rather than deterrence, the appropriate response to CBW threats was to strengthen and effectively

implement the CWC and BWC (Canberra Commission off., 1996).[11]
The Howard government has otherwise avoided direct attacks on the
U.S. CBW deterrence posture, including the aggressive antiproliferation deterrrent tone set by President George W. Bush, but at the same
time it has not gone out of its way to be supportive.

CASE STUDY: BIOLOGICAL WEAPONS

Capability-Denial

National Export Controls

Australian exports of biological material and BW-related equipment
were totally unregulated prior to the AG adopting applicable multilateral guidelines in the early 1990s (Australia Group off., 1990; DFAT
off., n.d.a, 1991k). Canberra quickly implemented new AG requirements once they were agreed to; for example, distributing the Group's
1990 BW Warning List widely to relevant domestic industries (AG off.,
1990). But it has only imposed specific BW-related licensing requirements in strict accordance with the agreed AG lists.

Multilateral Export-Control Regime: Australia Group

In contrast to Australia's leading role in establishing multilateral
export controls on CW-relevant items, Canberra did little more than
follow the American lead in expanding the scope of the AG to include
BW nonproliferation ([State] int.). Canberra did support the original
U.S. initiative in early 1990 to address BW proliferation through warning
guidelines to facilitate voluntary corporate vigilance (DFAT off., 1990a).
Although having little choice but to relent under intense U.S. pressure,
even this mild step engendered pronounced caution. Australia informed
the AG that, consistent with its position regarding the CWC, it considered this to be a strictly temporary measure pending negotiation of a
BWC verification protocol, although it recognized that unlike the CWC
this was still a distant prospect (DFAT off., 1990a; [DFAT] int.).

Australia responded warily to subsequent U.S. efforts to enact actual controls on BW-relevant items following the onset of the Gulf War.
In bilateral disarmament consultations in November 1990 Australian
officials voiced deep skepticism about trying to go beyond voluntary
industry guidelines. They asserted that an informal organization like
the AG could not regulate such heavily dual-use exports, and that therefore the best solution to the BW problem would be to enhance the BWC
by negotiating a verification protocol (Fox off., 1990). In the face of
U.S. determination, however, Canberra accepted that some BW-related
controls could be useful, and that this was not necessarily incompat-

ible with its higher-priority goal of strengthening the BWC (DFAT off., 1991j).

Once real prospects for enhancing the BWC emerged in late 1994, Australia and its AG partners once again faced the threat that the NAM would hold this process hostage to demands that the AG be disbanded once and for all. Throughout the VEREX process to explore the feasibility of BWC verification, a number of Third World states repeatedly expressed displeasure with AG members' failure to make good on the implied promise of the O'Sullivan Statement. Iran sought to insert the issue of cooperation and assistance into any new negotiating process by having it noted in the final VEREX report. Like most other Western governments, Australia opposed this move, but backed down when Iran threatened to derail a negotiating mandate by blocking consensus on the VEREX report (DFAT off., 1993i, 1994c).

The future of the AG was squarely on the table throughout the AHG negotiations in Geneva, with hard-line NAM states demanding its total elimination as a quid pro quo for supporting a compliance protocol. Because the United States shut down the endgame stillborn, however, this issue never posed a true negotiating crisis. Canberra's endgame strategy was to hope that, when the real crunch came, moderate nonaligned states ultimately would prevail on the others to pull back from a showdown ([DFAT] int.). It therefore made no formal effort to consider bottom-line positions during the negotiations. Informally, the prevailing mood was that additional concessions would be needed ([DFAT] ints.). As one official noted when the endgame seemed imminent:

You can't ignore the fact that a lot of countries are only in this process because they want to get out of it something on the technical cooperation side. And that probably isn't our priority, but for a number of countries it is, and we're going to have to be a bit more forthcoming on those sorts of issues if we're going to get the powerful disarmament side and the verification side that we want. ([DFAT] int.)

Precisely how far Canberra would have gone to address the NAM's demands is unknowable. However, Australia vigorously rejected U.S. explanations for rejecting Chairman Toth's text, which Washington believed went too far in undercutting AG export controls (*Sydney Morning Herald*, 7/27/01; *Canberra Times*, 7/27/01; *Washington Post*, 7/26/01).

Wider Export-Control Norms

Australia's reluctance to promote the AG as a wider export-control norm in the CW sphere has, if anything, been more pronounced for BW. To the extent that Canberra has been at all willing to promote wider export-control norms, it has been almost exclusively in the context of taking note of BWC Article III (Evans off.). Even in this, however, classified internal documents prior to the pivotal post–Gulf War BWC 1991 RevCon reveal significant skepticism about trying to bolster implementation of Article III. DFAT assessed that robust measures like those that Washington envisioned were of dubious value given the dual-use nature of the technology involved, and also unlikely to garner Third World support (DFAT off., 1991l; Starr off., 1991b). In this context, the Australian delegation to pre-RevCon consultations in the WEOG was instructed to express only conditional support for U.S. nontransfer ideas (DFAT off., 1991l). Following this guidance, the Australian delegation opted merely to support encouraging participants to exchange information on all of their national BWC implementing measures (including by implication those relevant to Article III). Even this unmistakably meek proposal was further diluted by being couched in an extremely restrictive interpretation of Article III; namely, that it forbids the transfer of BW per se, but does not address dual-use items (Starr off., 1991b). In other words, Australia declined to support any concrete measures to urge BWC members to regulate transfers of BWC-related equipment or technology. Moreover, the instruction cable to the delegation explains that Australia had decided to take even this patently milquetoast stance only due to "our role as Australia Group chair and consequently expectations from other Australia Group members that we would support strong non-proliferation rhetoric and measures" (DFAT off., 1991m, p. 5).

An internal DFAT paper explains the basis for this reluctance to support U.S.–led efforts to strengthen Article III: "We recognise the need to give support in principle to non-proliferation action in the BWC framework. In our view the question of the effectiveness of non-proliferation measures is critical. We do not see value in supporting measures which only serve to alienate the Third World parties to the Convention without constraining the spread of BW" (Starr off., 1991b, p. 5). A mid-level official at the time publicly made the same point in more biting language:

Of course non-proliferation measures are the instinctive U.S. response to any arms control issue. . . . Export controls in whatever framework tend to make Third World countries jittery. . . . There is a danger that in emphasising controls on proliferation of overwhelming the treaty which is about in the first instance disarmament. Non-proliferation is a sub-objective of disarmament and the two objectives cannot be pursued as if they are compatible. (Fox off., 1991, p. 9)

During the VEREX process that followed the 1991 RevCon, Australia expressed modest support for using future protocol negotiations to strengthen Article III, possibly by linking export controls to an illustrative list of items that would be banned under Article I (DFAT off. n.d.c.; Dauth off., 1992b). However, this does not appear to have been an active Australian priority during the actual protocol negotiations.

National Enforcement Mechanisms

As with CW denial, Australia has conspicuously refrained from undertaking enforcement actions; if anything, its actions vis-à-vis BW transfers have been even more low key. There does not appear to be even a single case in which Canberra has attempted to interdict specific transfers, or even to express concern after the fact. Again, Australia has not implemented any nonproliferation sanctions other than those required under international law.

Other Capability-Denial Responses

There have been no apparent cases where Australia has used other denial measures against BW programs.

Nonpossession Norm-Building

Global Nonpossession Norm: Biological Weapons Convention

Australia's participation in the 1980 First BWC RevCon was extremely low key. But by the next RevCon in 1986, Australia's growing involvement in CW disarmament led it to take a more activist role as a complement to its efforts in the CWC negotiations.

Although Australian officials regarded the Convention as grossly inadequate due to its lack of verification, they also recognized that implacable opposition to BWC verification by the two superpowers and many Third World countries meant that there was virtually no prospect for rectifying this perceived shortcoming. Instead, Australia set out to promote the more achievable outcome of promoting voluntary, modest CBMs (e.g., data declarations). A secondary aim was to work to ensure that U.S. allegations of Soviet noncompliance did not distract from achieving such positive goals, by neutrally stressing that the dispute highlighted the need for some type of verification (Walker int., 1998; Gee int., 1998).

Australia played an active role during and after the 1986 RevCon in instituting voluntary CBMs, proposing specific measures, and nominating the U.N. Department for Disarmament Affairs to coordinate data exchanges. Australian Disarmament Ambassador Richard Butler shepherded these proposals forward in his pivotal role as chairman of the drafting committee (DFAT off., 1990b). The Australian delegation also was responsible for crafting a compromise that sidestepped an attempt by India and other nonaligned states to hold CBMs hostage to creating a new organization to implement the peaceful cooperation obligations provided for in Article X (Sims, 1990b).

Following the 1986 RevCon, Australia played an active role in the intersessional working group that developed formats for data exchanges (Starr off., 1991a). Later, concerned that it was one of only a handful of States Parties that had made any declarations, Australia cosponsored a resolution at the UNGA in late 1989 asking the secretary general to report on participation in the voluntary BWC CBMs (CWC Bulletin [7], 1990).

In June 1990, Australian diplomats met with the Austrian disarmament officials who would preside over the September 1991 RevCon to discuss preparations well in advance. Australia indicated that it saw little point in aggressively promoting verification, given continuing superpower opposition and competing priorities: "A thoroughgoing attempt to reform the BWC could not be sustained and may dissipate energies best devoted to the CWC. Modest progress on the BWC . . . has more chance of success (both for the BWC and in terms of not undermining the CWC negotiations)" (DFAT off., 1990b, p. 6). Canberra therefore indicated that it would prefer to see the RevCon focus on improving the scope and implementation of existing CBMs and other modest, incremental measures.

The swift changes in the international climate brought about by the 1990–1991 Gulf War, as well as Moscow's decision to drop its categorical opposition to BWC verification, dramatically energized Australian aspirations on BWC verification. By November 1990 Canberra had concluded that "the pressures for work on BW verification are mounting" (DFAT off., 1990a). Although still mindful of the risk posed by distracting attention from the CWC negotiations and aware that Washington's unyielding opposition would be difficult to overcome, senior DFAT officials decided cautiously to pursue a more ambitious agenda for the September 1991 RevCon. During senior-level bilateral disarmament talks with the United States that month, Australia stated that although it was aware of the difficulties involved, it nonetheless wanted to use the RevCon to explore verification options (Fox off., 1990).

Australia was less circumspect during bilateral meetings with other Western governments. It lobbied for concrete action on verification at the upcoming RevCon, calling for states to use the intervening period to examine the feasibility of negotiating a new verification instrument. The instructions for these meetings explained, "A central objective of Australian policy . . . is to move U.S. thinking beyond confidence building measures (additional measures, improvements to existing measures) to support a BW verification regime, modelled on the CWC regime" (DFAT off., 1990a, p. 2).

Canberra went on record with this position at the beginning of 1991. Its "national position paper" for a Dutch-sponsored meeting to prepare for the Third RevCon stated, "Australia believes that a verification regime based on the CWC model should be technically feasible and appropriate" (Starr off., 1991a, p. 7). It went on to state that while Australia supported immediate steps such as strengthening existing CBMs, its main objective for the upcoming RevCon would be to take steps to set verification negotiations in motion, specifically by creating an ad hoc group with a mandate to negotiate a full-scope verification protocol in time for the subsequent RevCon in 1996. A later internal background paper noted that the primary obstacle to moving this position forward would be the U.S. position characterizing BW verification as technically impossible (DFAT off., 1991e).

Having staked out an aggressive diplomatic position, Australia moved to raise the political profile of the verification issue. In a May 1991 speech to a U.N. disarmament conference, Foreign Minister Evans not only called for the RevCon to approve a negotiating mandate, but also launched a thinly veiled attack against the United States: "At the Third Review Conference . . . a central issue will be to make progress on verification against the belief held in some quarters that verification is not possible. I believe it is possible, particularly if the sources of ambiguity in the text of the Convention—which allegedly make it unverifiable—are resolved through explication and elaboration" (Evans off., 1991b, pp. 8–9).[12]

Despite this uncompromising public rhetoric, Australian officials revealed in private talks with New Zealand several weeks later that they were already planning a tactical compromise. Given that the United States and others were certain to reject its calls for a negotiating mandate, Canberra would instead seek a technical experts group with a mandate to examine feasibility and options. This more palatable step could then lead more or less automatically to bone fide negotiations. In order to ensure progress along these lines after the RevCon, Australia would also push to establish a separate working group to develop lists to elaborate Article I, and an intersessional oversight committee to oversee these working groups and implementation of CBMs (DFAT off., 1991d).

At about the time when Australia was finalizing its position in late July, Washington informed Canberra that it could reluctantly go along with an intersessional group provided that it had only a narrow mandate to examine the technical feasibility of verification. Australia responded during senior-level bilateral consultations in August that it viewed this concession as inadequate, telling the United States, "We believe that progress on verification is a major—if not the major— issue facing the Review Conference. We will argue for the establishment of an expert working group on verification to examine not just questions of feasibility but to develop verification options. Unlike the U.S. we are not convinced at this stage that the group should not be given a negotiating mandate" (DFAT off., 1991g, p. 1).

Foreign Minister Evans signed off on a final negotiating position for the RevCon following this bilateral exchange. Canberra would oppose U.S. suggestions to make the existing voluntary CBMs legally binding on the grounds that "they may be superseded in due course by a verification package" (DFAT off., 1991l, p. 8). Instead, it would sponsor a comprehensive package of proposals:

Advancing the issue of BW verification is our most important objective. We have therefore given priority support to a proposal to initiate a process which addresses verification from the feasibility study stage to the negotiation of a verification protocol or annex. Any verification regime will be modelled on the CWC verification regime and will contain the same components of annual data reporting and various kinds of inspection. As well as a process which would set in train serious examination of BW verification, we have also given priority to putting in place as confidence building measures the components of a future verification regime. Linking these proposals is a measure for the establishment of an inter-conference BWC organization. (Starr off., 1991b, p. 1)

The classified instruction cable to the Australian delegation explained that this package was designed as "a workable compromise" to bridge the unresolved differences between the preferences of Australia (and other Western states) for a negotiating mandate "versus the more limited objective of a study group on the feasibility of verification" (DFAT off., 1991m, p. 2). The heart of this compromise was a set of interrelated proposals that would lead quickly and more or less automatically from an initial feasibility study to a follow-on negotiation. The cable bluntly tells the delegation to use Australia's institutional influence as RevCon vice president to promote this national agenda, as well as to deflect U.S. attempts to raise concerns about Soviet compliance that might distract attention from it.

In the event, Australia did not achieve most of its goals. Its proposals both for an intersessional working group to elaborate Article I with lists and thresholds and for an interim oversight organization were blocked. Its proposal to significantly expand the scope of CBMs in a way that would lay the groundwork for a full-scope verification regime was also largely unsuccessful (DFAT off., 1991n). However, it did succeed in leaving the door open to a Special Conference of States Parties in the event that VEREX concluded that verification might prove feasible. In this regard, Australia stated during the RevCon that it fully anticipated that the VEREX process would confirm the need for intrusive verification measures (O'Sullivan off., 1991).

Throughout the VEREX and subsequent AHG processes, Australia's purpose for any new protocol was only secondarily that it should be able to detect noncompliance with any significant degree of certainty. The main benefit that Canberra ascribed to a BWC verification regime was rather to enhance the normative value of the Convention. Australia believed that a verification protocol would contribute to this by requiring States Parties to participate in the political acts of negotiating, signing, and ratifying what would amount to a new treaty, and by creating an ongoing process through which members could cooperatively affirm their compliance and gain confidence from others doing likewise. From this norm-building perspective, Australia was confident in its conviction that even highly imperfect verification was better than no verification, and that the goal therefore was simply to get as much verification as possible (Bird off., 1994b; Butler, 1998; [DFAT] int.; Starr off., 1991b).

Canberra faced an uphill struggle in the VEREX process, with the United States, China, and key developing states such as India united in staunch opposition to moving ahead with verification (DFAT off., 1993f). As the 1993 deadline for a final report loomed, Canberra intensified bilateral efforts to convince key opponents not to block consensus on a positive outcome (DFAT off., 1992a, 1993e). Australia was therefore extremely gratified when the new U.S. administration dropped its categorical objections to a positive report at the final VEREX meeting in September 1993, although it remained frustrated by the persistence of what it saw as unwarranted U.S. concern about protecting sensitive commercial and national security information (Bird off., 1994b; DFAT off., 1993i).

Having unexpectedly obtained a reasonably positive VEREX outcome, Australia lost no time in making the most of it. It delivered a strong statement at the UNGA calling for a BWC Special Conference to be convened rapidly in order to move the process forward (DFAT off., 1993h). Canberra then launched a concerted bilateral effort at the foreign minister level to persuade key States Parties to support a formal request for such a meeting, reinforcing this ministerial effort with diplomatic démarches to all States Parties (DFAT off., 1993g, 1993j).

In the lead-up to the September 1994 BWC Special Conference, Foreign Minister Evans approved yet another coordinated bilateral campaign targeting all Western states, and in particular the United States as well as states in its region, to encourage support for a negotiating mandate for a full-scope verification protocol. The aim of this campaign was to avert consideration of any lesser outcomes; for example, a mandate merely to strengthen CBMs (Bird off., 1994b; DFAT off., 1994d). It also volunteered Disarmament Ambassador Richard Starr, a highly respected diplomat, to serve as the vice chairman of the Special Conference to facilitate this outcome.

Australia from the start played a central role in the resulting AHG negotiations, serving as AHG vice chairman, Western Group president, and "friend of chair" for legal issues. Unlike Washington,

Canberra's enthusiasm for BWC verification was not dampened by revelations at the start of the AHG process about the failure of UNSCOM to detect Iraq's residual biological weapons programs despite scores of highly intrusive inspections over several years, nor by the parallel failure of the U.S.–U.K.–Russia Trilateral Process to resolve concerns about Russian compliance ([DFAT] ints.).

Throughout the ongoing AHG talks, Australia refused to back away from its support for intrusive routine and challenge inspections. Taking a page from its CWC playbook, in early 1996 it conducted a national trial inspection at a corporate biotechnology facility, submitting a report to the AHG that concluded that managed access could adequately protect proprietary information, and that routine inspections of this type would significantly deter BWC violations (Pearson, 1997). A classified internal document in mid-1997, while noting that many key issues remained unresolved after nearly two years of negotiations, firmly ruled out any compromise that did not include at an absolute minimum compulsory declarations of relevant facilities and activities, infrequent routine visits to declared sites, and short-notice challenge inspections (DFAT off., 1997b).

The next year saw some progress, including adoption of a rolling text in July 1997 and what appeared to be a renewal of U.S. political commitment in President Clinton's January 1998 State of the Union speech; but dramatic breakthroughs remained elusive. Foreign Minister Downer therefore announced on 2 March 1998 that Australia would henceforth consider spurring progress in the AHG as one of its top priorities, citing Australia's role in the CWC negotiations as a model. The centerpiece of this initiative was a call for a meeting of all BWC foreign ministers to give political momentum to the AHG negotiations ([DFAT] int.; Downer off., 1998). In an unmistakable reference to Australian frustration at the continuing absence of a sincere U.S. commitment, a senior official explains that this initiative was motivated by "a feeling that the BW negotiating process was drifting, and importantly some key countries, friendly countries, were content with that" ([DFAT] int.).

Downer's BWC ministerial meeting was held in New York in September 1998.[13] It achieved its core objectives to the extent that it was widely attended and focused high-level political attention on the AHG process. Participants reaffirmed their commitment to negotiating an effective compliance instrument, and pledged to hold additional such meetings to review progress. Despite attempts by Downer, however, no additional meetings took place.

Australia persisted until the very end in holding firm on its core positions for achieving its negotiating objectives. Australia (and most other Western states) remained at an impasse with both the NAM and the United States on the crucial issue of routine inspections. Although the gap was narrowed—with Australia referring to "random visits" rather than "routine inspections," and Washington having been willing to at least consider voluntary no-cause visits—a workable Western compromise was not found because Australia and a few other WEOG states continued to insist on the need for mandatory no-cause inspections to validate declarations (int.). In addition, while Canberra bowed to U.S. objections and abandoned its earlier insistence on developing lists to elaborate Article I, Australia and some others continued to insist on far broader declarations and lower threshold quantities than the United States was willing to consider (ints.).

The apparent hostility of the Bush administration to compromise in the Ad Hoc Group put high level strains on the Australian relationship with its primary ally. Although the Howard government generally welcomed the advent of an ideologically compatible U.S. administration, Washington's reinvigorated skepticism about the BWC talks was an early source of significant bilateral tension. This was particularly true in the case of Foreign Minister Alexander Downer, who had long been the government's most ardent advocate of supporting American foreign policy, but who also had, early in his tenure, adopted the BWC protocol as something of a pet project (much as the CWC had been for his predecessor). Downer therefore lobbied the new U.S. administration to reconsider its stance, even going so far as to hint that U.S. intransigence on the protocol might undercut the willingness of allies like Australia to support President Bush's missile defense priorities (*Australian Financial Review*, 7/9/01).

The July 2001 U.S. decision to reject the AHG chairman's compromise text and effectively walk away from the negotiations was a not unexpected but nevertheless shocking blow to Australia. The AHG negotiations had, after all, been a primary focus of Australian bureaucratic energies and political capital for over six years. With press coverage widely characterizing the U.S. move as nothing less than a humiliation for Australia generally and Alexander Downer in particular, the foreign minister condemned Washington's decision in uncharacteristically harsh terms (*Australian Financial Review*, 7/9/01; *Canberra Times*, 7/27/01; *Sydney Morning Herald*, 7/27/01). Although Foreign Minister Downer has vowed to fight on for a protocol, in practical terms it is unclear that Australia and other Western protocol supporters such as the EU countries have any options except to keep trying to convince Washington to change its mind, or at least to offer alternative proposals.

Other Nonpossession Responses

Although in many respects Australia's approach to BWC enhancement followed its basic CWC script, it never attempted to replicate its

CW regional initiative. That said, it has actively tried to promote comprehensive regional adherence to the BWC, particularly in the aftermath of the 1990 Gulf Crisis. For example, in late 1990 Foreign Minister Evans wrote letters to the foreign ministers of regional states that had not yet signed and/or ratified the BWC, including Indonesia, Malaysia, Burma, and Brunei, urging them to fully accede. The initial effort was supplemented by raising the issue in diplomatic démarches, bilateral ministerial meetings, and finally a second round of ministerial letters to an expanded list of governments (Dauth off., 1992a; DFAT off., 1991h; Evans off., 1991a; Starr off., 1991a). It remains to be seen whether Australia will turn to regional demand-side initiatives now that the BWC protocol talks are collapsing.

Consequence-Management

Counterproliferation

Before the mid-1990s Australia did not have any research programs on BW defense. Moreover, other than those coincident with CW defense, Australian forces had no operational equipment or training to defend against BW (Ray tst., 1991). Indeed, DOD capabilities at the time were so limited that it could not furnish a single technical expert to advise DFAT prior to the 1991 BWC RevCon (Starr off., 1991b).

DSTO was authorized in the early 1990s to initiate limited research on defenses against toxins, but this still did not involve living biological agents (Brabin-Smith tst., 1997). This charter was expanded to cover living agents in early 1995, although only on a very modest scale (Punch tst., 1995). It does not appear that this program has ever involved the use of actual BW agents.

Australia has advocated positions that do not support the BW defense programs of the United States and others. At the 1991 BWC RevCon, it unsuccessfully sought an interpretive declaration that Article I prohibited either modification of existing BW agents or development of new agents for defensive purposes (Australia off., 1991). In the mid-1990s, Australia refused to support U.S. and British attempts to reverse or, failing that, delay a WHO decision recommending destruction of the last acknowledged samples of smallpox. Canberra rejected claims that these samples were needed for counterproliferation purposes. Indeed, an Australian official recalls making an off-the-record telephone call to a sympathetic Clinton NSC staffer to argue the case for destruction, which he believes directly led to a White House attempt to overturn the Pentagon's objections ([DFAT] int.). Australia continued to argue against continuing delays, including most recently at a special WHO meeting in May 1999 (*Washington Post*, 5/25/99).

Deterrence

Australia has taken the same generally nonsupportive stance on BW deterrence as it has on CW deterrence.

CASE STUDY: MISSILES

Capability-Denial

National Export Controls

Australia did not institute any nonproliferation export controls on missile technology prior to joining the MTCR in 1990.[14] At that time, it simply promulgated new regulations under the legislative authority of the Custom's Act, requiring individual export licenses for all items listed in the MTCR Annex, with decisions based on the MTCR Guidelines. There have been no preferential procedures for exports to other Regime members (DFAT off., 1993c). Although Australia has not been a significant exporter of relevant items (e.g., far less so than in all of the other WMD proliferation areas), it is widely perceived to have a solid record of implementing the MTCR conscientiously.

Multilateral Export-Control Regime: Missile Technology Control Regime

Australia has been extremely ambivalent about participating in the MTCR throughout its involvement, far more so than other nonproliferation suppliers groups. According to officials involved at different times throughout the 1990s, this discomfort has been based on the absence of a relevant global norm, which is seen to call into doubt the legitimacy of the entire missile nonproliferation enterprise (Courtney int., 1998; Dorling int., 1998; [DFAT] ints.). As a former official directly in charge of missile nonproliferation issues observed, "A global norm makes suppliers regimes less discriminatory clubs and more complementary, acceptable bodies" (Courtney int., 1998). A current official with similar responsibilities explained Australian reservations about the MTCR as follows: "Its got an air of ad hoc–ery and almost Cold War–ishness about it which the others don't have. . . . It began in a much more limited way than the Australia Group or NSG. Both of those . . . despite the attacks on their credibility and their right to exist, they can stand very firmly on long established international norms" ([DFAT] int.).

The perceived flaw of having no legally enshrouded normative basis has been exacerbated by concerns about specific features of the

MTCR, including its overtly discriminatory "have, have-not" structure. Australia sees this reflected in many aspects: All the AG members have renounced CBW through the BWC and CWC, and even before the CWC had renounced CW use and were at least in the process of addressing possession; its narrow Western-oriented membership; its explicit refusal to distinguish between civilian (i.e., SLV) and military technology; and (initially) its failure to cover CBW-related delivery systems (Courtney int., 1998; Dorling int., 1998; [DFAT] int.). Indeed, a former official speculates that these considerations would probably have posed more serious obstacles to Australian participation if top officials had ever bothered to pay more attention to the issue (Dorling int., 1998).

Australia did not participate in, and indeed was unaware of, the protracted negotiations that led to the MTCR. Soon after the G-7 states publicly announced the new Regime, the United States bilaterally approached Canberra to urge it to adhere unilaterally. Despite such pressure, the Australian response was noncommittal, saying that careful interagency study would be needed (DFAT off., n.d.d; Walker off., 1987). More than two years later, when the issue was raised during ministerial talks in Washington, Foreign Minister Evans told Secretary of State Baker that Australia still had not made a formal decision about adhering unilaterally, but that it was favorably inclined (DFAT off., 1989). Before any further action was taken, though, the idea of unilateral adherence was overtaken by an implicit invitation to join the Regime.

DFAT has blocked release of documents pertaining to Australian deliberations immediately before and after it became a Regime member, either in whole or part (DFAT off., 1998). It is therefore unclear whether Australia considered turning down the invitation to join the MTCR. Interviews certainly suggest that Canberra had serious qualms, and the very fact that this material has been singled out for declassification denial at least hints that it may allude to reservations that would be inconsistent with Australia's current status as a Regime member. Another issue that may still be regarded as sensitive is that Australia had an ulterior economic motive for joining the MTCR; namely, securing access to commercial SLV technology.[15] As then First Assistant Secretary Kim Jones (int., 1998) notes, while the desire for MTCR items was not the primary factor in Australia's decision to join, it was certainly a relevant factor.

Canberra's July 1990 public announcement that it would join the MTCR appears to have been intentionally designed to play down the significance of the decision, characterizing it merely as part of Australia's larger nonproliferation involvement. Moreover, the final press release put out jointly by the foreign and defense ministers was markedly more understated than an early draft prepared by the disarmament staff, to the point that it was ambiguous about whether Australia was actually becoming a full-fledged member (DFAT off., 1990d, 1990e). This downplaying theme is also apparent in Foreign Minister Evans's talking points to respond to questions from the press, which noted, "Australia currently manufactures for export little that would be covered by the MTCR" (DFAT off., 1990c, p. 1).

Once it joined the Regime, Australia set about to address its various specific concerns. Its first initiative was to promote expanding the Regime's objectives to cover CBW-related missiles. This was achieved in principle at its very first meeting in July 1990, thanks to a parallel U.S. initiative (Courtney int., 1998; DFAT off., 1990f; Evans off., 1993a). Australia also began a low-key effort to promote other reforms in the Regime's structure and policies; for example, broadening membership and clarifying the Guidelines (DFAT off., 1990g; Evans off., 1991b; Jones off., 1991). Canberra in particular wanted clarification that the MTCR was not intended to impede civilian SLV programs proposing that the "strong presumption of denial" on Category I items should be "qualified" for the civilian programs of Regime members. An internal paper comments,

At the [March 1993] Canberra Plenary we argued that consistent with the intent of the MTCR Guidelines, transfers of controlled items for space launch programs should be allowed, particularly to Partners, on a case-by-case basis with a country's nonproliferation credentials an important determinate. This preserves the Australian Space Office interests in transfers of technology and equipment for Australian space launches. The U.S. has in the past not accepted this interpretation. (Starr off., 1993, p. 3)

Although Australia was unable to get U.S. support for this reform, it successfully lobbied the Bush administration bilaterally to drop its opposition to the Cape York spaceport project now that Australia had joined the MTCR, which de facto had much the same effect by setting a precedent (Speier int., 1998). (Some argue that this precedent has greatly weakened the Regime's effectiveness as a technology cartel.) Australia pushed for consideration of further minor reforms prior to the November 1993 Interlaken plenary. At the same time, it reacted warily to the ambitious package of proposals brought forward by the new Clinton administration. For example, although it did not support automatic access to technology for members, Australia also opposed U.S. efforts to add new restrictions on interpartner trade that might impede its own access to SLV technology and Category I Tomahawk cruise missiles (Courtney int., 1998; DFAT off., n.d.b; Dorling int., 1998; Evans off., 1994a; Starr off., 1993). Australia also was wary of Washington's restrictive membership requirements, fearing that they would impede regional diversification (Courtney int., 1998; Dorling int., 1998; [DFAT] ints.; DFAT off., n.d.b; Starr off., 1993).

Even when Australia took firm positions, it did not play a leading role on any of these issues. Australia's involvement in the Regime's debates was markedly low profile, as Canberra had consciously decided to avoid trying to play a prominent role. Since the mid-1990s this already modest involvement has been scaled back even further, with Australia offering no significant national proposals for political, structural, or technical reforms pertaining to the Regime's core supply-side mission. Beginning in 1996 Australia also downgraded its level of representation at plenary meetings from an assistant secretary to a much lower ranking section head.

Wider Export-Control Norms

In principle Australia has supported encouraging non-MTCR states to adhere unilaterally to MTCR standards. However, its position has been that this objective should be pursued on a national basis by individual members according to their own strategies and interests, rather than for the Regime as such to push for this, as the United States and some others would prefer (Courtney int., 1998; [DFAT] int.).

For its part, Australia occasionally has encouraged governments to adhere to the MTCR during bilateral meetings, especially key Asian states like China and Singapore (DFAT off., 1991c, 1992d, 1993b; [DFAT] int.). However, interview data and documentary evidence suggest that Australia has limited this effort to just a few key governments, and even then has tended not to highlight the issue (DFAT off., 1993d, p. 1). As one official sums up Australia's reservations about vigorously promoting wider MTCR adherence, "It is not realistic or fair to expect states to adhere to regimes of which they are not members and which they have not been permitted/invited to join" (Courtney int., 1998).

National Enforcement Mechanisms

Consistent with its actions in the other proliferation areas, Australia has shied away from raising concerns about missile-related transfers with other governments. This has sometimes necessitated resisting explicit U.S. requests for Australia to undertake such efforts based on specific intelligence in order to reinforce its own interdiction efforts ([DFAT] int.).

On at least one occasion, probably in 1991, Australia does appear to have expressed concern at a high level in Beijing about press reports that China was planning to export complete MTCR-class missiles to Pakistan and the Middle East. This relatively uncharacteristic action was apparently the result of bilateral prompting from Japan, which explicitly asked Canberra as the only other Asia–Pacific member of the MTCR to reinforce its own bilateral protests (DFAT off. n.d.e). Australia has also expressed concern to Moscow about press reports concerning ongoing missile assistance to Iran, although without taking any position on the veracity of the allegations ([DFAT] int.). Such cases are exceptional, however, involving wide press coverage of flagrant violations of those countries' stated commitments.

Australia has no missile-related nonproliferation sanctions. It has also been especially wary of U.S. missile sanctions, because they are tied directly to the MTCR, albeit unilaterally. Australia has taken a firm position that sanctions should not be associated with any of the export-control regimes ([DFAT] int.; Starr off., 1993). It therefore never even considered U.S. calls to have the MTCR emulate its national sanctions, or for individual members to endorse them nationally. After the United States passed its sanctions law, Australia expressed displeasure bilaterally that Washington had instituted sanctions tied to the MTCR without obtaining the Regime's approval (Courtney int., 1998; [DFAT] int.).

Other Capability-Denial Responses

As with CBW, there have been no apparent cases where Australia has used other denial measures against missile programs, such as targeted denial or sabotage or destruction.

Nonpossession Norm-Building

Global Missile Norm Proposals

Australia has been at the forefront of efforts to explore the scope for a treaty-based global missile norm since becoming a member of the MTCR in 1990. Just months after joining the Regime, Canberra privately noted to Washington, "In the longer term the constraint on proliferation of missile technology will require a broad approach . . . [including] verification (e.g., on-site inspections) for states who wish to conform with the objectives of the MTCR" (DFAT off., 1990g, p. 7).

While using such oblique references with others, Canberra had initiated internal deliberations to consider whether to push openly for a global treaty norm to underpin the MTCR. The cognizant section director at the time within DFAT recalls, "I argued the case for a global norm strongly and that view prevailed." At the same time, she notes, "We were aware, however, of the complexity and unlikelihood of getting far with it" (Courtney int., 1998). Former Foreign Minister Evans (int., 1998) likewise recounts that he strongly supported exploring this issue, but did not make it a high priority because of the dim prospects for success.

Modest expectations notwithstanding, Australia cautiously decided to test the multilateral waters, beginning with its MTCR partners. In a carefully balanced speech to the March 1993 Canberra plenary meeting, Foreign Minister Evans called for consideration of a global treaty norm to ban missiles to underpin the MTCR. While acknowledging the complexities that such a negotiation would entail, he noted that efforts to establish global norms were "centrally important" in the battle against proliferation (Evans off., 1993a). Canberra followed up this initiative several months later with a statement to the UNGA in New York. Although Disarmament Ambassador O'Sullivan had wanted to explicitly call for a global missile ban, he was instructed to make a less-specific statement, urging "comprehensive international action on missiles" (DFAT off., 1993g, p. 4). The tactical reason for this circumspection was explained afterward in an internal paper that noted that although Australia had opted to promote a global missile ban, this "could only be realised in the long term and after complex negotiations (Starr off., 1993).

Canada took up the high level Australian initiative from the year before at the 1994 MTCR meeting, tabling a formal detailed proposal for the Regime to endorse negotiations for a global ban on medium-range missiles, essentially a proposal to globalize the INF treaty (Canada off., 1994; Sinclair off., 1995).[16] In response, Foreign Minister Evans approved pursuing negotiations on a global missile treaty as a matter of Australian policy. However, Australia had objections to the precise Canadian formula. Specifically, because the proposal was limited to medium-range systems it excluded ICBMs and therefore would codify a de facto discriminatory "have, have-not" status quo. Recognizing that a more comprehensive ban on possession stood no chance of even being considered by the United States and other "haves," Canberra opted to champion a ballistic missile test ban treaty using the CTBT as a model rather than the CWC, BWC, and NPT. DFAT concluded that this approach would effectively establish an antimissile norm, impede missile development (particularly for rudimentary programs), not impinge on dual-use transfers for civilian space programs, allow for verification mechanisms, make use less likely by undermining confidence in the effectiveness of existing systems, and achieve all of this in a utterly nondiscriminatory manner (Cousins off., 1994; Dorling int., 1998).

Rather than tabling a counterproposal to the Canadian initiative, Australia privately raised the idea of a missile test ban treaty with Washington. However, in a series of bilateral discussions the United States categorically rejected any proposal along these lines (Dorling int., 1998). Faced with this implacable opposition, Canberra pragmatically retreated to a less-ambitious alternative. At a January 1995 MTCR intersessional meeting, although Australia vigorously defended the Canadian initiative against scathing U.S. criticism, it suggested that a compromise might be to consider a global missile–SLV launch prenotification agreement, noting that this mirrored a 1993 French proposal in the CD (Australia off., 1995).

Australia had intended to send a team afterward to Washington in order to lay the groundwork to secure U.S. support for this alternative as an acceptable compromise. The plan was to feel out divisions within the interagency, assess how far the United States might be willing to go, and then tailor a formal proposal that Washington would at least consider. But at precisely this juncture, France announced that it would resume nuclear testing in the South Pacific, sparking a major, protracted crisis for the Australian disarmament bureaucracy. As a result of this distraction, DFAT was unable to lobby Washington prior to the special August MTCR meeting to consider the Canadian proposal (Dorling int., 1998). Although Australia continued to promote its idea in MTCR channels, convinced Canada to add consideration of a launch notification agreement to the meeting agenda, and then tabled a detailed proposal at the meeting itself, the proposal did not receive any serious consideration (Australia off., 1995; DFAT off., 1995a; Dorling int., 1998; Sinclair off., 1995).

Australia remained interested in promoting some type of global missile treaty after this setback. However, given the shrill opposition engendered by the Canadian proposal and the disinclination of others to consider even the extremely modest Australian alternative, a political decision was made afterward to abandon any active efforts until and unless the international climate improved ([DFAT] int.). This remains the position of the current government ([DFAT] int.). That said, in June 1998 the opposition Labor Party's "shadow" foreign minister gave a Parliamentary speech urging the government to reinvigorate its efforts to promote a multilateral missile treaty, asserting that the South Asian nuclear crisis lent new urgency to this issue (Brereton tst., 1998). In the federal election later that year, Labor's foreign policy platform included only three disarmament and nonproliferation initiatives, one of which was to pursue a multilateral treaty to constrain ballistic missiles (Australian Labor Party off., 1998). Now poised to regain the next federal election, Labor has promised to press for a global launch notification regime and possibly a missile test ban (*Sydney Morning Herald*, 1/17/01).

Australia does not appear to have taken a formal position regarding Russian efforts since 1999 to sponsor negotiation of a Global Control System for missiles, again probably due to Howard government's reluctance to defy strong U.S. objections. However, Canberra has strongly supported Canadian-led efforts within the MTCR to develop a voluntary Code of Conduct Against Missile Proliferation to recommend to nonmembers (Assembly of WEU off., 2000; Smith, 2001). It is unclear whether Canberra will regard this conspicuously modest initiative as sufficient to satisfy its long-standing interest in instituting stronger global norms against missiles, particularly if Labour is returned as expected at the next election, sometime in 2001. Given its past pragmatism on the issue, much may depend on whether more ambitious proposals gain any multilateral traction.

Other Nonpossession Responses

Despite its support for a global missile norm, Canberra has opposed the U.S. strategy of promoting a targeted, de facto nonpossession norm by requiring new MTCR members to forgo MTCR-class missiles. Australian objections are based on two considerations. First, this unilateral U.S. requirement has hampered non-Western states joining, particularly Asian countries like South Korea. More important, Australia has been uncomfortable with the discriminatory character of this requirement (Courtney int., 1998; Dorling int., 1998; [DFAT] int.).

Because of the dim prospects for negotiating a global missile norm, DFAT has flirted with promoting a fallback regional arrangement (Starr off., 1993). Specifically, in the early 1990s it considered a Regional Missile Free Zone treaty, or if that proved infeasible, a less ambitious Regional Register of Missile Free Countries (DFAT off., n.d.b).

After the apparent collapse of any real prospects for global negotiations in 1995, Canberra began to consider more seriously whether to push for some type of regional missile ban, possibly through the existing ARF process. However, the Defence Department weighed in against the idea at senior levels, arguing that it would foreclose its missile acquisition options.[17] This led to a prolonged interagency dispute. As a result, a final decision on whether to pursue a regional alternative was delayed, until being overtaken by the revival of global efforts in the form of the MTCR Code of Conduct. However, there is little doubt that once it is completed, Australia will aggressively promote the Code regionally ([DFAT] ints.).

Consequence-Management

Counterproliferation

Australia opposed the U.S. SDI program in the 1980s, arguing that verifiable arms-control agreements represented the best means to prevent war and to ensure international stability (Evans tst., 1987). However, when the United States began to reorient its missile defense efforts from strategic defense to counterproliferation after the Gulf War, Australia dropped its unconditional opposition. In 1992 the Australian Defence Department quietly began to consult regularly with SDIO in order to monitor developments and explore the scope for cooperation (*Sydney Morning Herald*, 5/19/95). The 1994 Defence white paper formally codified that the growing threat of missile proliferation raised the potential for cooperation with the United States on missile defenses.

In April 1995 Australia agreed to a high-level U.S. request to cooperate in this area. However, Australia specified in writing that this cooperation would be modest, that it would be consistent with its opposition to any activity that would violate the U.S.–Russian ABM treaty, and that it would be based on its own national needs and priorities. Examples specified included the exchange of a single scientist and conducting joint space tracking of civilian NASA launches for purposes of missile defense research, with total costs anticipated at under A\$500,000. In explaining this policy to Parliament, the Keating government noted that its motive was not to acquire missile defense capabilities for Australia, but rather to demonstrate that Australia was a cooperative ally, as well as to attain spin-off technology for conventional military applications (Ray tst., 1995).

The Howard government expanded this cooperation in 1997 on a limited basis, agreeing to establish a test range in remote Western Australia for a series of four U.S. test launches over water so that BMDO could assess its ability to detect distant launches during the launch phase. Again, though, in announcing this initiative the government stressed that it was not acting out of any interest in supporting missile defense, but rather to demonstrate alliance cooperation (McLachlan off., 1997).

The Howard government has stoutly tried to support the new Bush administration's call for antiproliferation missile defenses within the international community. Indeed, Australia has been among Washington's most helpful allies in this regard. However, Howard has resisted any further involvement in missile defense activities by Australia itself, despite strong interest by the new Bush administration in closer Australian cooperation. Specifically, Canberra has been openly noncommittal about letting Washington use the joint U.S.–Australian Pine Gap space tracking facility to support missile defenses. For its part the Labor Party, which polls show is poised to reclaim power, has categorically ruled out any such direct Australian involvement in U.S. missile defense programs (*International Herald Tribune*, 2/22/01). Labor has added an antimissile defense plank to its national platform and has loudly attacked the Howard government for giving the Bush administration aid and comfort by not condemning the concept (*Sydney Morning Herald*, 8/4/00, 1/17/01, 3/30/01, 5/14/01).

SUMMARY AUSTRALIAN FINDINGS:
CROSS-CASE PATTERNS

The Australian response to proliferation has consistently accorded unambiguous primacy to the nonpossession norm-building approach. Canberra has favored using a full spectrum of nonpossession tools, including global and regional instruments. It has expended tremendous multilateral and bilateral energy to contribute to negotiating, strengthening, and effectively implementing a web of normative treaties. This has been the case over time and across the different proliferation areas, although at any given time it has tended to devote the most attention to areas where multilateral progress has appeared most promising. This reflects the general philosophy that a middle power like Australia is not in a position to set the international agenda, but that, by being pragmatic and opportunistic, it can shape it closer to its preferences.

In contrast, Canberra has been consistently ambivalent about supply-side regimes, and generally has refrained from embracing additional capability-denial instruments nationally beyond the least-common-denominator commitments of the multilateral suppliers regimes. Canberra has shown little or no inclination to take enforcement action against other governments, even in concert with its antiproliferation partners. Moreover, even this modest level of support has to some extent been based on ulterior motives: wider prestige and influence in the case of the AG, and access to technology in the case of the MTCR. At the same time, unlike some Western governments, it has been consistently diligent in policing its own exports to ensure that Australian firms do not contribute to proliferation directly. Australia has also eschewed all but the most humble national consequence-management efforts, as well as generally declining to cooperate with U.S.–led counterproliferation and deterrence efforts. In virtually every case where tradeoffs have existed between norm-building and capability-denial and/or consequence-management, Australia has opted to support the former.

Whereas Chapter 3 notes consistent patterns in U.S. behavior despite variations over time and across areas, Australia's consistency has been far more pronounced. Indeed, it has used what almost amounts to a single, unchanging script. Although it has often been forced to compromise in order to achieve results, its preferred outcomes have always remained constant. Moreover, there have been no meaningful internal bureaucratic or political divisions regarding these preferences. The closest would be bipartisan differences on missile defense, but these involve *not* whether Australia should seek to attain missile defenses as Washington is offering, but merely how strident it should be in opposing U.S. plans.

In summary, Australia has strongly favored the norm-building approach across the board, with sometimes reluctant support for capability-denial as a supplementary approach, and little or no support for consequence-management strategies.

NOTES

1. The Joint Facilities are jointly operated U.S.–Australian military intelligence-gathering installations in Australia integrated into the U.S. strategic warning system. In addition to being perceived by the Australian public as contributing to U.S. nuclear force posture, these facilities were thought (correctly) to be targets for a Soviet nuclear strike.

2. Australian officials other than the actual minister are career civil servants. This is in dramatic contrast to the U.S. system, where political appointees dominate senior levels and extend all the way down to the mid and even working levels. Consequently, the bureaucracy is far more influential in Canberra than in Washington.

3. Desk officers through section directors are generally referred to herein as working level, assistant secretaries as mid-level, and first assistant secretaries or above as senior level. Ministers and department secretaries are sometimes referred to as top or high level.

4. This has been in marked contrast to DOD's aggressive opposition to DFAT's activist inclinations on conventional issues such as supporting a global land-mine ban or curtailing conventional arms transfers where Defence has had actual assets at stake. Consequently, Australia has been far less forward leaning in these areas (Cheeseman, 1997; Evans int., 1998; White int., 1999).

5. The one technical exception was Canberra's implementation of "interim" controls on items that had been agreed by the AG but before this multilateral requirement formally had gone into effect (DFAT off., 1991k).

6. Gee (int., 1998) notes two very minor exceptions. One was an instance in the late 1980s when Australia expressed concern to Thailand about press reports that its companies were supplying workers to the Libyan CW program. The other was a case in which Australia, acting in its capacity as AG chairman, used a specific transfer as an example by which to clarify the Group's rules to a new member.

7. Several officials note that often Australia is not free to act on intelligence that it owns jointly with the United States or other friendly governments. However, these same officials concede that this merely requires asking permission through intelligence liaison channels, which would almost certainly be granted. Moreover, this explanation does not explain why Australia would turn down specific U.S. requests to take joint action on intelligence.

8. It seems likely that this greater focus on the "anytime, anywhere" reversal, rather than the security stockpile issue, was based on a pragmatic calculation that because the United States was completely isolated on the latter, it would eventually have to back down. By contrast, the new U.S. position on verification tracked closely with the views of many nonaligned CD members.

9. Among the concessions obtained by Australia, the United States had agreed to remove the most glaring restrictions that it had sought on challenge

inspections; for example, shortening the time between notification of an inspection and access within the perimeter from 228 to 168 hours. The United States had also expanded routine inspections to included all facilities capable of producing 100 tons of CW precursors annually, as opposed to only facilities that had actually done so in the past'(Findlay, 1992a).

10. That said, Australia hedged its position by recommending against the court rendering an opinion, as well as by acknowledging the necessity of a transitional period before nuclear weapons could feasibly by eliminated.

11. It should be noted that the report's "official" status is somewhat confusing. The Commission was initiated and sponsored by the government of Prime Minister Keating, and was intended as a government to government product. The Howard government continued this sponsorship, but did not identify the recommendations in the final report as expressing formal Australian government policy. Foreign Minister Downer appeared to walk a fine line on the report's status when he presented it to the CD in Geneva in January 1997, urging its consideration without formally endorsing its specific recommendations (Downer off., 1997).

12. One of the practical obstacles to verifying compliance with the BWC is that noncompliance is poorly defined because the treaty does not specify what agents are prohibited and allows possession of unspecified quantities of any agent for poorly defined allowable purposes.

13. Through an unhappy quirk of fate, Downer himself was unable to chair the meeting as planned, because for domestic political reasons Prime Minister Howard called a federal election for soon after the scheduled meeting. Australian law prohibits ministers from participating in such high-profile public events once an election has been called. Therefore New Zealand's foreign minister was asked to represent Australia as the meeting's chairman ([DFAT] int.).

14. Missiles per se would have been captured by general controls on sensitive military items (Walker off., 1987). However, since MTCR-class missiles are not produced in Australia, this would not have been relevant.

15. In 1989 the United States had blocked an export license for a U.S. firm to participate in an Australian project to build a commercial spaceport at Cape York, Queensland, citing the MTCR's prohibition on supporting space launch capabilities in non-MTCR countries (Speier int., 1998). The domestic importance of Cape York is revealed by the fact that Foreign Minister Evans was explicitly prepared to address this issue in announcing the Australian decision to join the MTCR (DFAT off., 1990c).

16. Except that the Canadian proposal lowered the 500-km INF range floor to the 300-km MTCR Category I range parameter.

17. It is unclear why DOD did not likewise oppose a global treaty, which presumably would have the same result.

Chapter 5

Comparative Findings
and Analysis

This chapter seeks to compare the findings from the two embedded sets of case studies in Chapters 3 and 4. It then analyzes possible causal explanations for the primary ensuing comparative finding.

COMPARATIVE NATIONAL FINDINGS

Comparison of the major patterns discerned in each of the two sets of case studies reveals considerable discord between the United States and Australia on numerous specific policy issues across proliferation areas over a period of nearly two decades. Indeed, instances where the two governments have agreed—for example, on the need to expand the scope of controls in the early years of the AG—have been relatively few, short lived, and far between. Ironically, the most notable case where they ostensibly saw eye to eye for an extended period on a major policy issue was during the 1980s regarding "anytime, anywhere" CWC verification. In reality, this agreement was based on such contrary motivations and intentions that it can be fairly characterized as the exception that proves the rule.

This discordant record has not been lost on either government. Interviews attest that past and present officials on both sides are widely aware that they have tended to disagree more often than they agree on specific policy questions. For example, a mid-level official from the first Bush administration notes, "There are a lot of important differences below the macro level objectives between Australia and the United States. In fact it doesn't take long for that to break down below the macro in terms of beginning to see the differences. . . . There is a definite difference of opinion in terms of how you implement achieving those objectives" (Inglee int., 1998).

Awareness of these differences seems to be perceived most acutely by working- and mid-level officials who have been immersed in the details of policy. But former Australian Foreign Minister Gareth Evans (int., 1998) notes that even at high levels, differences have been readily apparent, and that these differences have gone well beyond trivial contrasts in diplomatic style. Awareness of national differences is particularly strong on issues pertaining to individual treaty norms, such as CWC, BWC, and CTBT.

The organization of the case studies into two embedded sets based on a common conceptual framework reveals that these many instances of divergence fall into an unmistakable pattern of opposing national preferences toward the three major approaches to proliferation response. The United States has accorded primacy to the complementary approaches of capability-denial and consequence-management while treating norm-building as a subordinate approach. Australia has put norm-building above all else, treating capability-denial as subordinate and largely eschewing consequence-management altogether. This preference pattern is discernible for each actor across proliferation areas and over time. There has not been a single major case of deviation that contradicts this primary empirical finding.

An opinion survey of officials conducted in conjunction with research interviews shows that the national divergence revealed in the case studies is mirrored in corresponding differences in the underlying personal attitudes of officials. These include pronounced bias toward capability-denial versus nonpossession norm-building (Figure 5.1), and differing perceptions of the effectiveness of preventative nonproliferation generally (Figure 5.2). Survey responses also suggest that there is considerable frustration and bafflement on each side regarding the other's perspectives. Although not scientific, these survey results reinforce the major empirical finding that there has been a consistent, persistent, and pervasive divergence in U.S. and Australian proliferation-response preferences.

It should be noted that beyond the primary divergence detected, the empirical case studies also reveal a number of interesting secondary findings. For example, U.S. policies have displayed greater inconsistency, both over time and across the different proliferation areas.

Figure 5.1
Survey Question: Preferred Strategy

Hypothetically, if you had to choose, which of the following would you consider to be more important in promoting your country's anti-proliferation goals?

<u>Option 1</u>: Building and maintaining strong multilateral treaty-norms against possession of these weapons

<u>Option 2</u>: Preventing specific transfers of these weapons and associated equipment and technology to programs or countries of concern

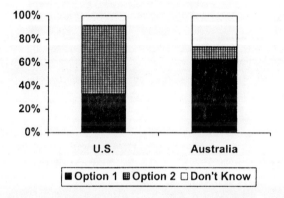

Although not central to the analytical objectives of the current study, such subsidiary findings may be useful for future research on the overall foreign policy behavior of these actors.

CAUSAL ANALYSIS

Analytical Objectives

Having empirically detected a significant and consistent divergence in how these two so-called like-minded actors have responded to proliferation, it remains to explain this primary finding. The remainder of this section seeks to utilize foreign policy analysis (FPA) and cognate international relations theory in order to explain the principal finding of the preceding chapters.

It is a firmly established FPA precept that "multicausal models" are needed in order to explain any aspect or pattern of foreign policy behavior (Hermann, 1978b; Kegley & Wittkopf, 1991; Rosenau, 1976; Steiner, 1983). Consistent with this paradigm, the present analysis

Figure 5.2
Survey Question: Nonproliferation Effectiveness

Do you believe that efforts by Western states to prevent proliferation over the coming 10-15 years will be effective?

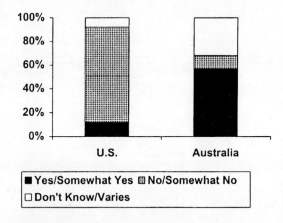

draws heavily on the environmental model of FPA suggested by Papadakis and Starr (1987). A salient feature of this model is that it synthesizes multiple FPA perspectives in order to take into account both structural (e.g., international system, international relations) and agent-specific (e.g., societal, governmental, individual) influences on foreign policy behavior. The fundamental aim in using this type of broad multi-causal approach is not to isolate one of these variables as the single explanation, but rather to assess their proportionate importance, with the expectation that the answer lies in a combination of factors.

Possible Explanations

National Attributes

At first glance, the most intuitively evident explanation for this or any other foreign policy difference between the United States and Australia would seem to be the dramatic difference in their national attributes. They certainly are very different in terms of size and power within the international system. But it is uncertain just how important this structural factor is in explaining divergent antiproliferation preferences. The theoretical predictions that can be derived from national attributes do not appear to go very far in explaining this difference.

The notion of American exceptionalism seemingly offers a logical explanation for any divergence. This concept holds that for a variety of reasons, some having to do with national attributes (e.g., its current status as the world's lone superpower), the United States is different from other states.[1] Accordingly, U.S. behavior on any issue can be expected to diverge from that of other states. However, this idea has not been well developed as theory, and certainly has never been convincingly demonstrated through rigorous empirical testing. Moreover, it is usually propounded in the context of comparative politics rather than international relations. Therefore, assumptions about foreign policy exceptionalism are merely extrapolated from differences in its culture, political system, and so on. Kegley and Wittkopf (1991) summarize this reasoning with the formula, "American foreign policy may be uniquely different from the policies of other states because the United States itself is different" (p. 249). Needless to say, while perhaps true, such an underdeveloped, untested hypothesis carries little presumption of credibility.

It is impossible to assess the explanatory relevance of this concept for the present two-actor comparison without additional empirical research. In order to reasonably consider this as a convincing explanation, it would be necessary at a minimum to demonstrate that Washington has been unique in its preferences. Anecdotal evidence from the case studies is indeterminate, offering numerous cases in which other Western states were arrayed together against U.S. preferences, but also cases where Australian preferences were at variance with the positions of other Western states. Moreover, the latter cases have involved instances in which other states were leaning further toward the capability-denial or consequence-management approaches than Canberra (e.g., British opposition to destroying smallpox samples), or further away (e.g., widespread initial resistance to establishing the AG). This suggests that there may be a spectrum of Western preferences among the approaches. To the extent that this is true, American exceptionalism cannot explain this wider variation. But this represents mere speculation based on insufficient evidence. Further research is needed in order to confirm that such wider variation exists, and if so, where U.S. and Australian preferences fall along such a spectrum.[2]

On the Australian side of the equation, the modest literature on small state–middle power behavior offers an alternative explanatory tool that is also based on national attributes. This theory suggests that regardless of whether U.S. behavior is exceptional, the behavior of a middle power such as Australia will diverge from that of a major power in predictable ways. However, this body of theory represents an extremely limited theoretical tool generally, and even more so in explaining the present case.

Generally, the national-attributes literature is divided on whether "smallness" affects merely the available quantity of the same means (e.g., diplomatic leverage, military power) with which to pursue the same types of national interests (e.g., prosperity, security), which is the traditional perspective, or whether it also influences the very nature of such interests (Thakur, 1991; Papadakis & Starr, 1987). Both perspectives accept that "smallness" causes different behavior. But traditional theorists such as Fox (1977), Handel (1981), Holbraad (1984), Rothstein (1968), and Vital (1967) tend to see this difference in terms of tactical accommodations necessitated by comparatively limited resources. This perspective therefore concentrates on the style rather than the content of middle-power statecraft. A more recent, ambitious school accepts these differences, but seeks to go further, suggesting that small and middle powers have manifestly different goals; for example, the desire to actively behave as "good international citizens" (Cooper, 1997; Cooper, Higgott, & Nossal, 1993; Hocking, 1997; Nossal, 1993; Papadakis & Starr, 1987; Wood, 1988).

The established body of middle-power theory, to which both schools subscribe, is able to provide only a few predictions. The most empirically validated of these is that such states prefer to work (either as leaders or joiners) through multilateral institutions or ad hoc coalitions of like-minded states, rather than pursuing interests on their own. This is seen as particularly true for global issues (Cooper, Higgott, & Nossal, 1993; Fox, 1977; Jensen, 1987; Keating, 1993; Nossal, 1993; Papadakis & Starr, 1987; Thakur, 1991; Wood, 1988). Following from this, they are also thought likely to be inclined to support multilateral institution- and norm-building generally, in order to maximize such opportunities (Cooper, Higgott, & Nossal, 1993; Nossal, 1993; Thakur, 1991). In doing so, they are thought to favor an activist approach, stressing entrepreneurial flair and technical competence in order to compensate for their relative lack of other sources of leverage (Cooper, Higgott, & Nossal, 1993; Nossal, 1993). At the same time, facing relatively constrained resources, they are also considered likely to concentrate on "niches" rather than trying to take on everything at once, again especially regarding global issues. These niches are chosen based on both national interests and the likelihood of being able to play an effective role in a particular process (Cooper, 1997; Hocking, 1997; Leaver, 1997a; Porter, 1996–1997). For a variety of reasons they are also thought more likely to embrace compromise positions and to facilitate others doing likewise (Cooper, Higgott, & Nossal, 1993; Fox, 1977; Lyons, 1995). All these predictions in essence relate to tactics by which middle powers seek to maximize their leverage in pursuing national preferences.

These tactical predictions help to explain some secondary comparative findings revealed by the case studies. Indeed, the style of Australian diplomacy has rather consistently displayed characteristic middle-power methods. For example, Cooper, Higgott, and Nossal (1993) note that Australia's role in the CWC negotiations typifies classic middle-power tactics. The enterprise involved multilateral institution- and norm-building. It featured opportunistic activism, using entrepreneurialism and technical expertise as well as mediating compromises. Niche tactics also explain national differences in the relative priority accorded to the different proliferation areas, with the Australian agenda being far more process driven.

However, middle-power tactics do not plausibly explain the consistent divergence in U.S. and Australian preferences between antiproliferation approaches. This is especially the case for differences regarding the two approaches to prevention: capability-denial versus nonpossession norm-building. Middle-power tactics could apply equally to either capability-denial or nonpossession norm-building. For example, the creation of the AG represents a classic example of Australia using middle-power tactics on behalf of capability-denial. Indeed, participation in suppliers regimes, in which all members participate as sovereign equals, is perfectly consistent with middle-power methods. The fact is that denial strategies of various types offer ample scope for multilateral institution- and norm-building and coalition action, which overall Australia opted to pursue less vigorously than it could have. Even in terms of unilateral and bilateral national enforcement actions (e.g., interdiction, sanctions), Australia has explicitly and consistently refused to act in unison with a coalition of supply-side partners. At the same time, Canberra frequently has been willing to employ aggressive bilateral means in furtherance of nonpossession norm-building interests, especially within its own region.[3] Australia has likewise frequently instituted unilateral, punitive sanctions on behalf of other issues like human rights (Nossal, 1994). In other words, Australia has not availed itself of available opportunities to use middle-power methods in furtherance of capability-denial, while at the same time it has been willing to depart from these methods in furtherance of treaty norms.

Given this failure of the traditional theory of middle-power tactics to explain satisfactorily the divergence, we would have to turn to the more ambitious school of middle-power theory, which asserts that national attributes can explain not only the manner in which middle powers pursue their interests, but also the type of interest they are likely to have. Unfortunately, it is precisely in this ambitious attempt to predict interests (*vice* tactics) that the fundamental soundness of the theory becomes highly dubious.

Thakur (1991) argues convincingly that similarity in attributes cannot provide even weak universalizable predictions about foreign policy preferences: "Instead, it is specific to the actor, context, issue, region, and time" (p. 279). He continues, "This is not to say that size can serve no explanatory purpose at all. . . . But the importance of size as an isolated factor should not be exaggerated: small countries are a heterogeneous group which do not have uniform behavioral characteristics and cannot be expected to respond the same way to similar stimuli" (p. 282). So while Australia, Argentina, Belgium, Indonesia, South Africa, and South Korea may all by some measures be roughly comparable in terms of their attributes, and indeed may evince certain tactical similarities compared to major powers in pursuing their separate interests (i.e., the traditional "smallness" prediction), it is difficult to discern that such similitude has extended to those interests per se.[4] Ravenhill (1998) notes, "Intra-category variation . . . [is] likely to vitiate the utility of the category for making predictions about the states' likely foreign policy behaviours" (p. 310). Thakur (1991) concludes specifically regarding Australia, "While the size of a state can be used to describe an actor in international relations as small, the concept of the small state lacks explanatory content and theoretical utility: analysis of Australian . . . foreign policies as small state behavior will confuse more than clarify" (p. 241).

This general explanatory weakness is especially pronounced when it comes to security issues, such as proliferation response. The proponents of ambitious middle-power theory, such as Cooper, Higgott, and Nossal (1991), readily acknowledge that commonality in middle-power behavior is most evident regarding elements of the economic and social agendas of international relations, rather than elements of the security agenda.

Proponents of expansive middle-power theory have sought to get around the problem of intracategory divergences by narrowing their focus to what Andrew Cooper (1997) terms "self-identified middle powers," citing as examples Australia, Canada, Sweden, and Norway. This seems a promising avenue, since it yields predictions that closely correspond with Australia's antiproliferation preferences. Specifically, these "self-identified" middle powers are said to have an unusually strong common interest in altruistic "good international citizenship." This interest is reflected in activism on global causes that reflect the interests of the international community as a whole rather than parochial national or block interests, and which emphasize cooperation rather than coercion as the basis for world politics (Cooper, 1997; Cooper, Higgott, & Nossal, 1993; Evans & Grant, 1991; Nossal, 1993).

The problem with narrowing the focus to this type of artificially delineated subset of the category "all middle powers" is that because the refinement is based on self-selection, it removes national attributes from the predictive equation. As Ravenhill (1998) observes, this boils down to defining middle powers not by quantitative factors (e.g., size, military power), but by how they behave. It is therefore at best a descriptive rather than a predictive grouping, based on shared inclinations more than common attributes. Therefore, while these states may well have common interests (e.g., promoting international cooperation), this could be explained by other underlying common factors. For example, the fact that these states are located in conspicuously safe and stable regions suggests that geopolitical commonality could be a factor. Alternatively, they are all members of what Findlay (1991b) describes as the "left wing" of the Western group of countries, suggesting that another explanation might be similarities in either worldview and ideology or national identity and political–strategic culture. Ravenhill suggests as much when he notes that following the election of a conservative government in the mid-1990s, Australia's enthusiasm for the predicted types of middle-power activism declined sharply.

Geopolitics

Another structural explanation for the divergence between U.S. and Australian responses to proliferation is geopolitical disparity. This can be thought of as the flip side of national-attributes theory, in that whereas national-attributes predictions are based on the relative distribution of power (e.g., economic and military capabilities) within the international system, geopolitical predictions are based on the relative distribution of threats (e.g., proximity, intentions) within the international system (Thakur, 1991; Walt, 1987).[5] Although less intuitively apparent than balance-of-power theory, balance-of-threats theory in fact proves to be a far more persuasive explanatory factor in the present case.

Theorists generally recognize that "one of the most important influences on a state's foreign policy behavior is its location and physical terrain" (Kegley & Wittkopf, 1991, p. 41). But as two continental, geographically remote states, it would not necessarily appear that Australia and the United States are sharply differentiated in this regard. After all, neither is threatened by WMD from within their region, leaving WMD-armed ICBMs as the only plausible direct military threats to their homelands.[6] And whereas the proliferation of WMD and long-range missiles is likely to expand this threat over time, China and Russia currently remain the only potentially hostile states with such capabilities. However, using a more dynamic conception of balance of threats, as the contemporary literature on critical geopolitics suggests, and taking into account all manner of threats and relationships, significant differences separate these actors (Dalby, 1996). More to the point, the empirical case studies manifestly reveal that such broadly conceived geopolitical divergence has been consistently apparent regarding proliferation threats specifically.

During the early to mid-1980s, geopolitical differences led the United States to focus on the Soviet threat in these areas more than the comparably minor threat of proliferation, and vice versa for Australia. However, even then, the proliferation threat was far greater in absolute terms for the United States than for Australia. For the entire period covered by the present study, particularly the 1990s, large numbers of U.S. military forces stationed permanently in the Middle East, Northeast Asia, and southern Europe and Turkey have faced potential WMD threats by hostile states. Some portion of globally deployed U.S. naval forces are likewise usually in harm's way. The immediacy of these threats has steadily increased over the past decade as proliferation has preceded apace in hostile states such as Iran, Libya, North Korea, and Syria—particularly in terms of effective delivery systems—and the U.S. military presence has grown in adjacent countries. In addition, the United States has close allies in proliferated regions who are under the gun of proliferation and that the United States is obligated to protect.

Beyond these immediate threats to allies and its own forces, proliferation globally threatens to degrade U.S. power projection capabilities by asymmetrically offsetting its conventional superiority. For example, Iran's WMD doctrine explicitly focuses on neutralizing U.S. military power in the Persian Gulf. This danger is exacerbated by the increasing percentage of U.S. mobility forces that are homeland based, and which therefore rely for crisis deployment on enroute and in-theater ports, airfields, and maritime chokepoints (e.g., Suez Canal, Strait of Hormuz) that as "soft targets" are especially vulnerable to CB/M disruption (Commission off., 1998; DeSutter, 1997; Larsen, 1995; Rauf, 1998; Starr, 1997). This consideration greatly broadens the existing geopolitical threat that proliferation poses to the United States.

In contrast, Australia has been described as "arguably one of the least militarily threatened states on the planet" (Dalby, 1996, p. 59). Even the lingering fears of prior generations, who saw their country as an isolated Western outpost in a potentially hostile Asia, had largely given way to benign perceptions of the region by the early 1980s (Dalby, 1996; Walker int., 1998; White int., 1999). This propitious geopolitical circumstance has been especially notable regarding proliferation threats. Australia has no significant forces permanently stationed outside its territory and has not significantly deployed outside its immediate vicinity since the Vietnam War. It therefore has little expectation of ever undertaking a large-scale deployment beyond its own strategic region (defined as including the eastern Indian Ocean, Southeast Asia, and the southwest Pacific), which has never experienced proliferation or even a real threat of proliferation (Defence off., 1987, 1994, 1997; DFAT off., 1997a; Dibb off., 1986; Evans & Grant, 1991; Reese int., 1998; White int., 1999).

Recall from Chapter 2 that at a purely conceptual level, the strengths and weaknesses of the different approaches to antiproliferation to a great extent depend on the nature of the threat envisioned. For example, proponents of the nonpossession norm-building approach do not claim that it is the most effective in countering active, determined proliferators in the short to medium term. Instead, they maintain that its strength is as a long-term prophylaxis, whose tangible impact on today's proliferation "hard cases" may take considerable time. In other words, the approach focuses in the present on preventing the emergence of new proliferators, rather than coping with the ones that already exist. By the same token, advocates of the denial and proliferation-management approaches do not claim that they offer permanent, stable, long-term solutions. Rather, they support these approaches as the best way to counter today's proliferators. Longer-term solutions are seen in terms of buying time for demand to be reduced through indirect means such as democratization, regional stability, or, indeed, even norm-building.

In a sense the different conceptual strengths of the two nonproliferation approaches can be compared to preventative and palliative medicine. Most would agree that some combination of both is desirable. The emphasis, however, would depend overwhelmingly on whether one actually had a disease. A patient with cancer would be ill-advised to rely primarily on a healthy diet rich in antioxidants. A healthy but perhaps at-risk patient would be equally ill-advised to undergo surgery or chemotherapy. To take this analogy a step further, a healthy patient at extremely high risk might consider preemptive surgery, but only if the risk was dire, and even then every effort would presumably be made to minimize the procedure and the primary emphasis would remain on preventative measures.

Although this medical analogy is imperfect, it does capture the logic of why one state actively imperiled by proliferation and another facing only a latent danger would logically emphasize different responses. Thus, during interviews, many U.S. officials complained that while treaty norms might be useful to contain the further spread of proliferation, they are ineffective when it comes to the clear and present danger posed by proliferant rogue states. At the same time, many Australian officials complained that while denial strategies may be a short-term necessity, relying on them as the primary response to proliferation is myopic, putting immediate concerns ahead of long-term solutions.

Australian officials (who are far more aware of U.S. motivations than vice versa) are fully cognizant that different geopolitical circumstances are a major reason for the contrasts between Australian and American antiproliferation preferences. One very senior, long-serving Defence official states, "I do think that a lot of the differences between our approaches can be quite easily traced back to differences in our strategic situation" (White int., 1999). A former senior, long-serving DFAT official interviewed notes that Australia's antiproliferation approach "reflects the situation that whereas proliferation anywhere is a threat to everybody, proliferation some distance from us doesn't present the same sort of national threat as it would if there was proliferation in Southeast Asia." It seems extremely telling that more than a few past and present Australian officials of various rank speculate that, *if a meaningful proliferation threat were ever to emerge in its region, then Australia's response would probably move closer to a U.S.–style approach* ([DFAT] ints.; [DOD] int.; Dorling int., 1998; White int., 1999). This is a compelling indication that threat perception represents a decisive explanatory variable.

Competing Subnational Interests

Competing subnational interests offers one of several plausible agent-specific explanations. Proliferation response often competes with other elements of national interest; for example, promoting trade and maintaining cordial diplomatic relationships. It is therefore possible that if the United States and Australia have different levels of relevant competing interests, this could influence their respective antiproliferation preferences. However, while such differences in competing interests clearly exist between these states, and probably have affected their antiproliferation behavior, the indications are mixed about whether this factor has contributed to the overall pattern of divergence in question.

Australia and the United States see antiproliferation as being in their national interest. Analytically, however, it is rather more complicated. The FPA literature generally recognizes that, notwithstanding its ubiquitous use by governments to explain their behavior, the concept of national interest is problematic as a conceptual tool. One problem is that the term is used variously to denote very different concepts; for example, the aggregate of a country's collective concerns, a fixed set of determinates outside the government decision-making process, or mutable government objectives. Although the first is what governments usually mean, it is also the most amorphous and therefore least theoretically useful sense of the term. FPA theorists therefore tend to focus on the latter meanings (Frankel, 1970; Plischke, 1988; Rosenau, 1980). In this context, they widely recognize that states do not have a single national interest, but rather a set of subnational interests. The literature generally divides these into three broad categories: security–military; economic–trade, and political–diplomatic (Frankel, 1970). Because they often cannot be obtained simultaneously, states constantly are forced to prioritize among them (Clinton, 1994).

Antiproliferation, first and foremost, represents a security interest. That said, the case studies provide frequent examples where it has explicitly competed with other rival security interests. It is thus possible to have competing intra-subcategory interests. In this respect, the United States has had rival security interests that would be undermined by treaty norms that Australia has not shared. The most conspicuous of these is that, unlike Australia, it has stood to lose existing weapons arsenals. In the CW area initially, and still in the missile area, the United States operated as a status quo "have." This was certainly a factor in U.S. wariness of the CWC, and remains a significant factor in Washington's opposition to trying to negotiate a global missile norm. As for Australia, it is naturally easier to support disarmament when it is others who do the disarming. Canberra's early opposition to foreclosing its nuclear options via NPT (Walsh, 1997), and more recently its reluctance to foreclose its missile options through a regional normative mechanism, and its wariness of the Ottawa Convention banning land mines as a new category of abhorrent weapon—the first time that its own existing weapons were at stake in any of its disarmament activities since the Washington Naval Talks in the 1930s—shows that this has been a tangible factor in its strong willingness to support nonpossession norm-building against things that it already does not possess and which it has decided it will never want.[7]

However, although differences in competing security interests based on possession (or lack of it) clearly have been a reinforcing factor on both sides, it does not appear on its own to be a decisive variable in explaining the overall divergence in preferences over time and across the different proliferation areas. After all, the United States had unilaterally renounced BW long before any of the contemporary debates on strengthening the BWC, had unilaterally decided to destroy the bulk of its CW stockpile and later to renounce in-kind retaliation in the midst of the CWC negotiations, and bilaterally gave up INF-range missiles before rejecting attempts to negotiate a global ban on such systems. Moreover, Australia has pushed for a global missile ban, notwithstanding its own missile aspirations.

A second asymmetric, competing security interest is the need to protect sensitive military and intelligence installations against intrusive challenge inspections. While both governments have such sites, Australia, unlike the United States, does not have super-secret weapons-development projects, so-called black programs, the very existence of which is highly classified. Also, with just a handful of sensitive sites, Australia can institute defensive precautions, such as training, on a scale that would be impossible for the thousands of sensitive American military sites around the world (Donadio int., 1998). Again, it is easier for Australia to insist on sweeping intrusiveness when it has relatively little to hide.

However, like possession, this factor does not explain consistently divergent preferences over time and across the different areas. Having reluctantly accepted "anytime, anywhere" managed access challenge inspections in CWC, the issue of challenge inspections was not an overriding concern for Washington in the BWC context because the vulnerability already existed from CWC. Moreover, given that combating proliferation has been considered a top U.S. security interest since the late 1980s and its very top national security priority in recent years, it would be illogical for Washington to sacrifice a proliferation-response option for the sake of competing security interests if it believed that that option was the best means to achieve its higher priority antiproliferation goals. Again, while these competing security interests in some cases reinforce each actors' divergent national inclinations, it seems unlikely that they represent a root cause.

In addition to intrasecurity tensions, antiproliferation competes with the other main elements of national interest. One analyst notes that proliferation response "is an extremely complex affair . . . because a delicate balance must be preserved between security concerns, matters of foreign policy, and commercial interests" (Van Ham, 1993, p. 5). U.S. officials, for their part, readily acknowledge these tensions. According to senior officials from the last two administrations, "There are frequently competing and legitimate interests at play—national security, foreign policy, and export promotion, to name three. The result is a balancing act" (Clarke tst., 1991, p. 99), and "We very much appreciate [that] the complex nature of the task of promoting nonproliferation . . . deals with tough and interrelated issues of security, economics, jobs, and trade" (Davis tst., 1993, p. 4). In other words, proliferation response can damage other subnational interests, and vice versa.

There are dramatic differences between the United States and Australia in their levels of competing economic interests. Industries relevant to missiles, CW, and BW each comprise major export sectors of the U.S. economy. In contrast, Australia has no significant aerospace industry. Its small chemical industry does not represent a significant export sector of the Australian economy. Even its robust biotechnology sector, while a significant exporter, does not begin to approach its U.S. counterpart as a percentage of GDP. Put bluntly, the United States has far more at stake in terms of competing economic interests across all of these areas.

Despite this disparity, there is nothing to suggest that this helps to explain the main comparative finding in question. If anything, indications point toward a contravening explanation in this regard. It is widely acknowledged that the economic costs of supply-side strategies are far higher than for treaty norms. One analyst notes that the costs of export controls are especially onerous for the technology-driven U.S. economy:

Although the United States has an interest in controlling the proliferation of weapons technologies through export controls, current export controls also have an adverse effect on the ability of U.S. industries to export these technologies for peaceful purposes. . . . U.S. corporations are limited in their ability to promote international sales of cutting-edge technologies and to tap into the global technology market because of . . . export controls on "dual use" technologies. (Hiestand, 1995)

Indeed, studies by the National Academy of Science estimate that in 1985 (before sweeping nonproliferation restrictions had been enacted) controls on high-technology exports were already costing the U.S. economy $9 billion and nearly 200,000 jobs annually, and that by the mid-1990s with the introduction of nonproliferation restrictions these figures had more than doubled (Moodie, 1995; Hiestand, 1995). Nonproliferation sanctions further spike the economic costs of supply-side nonproliferation. Whereas missile sanctions could cost the U.S. economy millions or even billions in trade, treaty norms conversely tend to facilitate trade, either implicitly or explicitly. In contrast, we have seen that Australia has had positive economic incentives to join suppliers regimes in order to get access to trade.

Higher levels of competing economic interests are a likely explanation for greater U.S. inconsistency in implementing capability-denial strategies (e.g., uneven licensing or sanctions decisions). This factor does not, however, explain the fundamental divergence in preference. Given the steep trade costs associated with supply-side strategies compared to treaty norms, the higher U.S. economic stakes would lead one to expect Washington to be less enthusiastic about supply-side measures than Canberra.[8] Since the actual empirical finding is the opposite, this suggests that the divergence has occurred not because of different levels of competing economic interests, but in spite of them.

Of course, verification provisions associated with treaty norms pose the counterbalancing economic threat of industrial espionage. U.S. biotechnology industries have maintained significant technical advantages over their counterparts in other advanced industrialized states. This advantage puts them at particular risk from industrial espionage in that they have relatively more to lose. This indisputably has contributed to U.S. reservations about intrusive BWC measures. However, this was far less of a consideration for the CWC, where the chemical industry was less at risk and, in fact, at some junctures during the negotiations supported stricter measures than the U.S. government. Such commercial concerns would also be a negligible factor for any potential missile ban. On the Australian side of the equation, although it faces much higher economic risks in this regard for its well-developed biotechnology sector than it did in the chemical area, it pursued virtually identical verification policies for both the CWC and the BWC. This factor has therefore reinforced U.S. wariness of BWC verification, but it does not offer a persuasive explanation for divergent U.S. and Australian preferences across the board. At best, therefore, the evidence about the impact of differences in competing economic interests is inconsistent.

Assessing the causal relevance of competing foreign policy interests likewise yields an indeterminate prognosis. This factor is relatively unconvincing in the case of the United States. The fact that the United States has had strong bilateral ties to some countries of proliferation concern (e.g., Israel, Pakistan, South Korea) certainly explains any inconsistency in its application of universal nonproliferation standards in these cases. But it does not explain its larger proliferation-response preferences. Again, capability-denial generally tends to be more costly than norm-building in terms of bilateral diplomacy, because it is inherently more coercive. For example, U.S. efforts to compel and enforce Russian and Chinese compliance with export-control norms has been a major irritant to two of Washington's most important bilateral relationships. Therefore, as with its trade interests, Washington leans toward capability-denial despite, rather than because of, its relatively high level of competing diplomatic interests.

On the Australian side, this factor appears to be more significant, although the assessment remains mixed. On the one hand, Canberra has a disproportionate interest in maintaining good relations with certain nonaligned governments that are hostile to discriminatory, coercive denial strategies. Whereas relations with Indonesia and Malaysia have been high on Canberra's foreign policy priorities, such states are far less important in Washington's international relations. Indeed, one of the main reasons that Australia feels more secure today than it did a few decades ago is that it has been able to forge stable, cooperative strategic relationships with its neighbors. Therefore, pursuing discriminatory approaches is potentially damaging to Australia's core bilateral interests (Walker int., 1998).

On the other hand, maintaining strong bilateral relations with the United States has been at least as important to Australian diplomacy as relations with its neighbors. This would seem to balance out the equation. Moreover, even in terms of currying favor with the Third World, the norm-building approach cuts two ways. Nonaligned states' vehement opposition to intrusive verification—which has often seen them arrayed with the United States against Australia—has not inhibited Canberra from fighting hard for tough verification of global treaty norms, including through aggressive bilateral diplomacy with Indonesia and Malaysia. Moreover, the Howard government has to some extent reoriented its foreign policy away from supporting cooperation for its own sake, and toward bilateral diplomacy based on specific national interests.

Overall, the different levels of competing interests offer an assortment of influences pushing and pulling for and against the divergent antiproliferation preferences of these governments. It is therefore difficult to assess whether these influences collectively do more to explain or to confound the main comparative finding. But none of the factors that would explain the divergence appears to apply consistently for both actors over time across all of the areas. They therefore do not appear to be decisive variables, at least on balance.

Worldview

There is an undeniable link between the discernible differences in worldviews between U.S. and Australian decision-making elites and the observed divergence in proliferation-response preferences. It is unclear, however, whether worldview is an independent causal variable, or simply a manifestation of more fundamental factors.

It is widely recognized within FPA literatures that agent-specific perceptions of the external environment (i.e., objective and subjective awareness) are as important in influencing foreign policy as the actual systemic reality of that environment. At the basic level of objective awareness, this suggests that divergent understandings of the proliferation problem could explain differences in national responses to it. However, the extensive intelligence sharing between Australia and the United States in these areas would appear to minimize differences in objective knowledge as an explanatory factor in the present comparison (although it might be highly significant in other cases where intelligence disparities exist).

Beyond straightforward objective awareness, a number of subjective factors are thought to affect the outward-looking perceptions of foreign policy elites, such as belief systems, ideology, and psychological influences. International-relations theorists remain sharply divided about the importance of these perceptual lenses in shaping foreign policy behavior. For example, traditional systemic and rationalist perspectives inherently disregard such considerations. But even within theoretical orientations that stress these very considerations (e.g., constructivism, FPA), there are dozens of subliteratures pointing in different analytical directions and offering any number of typologies for categorizing the internal filters that can affect decision makers' external perceptions (MacLean, 1988; Ripley, 1993; Smith, 1988).

206 / Competing Western Strategies Against Weapons of Mass Destruction

For the present case, however, most of these perceptual factors can safely be set aside, because they are not helpful in distinguishing American and Australian leadership elites. For instance, there are no competing civilizational (e.g., Islamic) or metaideological (e.g., Communist) belief systems, and the various psychological determinants on decision making are unlikely to be especially different for American and Australian elites. Given this relative similarity in other respects, the appropriate focus for differences in worldview would appear to be ideology, as the term is used within the mainstream political parameters of Western democracies. However, the familiar domestic political concepts of "conservatism" versus "liberalism" (the latter to include democratic socialism) are ill-defined and frequently misleading when applied to foreign policy. Instead, it is more useful to think in terms of the mainstream Western perspectives on the nature of international relations, realism–neorealism versus liberalism–neoliberalism, recognizing that these are loosely identified with conservatism and liberalism, respectively. The focus then is not on neorealism and neoliberalism as predictive scholarly theories by which to analyze and explain events, but rather as descriptive (and therefore implicitly prescriptive) worldviews internalized by foreign policy decision makers (knowingly or otherwise).

Prior studies suggest that during the time period in question since the early to mid-1980s, there have been discernibly different national leanings in this sense of worldview between the foreign and national security policy elites in Washington and Canberra. The American foreign and national security policy establishment has been steeped in neorealist perspectives, evolving from classical realism of the Kissinger ilk. This has been the case under both political parties, although the Democratic Carter and Clinton administrations have been seen to flirt with tinges of liberalism (Olson & Onuf, 1985; Haas, 1995, 1997). However, because these impulses have been episodic and limited within these administrations, and also usually tempered by divided government (i.e., Republican control of at least one part of Congress), realist–neorealist perspectives have always remained predominant. The new Bush administration has been particularly direct in stressing the need to reassert "realism" in foreign policy.

In contrast, Australian foreign policy circles during the Labor period embraced a self-consciously neoliberal worldview, evolving from the English school of Grotian rationalism (George, 1997; Kerr, 1999; Mathews & McCormack, 1995).[9] Although Kerr (1999) notes that in contrast to the foreign policy establishment the Australian defense establishment has infused a strong dose of realism in its worldview, this is not especially relevant in light of DFAT's virtual policy monopoly in the proliferation response arena. Likewise, while the conservative Howard government has adopted a more realist tone over the past few years, it does not appear that this has shifted the fundamental neoliberal tilt of Australian foreign policy.

The neorealist and neoliberal paradigms paint very different pictures of the nature of the international system and relations within that system. At the most general level, "Neo-realists concentrate on capabilities rather than intentions, whereas neo-liberals look more at intentions and perceptions" (Smith, 1995, p. 23). Reflecting the inheritance of the classical realism of Carr, Morgenthau, and Kissinger, neorealism is especially concerned with states' innate pursuit of power in the form of military capabilities. As regards international norms and institutions, Wendt (1994) observes that neorealists see these as reflecting state interests, whereas neoliberals see them as affecting states' conceptions of their interests over time. Therefore, he notes that in the neorealist worldview, "Any international institutions which are created will be inherently unstable, since without the power to transform identities and interests they will be 'continuing objects of choice' by exogenously constituted actors constrained only by the transaction costs of behavior change" (pp. 403–404). In other words, the two perspectives fundamentally disagree on the ability of constituted norms and institutions to alter or constrain state behavior, especially in the long term.

Even at this level of gross generalization, the two perspectives point to obvious prescriptive preferences vis-à-vis the three broad approaches to antiproliferation. As the term suggests, capability-denial is all about inherent capabilities, with intentions considered secondarily or not at all. For example, a state might have perfectly peaceful intentions for its SLV program, but the MTCR Annex would see it as a Category I system by any name. As one analyst states, the U.S. emphasis on denial strategies reflects a "realist worldview that linked national security to military strength and military strength to dominance in science and technology" (Wright, 1993, p. 141). Consequence-management likewise focuses overwhelmingly on capabilities rather than intentions (although obviously these tools are ultimately only used against enemies). In contrast, intentions are embedded in the cooperative norm-building formula, where states are explicitly or implicitly granted access to capabilities in return for promising not to misuse them (and possibly demonstrating this benign intention through transparency measures or verification).

A neoliberal looking at the norm-building project can comfortably overlook short-term weaknesses in deference to the expectation of a slow, ongoing synthesis of interests that over time promises to solve the problem permanently. For a neorealist on the other hand, what time lends to a norm is the ever-greater possibility of breakout as real capabilities accumulate behind a lulling veil of good intentions. Thus, a neoliberal would see capability-denial as at best a temporary necessity to hold the line while the effects of norm-building are taking root. As a primary long-term approach, however, a neoliberal would see it as inherently shortsighted, locking in an indefinite, ineffective, costly, and ultimately unnecessary struggle between suppliers and recipients. As for consequence-management, neoliberalism would regard this as just an additional long-term cost necessitated by the gormless insistence of relying on denial strategies, which would not be needed if normative strategies were used to good effect. The neorealist would not necessarily dispute the imperfection of denial strategies, but without norm-building as a viable alternative the only realistic option is to make preventative denial as strong as possible, while in parallel taking steps to manage the consequence of unavoidable residual proliferation. In the present case, the dramatic differences in long-term U.S. and Australian optimism about being able to prevent proliferation depicted in Figure 5.2 are fully consistent with these two very different sets of expectations.

Ideological orientation influences more than just opinions about the efficacy of one or the other antiproliferation approach. To the extent that antiproliferation represents a high priority on the international agenda, the approach chosen will bolster different visions of world politics. Norm-building fits in neatly with an international system based on collective security, whereas capability-denial and proliferation management represent what amounts to a concert-of-powers or occasionally even unilateralist approach to international relations. Ergo, in explaining the ideological basis of criticism that is often leveled against supply-side strategies, Karp (1996) observes, "The challenge ultimately is a question of world order: Will future international security affairs be dominated by the pursuit of distinct national interests organized through us-against-them alliances, or will they give a greater role to collective security organizations based on universal principles? Most supplier governments are divided on such issues" (p. 27). Roberts (1993) argues along the same lines that supporting the CWC is important not only to address CW threats, but also as a means to bolster the larger U.N. system. Thus, the prescriptive implications of these competing worldviews apply not only to proliferation per se, but to the wider political agenda of world order. It is presumably in just this sense that one analysis of Australian disarmament policies concludes, "In the context of Australian foreign policy as a whole, disarmament and arms control policy has thus far been overwhelmingly shaped by political objectives rather than security or economic objectives" (Findlay, 1991b, p. 16). Indeed, a number of observers suggest that Australia's disarmament policies during the Labor period were driven to a significant extent by its commitment to a wider ideological agenda for world politics (Butler int., 1998; Evans, 1997; Leaver, 1997b; Mathews & McCormack, 1995).

Since each of the two subject actors has evinced a marked leaning toward different competing worldviews, and these in turn correspondingly augur for the different antiproliferation approach favored by each—both narrowly in terms of how best to curb proliferation, and more broadly in terms of contributing to broader formulas of world order—it would seem that there is a strong link between worldview and antiproliferation behavior. The question that remains is whether this is a causal connection. Although U.S. and Australian elites are seen to subscribe to different worldviews, extant theory is unclear about why this should be so. Consequently, it is difficult to know whether their divergent worldviews represent an independent causal variable, or merely are secondary manifestations of other primary factors.

Assuming that foreign policy worldview is in fact derived from political ideology with realism on the right and liberalism on the left, as is typically assumed, then it could represent a key explanation in the present case. If so, this would mean that U.S. decision-making elites have been more conservative (i.e., neorealist) than their Australian counterparts, to the extent that not only were the center-right Reagan and Bush administrations to the right of the center-left Hawke and Keating governments, but less intuitively that the centrist "new Democrat" Clinton administration remained to the right of the center-right Howard government (albeit likely with a narrower gap). There is certainly nothing in our empirical findings that is inconsistent with this interpretation.

The idea of a relatively static comparative balance between U.S. and Australian ideological perspectives is not as improbable as the changes in the ideological orientation of their regimes over the past two decades might suggest. On the Australian side, Miller (1988) argues that the foreign policy differences between the two major Australian parties are more rhetorical than real. In addition, the conspicuous influence of the Australian career bureaucracy is a force for continuity in changing political winds. This latter factor is especially pertinent in the present case, because antiproliferation policies have generally been formulated and implemented well below the overtly political ministerial level. Another source for Australia's enduring neoliberal penchant relates back to its status as a "self-identified" middle power. Whatever flaws the concept of middle powerdom may have as a predictive national-attributes theory, there is no doubt that Australian foreign policy elites have embraced it as prescriptive orthodoxy. One observer notes, "The Australian government under the leadership of [Labor Prime Ministers] Bob Hawke and Paul Keating has projected the notion of middle powerdom as the conceptual foundation of its foreign policy" (Hocking, 1997, p. 134). Middle-power theory's prescriptive emphasis on cooperation over coercion, and international law over ad hoc structures, correspond neatly with the neoliberal outlook. Given that this foreign policy doctrine has been closely associated with Labor governments, it is not necessarily distinct from ideology, but can be seen as a reinforcing factor which, to some extent, may also have seeped into the Coalition Party's worldview (and which, in any case, underpins the training of the career bureaucrats and external policy influencers in academia and the press).

On the U.S. side, despite speculation about the erosion of the bipartisan national security consensus that prevailed during the Cold War and increasing Congressional partisanship on these specific issues, there is still a significant center that shares fundamentally the same worldview. On proliferation response in particular, while Congressional support for treaty norms has tended to divide somewhat along party lines, although not strictly—recall that it was in a Democratic Senate that concerns about the CWC initially delayed ratification—there has also been strong bipartisan support for tough supply-side (e.g., export controls, sanctions) and counterproliferation policies. There is likewise no evidence of deep schisms within the broader U.S. national security establishment from which many political appointees are drawn. Moreover, to the extent that ideological differences have existed, divided government has hindered either branch of government from successfully acting on any radical shifts in worldview (particularly to the left).

The preceeding discussion shows that a causal link between domestic ideology and divergent worldviews is plausible, and that differences in worldview therefore may represent an important causal (versus merely symptomatic) factor. However, there is still reasonable room for doubt. Another viable explanation is that the difference in U.S. and Australian worldviews is merely a secondary symptom of geopolitics. For example, is Japan pacifist for ideological reasons, or because it can afford to be by virtue of having the United States provide its security? It has already been observed that countries associated with neoliberal worldviews are often those facing low geopolitical threats. If geopolitics rather than ideology is the root cause of the divergence in U.S. and Australian worldviews, then these different worldviews are nothing more than secondary effects of this root cause. The credibility of this alternative explanation highlights the common inability of extant FPA theory to distinguish between intertwined primary causal factors and their subsidiary manifestations. Thus, while it can be inferred that there is a strong link between worldview and antiproliferation preferences, the causal significance of this is open to interpretation.

Governmental–Bureaucratic Structures

Differences in government systems and in bureaucratic decision-making structures doubtless contribute to the marked differences in the style and consistency of U.S. and Australian proliferation-response policies, but it is difficult to discern a causal variable between these factors and these actors' overall preferences for different antiproliferation approaches.

The causal relevance of governmental and bureaucratic structures and processes on foreign policy behavior represents a mainstay of FPA theorizing. Even among Western democracies, differences between presidential and parliamentary cabinet systems can yield significant foreign policy differences. The constitutional division of powers within the U.S. system gives Congress far more power over foreign and national security policy than most parliaments, especially regarding treaty making.[10] The U.S. president, moreover, does not exercise explicit control over members of his political party in Congress. Thus, even when the same party controls the White House and both sides of Capitol Hill—a rare and usually brief occurrence in recent decades—Congress is prone to act independently. At the same time, most prime ministers have far less control over the ministers in their own cabinet than is the case for the U.S. president. The American cabinet, serving at the pleasure of the president, does not fulfil the collective decision-making function by which the term is understood in a parliamentary system. But cabinet secretaries in the United States are able to exert extensive control over their departments through a network of political appointees throughout the hierarchy, whereas ministers themselves are the only personnel that automatically change with the government in the Australian system (Blechman, 1990; Halperin, 1974; Nathan & Oliver, 1983; Rosenau, 1976; Verney, 1992; Wilson, 1989).

These differences in system of government suggest that the style of U.S. foreign policy decision making is likely at any given moment to be more cumbersome, fragmented, and unpredictable than that of Australia. As for continuity over time, the result is somewhat mixed. On the one hand, the dominance of senior bureaucrats in Australian policy making minimizes political interference within departments. At the same time, the need for any U.S. administration to find mutual accommodation with Congress mitigates against radical policy shifts, whereas a new Australian government faces no comparable direct external political constraints.

The case studies reveal that such differences in foreign policy style and consistency are readily apparent in U.S. and Australian antiproliferation policies. It is unclear, however, how much, if at all, these factors explain the divergence in their overall approaches.[11] Of course, one cannot validate a hypothetical negative, but there is nothing to suggest that fundamental U.S. preferences would have been different if Congress had not played a significant role. For example, although the Senate can exercise a negative pressure on norm-building through its scrutiny in the treaty-ratification process, Congress under both parties has also been the driving force in ensuring that administrations of both parties have enforced capability-denial rigorously. On the other side of the equation, if the Australian Parliament had had a larger role, there is no indication that it would have interjected any meaningful skepticism about nonpossession norm-building. If anything, circumstantial evidence suggests that greater Parliamentary involvement might have further dampened support for supply-side instruments. Likewise, there is no indication that a stronger prime minister, or a foreign minister with more politically appointed deputies, would have imposed different preferences.

Since the seminal works of Allison (1971) and Halperin (1974) first challenged the conception of states as unitary, rational actors, foreign policy influences at the bureaucratic level have been seen as equally or more important than overall governmental systems. Although views on the particulars are diverse, it is widely held that "decision structures and their procedures exert a powerful influence on the substance and form of foreign policy behavior. If different decision structures or processes are employed, then frequently the nature of the resulting foreign policy can be expected to change" (Hermann, 1978a, p. 70).

Here, too, differences between Washington and Canberra are readily apparent at the basic structural level. Whereas the National Security Act of 1947 institutionalized bureaucratic fractionalization within the U.S. executive branch, Australia has no such institutionalized interagency process to coordinate disparate elements of foreign and national security policy on a day-to-day basis (Ball & Kerr, 1996). Consequently, control over issues is far more concentrated within single government departments in Canberra, whereas in Washington a complex, multilayered, regularized interagency process ensures that the role of any particular agency is limited to interagency "lead" for a given issue.

These bureaucratic differences reinforce the outcomes suggested by governmental differences; namely, that any aspect of U.S. foreign policy should be more cumbersome, fragmented, and inconsistent when compared with Australia. But the only bureaucratic factor that might explain consistently divergent antiproliferation preferences is the consistent involvement of a mix of agencies on each side with different collective preferences. For instance, the strong anti-norm, pro-denial influence of the Pentagon in the U.S. interagency process, compared to the passivity and neutrality of the Australian Defence Department, could account for "national" differences. On the surface, this appears to be a promising line of analysis.

Interview surveys reveal sharply different attitudes among U.S. agencies. If U.S. and Australian attitudes are compared by agency rather than collectively (i.e., nationally), State Department and DFAT officials are seen to share roughly comparable biases toward norm-building (Figure 5.3). At least by this simplistic measure, if antiproliferation policies were left exclusively to the State Department and DFAT, national divergence would all but vanish. Given that DFAT does in reality control relevant Australian decision making, whereas the State Department must reach accommodation with other agencies in a consensus process supervised by the NSC staff, this implies that national variations in bureaucratic involvement could be a decisive causal factor.

Here again though, there is a question of primary cause versus secondary effect, with the overwhelming probability in this case being that bureaucratic differences represent the latter. In other words, variance in bureaucratic involvement does not explain the divergence so

Figure 5.3
Survey Question: Preferred Strategy (by agency)

Hypothetically, if you had to choose, which of the following would you consider to be more important in promoting your country's anti-proliferation goals?

Option 1: Building and maintaining strong multilateral treaty-norms against possession of these weapons

Option 2: Preventing specific transfers of these weapons and associated equipment and technology to programs or countries of concern

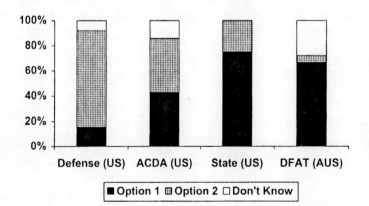

much as do the factors that explain this variance. Specifically, national interest theory, as well as most bureaucratic politics models, to a greater or lesser extent recognize that, in addition to various intermediary factors (e.g., organizational processes, personal interests) different agencies "rationally" represent different components of the national interest (e.g., security, diplomacy, and trade) (Frankel, 1970; Halperin, 1974; Hilsman, 1990; Nathan & Oliver, 1983; Rosenau, 1976). The level of a given agency's participation, therefore, can in large part be seen as a reflection of the subnational interests at stake on a given issue. For example, the U.S. Commerce Department has been a major player in all aspects of nonproliferation, which involves both export controls and verification measures on dual-use commodities that impact commercial interests, but it has not participated in traditional arms-control processes (e.g., CFE, START). Similarly, the U.S. Energy Department has participated actively in the interagency process on CBW treaty norms, because intrusive challenge inspection measures might impinge on the security of its nuclear laboratories, but has been totally uninvolved in the missile area, where no such policies have been in the offing (Allessi int., 1998).

This logic suggests that the Pentagon is involved in proliferation response, and by extension that it embraces its particular preferences, because the United States faces a clear and present geopolitical danger from proliferation. Likewise, the reason that the Australian Defence Department has been voluntarily passive and, by extension, content with DFAT's approach, is because it perceives no direct proliferation threats. This inference is supported by the finding that the Australian defense establishment's worldview incorporates realist assumptions (Kerr, 1999), and officials' assertions that Defence would unquestionably seek to assert its influence to reshape Australian antiproliferation policies if an explicit proliferation threat were to emerge ([DFAT] int.; [Defence] int.; White int., 1999). The same is demonstrably true if it were to have specific military equities threatened. For example, the aggressive Defence reaction to the anti-land-mine negotiations, and its moves to block consideration of a regional missile arrangement, indicate that it is willing to intervene against nonpossession norm-building when its interests are at stake (and that this intervention can be effective in influencing Australian policy). It therefore seems very likely that differences between U.S. and Australian interagency involvement have not been a major causal variable in the divergence of U.S. and Australian responses to proliferation, but rather a reflection of differences in the geopolitical balance of proliferation threats, reinforced by the lower level of competing subnational interests on the Australian side.

National Identity–Political-Strategic Culture

National identity is one of several other agent-specific factors that do not appear to offer compelling explanations for the fundamental divergence of U.S. and Australian strategies against proliferation. It is often espoused as a material variable that impacts a given actor's foreign policy and security interests and policies (Jepperson, Wendt, & Katzenstein, 1996; Kowert, 1998–1999; Sampson, 1987). Whereas the concept of worldview entails outward-looking perceptions, national identity and the related concept of political-strategic culture pertain to societal self-image. An obvious parallel is the operative assumption in psychology that an individual's self-image explicitly affects their behavior in predictable ways. But as Chafetz, Spirtas, and Frankel (1998–1999) note, identity theory continues to suffer from two profound flaws: "First, it offers too many vague and imprecise definitions—which means that it offers none—of the concept that stands at its very core; second, most of this scholarship does not go much beyond the mere assertion that identity is important and that, somehow, in one way or another, it plays a role in how states define and pursue their national interests" (p. vii). Therefore, while perhaps perfectly valid, the concept at its current stage of theoretical development is too vague to explain the specific finding at hand.

Beyond the general explanatory weakness of identity theory, the relative cultural and political similarity between the actors in question would appear to minimize the applicability of this factor in the present case. For example Siracusa and Cheong (1997) and Spillman (1998) argue that Australia and the United States have shared strong similarities in their national identities throughout their histories relative to other sets of countries. These include Anglo-American culture, settler nations, vast geographic territory, multiethnic–immigrant societies, urbanized, democratic, capitalist, and federated systems of national organization.

Spillman (1998) finds that the one appreciable difference is that Australian national identity is more informed by how it is perceived by the rest of the world, whereas American national identity focuses on internal integration of national values and ideals. While this raises the tantalizing prospect that Australian society's greater desire for external approval—in effect, a psychological need to be liked, whether within the society of states or international civil society—might impel its government to embrace cooperative rather than coercive international relationships, this hardly seems a tangible basis on which to suggest causal inference regarding specific patterns of proliferation-response behavior.

Domestic Politics

Extant theory on domestic political influences on foreign policy does not offer a particularly useful explanatory tool for the present comparative analysis. On the one hand, there is a wide consensus among FPA theorists that at the highest decision-making levels, domestic and international pressures are weighed simultaneously in any foreign policy decision (Putnam, 1988). Flank (1994) specifically argues that this has been overlooked as an important influence on the antiproliferation policies of Western states. At the same time, political variables are extremely complex, involving the governing regime, opposition parties, and various interests groups (Hagan, 1987; Salmore & Salmore, 1978). Most attempts to isolate domestic political factors for comparative purposes therefore tend to concentrate on the sole variable of accountability (democratic versus authoritarian systems of government), which obviously is not a distinguishing factor in the present case. Halperin (1974) notes that analysis is further complicated by the frequent reluctance of governments to acknowledge the intrusion of domestic considerations on foreign and national security policy.

Turning specifically to the present case, there are no obvious differences between the pressures faced by successive U.S. and Australian regimes that would explain their consistent divergence in antiproliferation preferences. Some of the differences in domestic political pressures that have existed reflect other explanatory factors, such as ideology and competing subnational interests. For example, political pressure from domestic U.S. industry, in the form of PhRMA's opposition to BWC routine inspections, is a reflection of the high economic stakes involved. But other factors—for instance, so-called ethnic politics—represent truly independent variables. In this regard, Washington is generally thought to be unusually subject to ethnic pressures on foreign policy, particularly from groups concentrated in key electoral states for the presidential election system (Halperin, 1974; Kegley & Wittkopf, 1991). Although Australia as a multiethnic immigrant society is probably more similar in this respect than most countries, U.S. foreign policy has been more prone to ethnic "pork barreling." However, while this might contribute to U.S. inconsistency in implementing global antiproliferation policies (e.g., going easier on Israel or tougher on Cuba), it is hard to imagine how ethnic interests would shape its overall antiproliferation approach.

In addition to special interests, domestic pressures can take the form of generalized public concern. On the Australian side of the equation, this was clearly a major factor in the Hawke government's activism on nuclear disarmament in the early 1980s. However, while this policy had a spill-down effect in the other areas, there was never any significant concern by the Australian public or, for that matter, Labor Party activists, about CB/M proliferation. Indeed, public awareness and concern regarding these areas has been a markedly stronger factor in the United States. Here again, while this is an obvious explanation for the higher priority given to responding to proliferation in Washington versus Canberra, it does not appear to bear on the nature of that response. This leads to the conclusion that various strands of domestic politics may have affected the relative consistency and priority of each actor's proliferation response, but domestic pressures have been relatively neutral regarding overall approaches.

Idiosyncratic Leadership

One of the most controversial and undertheorized variables in foreign policy making is the impact of idiosyncratic personality. While decision makers play a key role in many FPA perspectives, the focus is usually on psychological factors in decision-making processes, or on their institutional roles, which are seen to set parameters that nullify, or at least minimize, the impact of personality. Thus, advocates of the importance of idiosyncratic leadership assume that certain leaders have qualities that are resistant to molding and modification by process and role variables. However, even supporters of this view acknowledge that such factors do limit the impact of personality. Specifically, the influence of personality is seen to increase with the level of the individual within decision-making structures and the intensity of their personal involvement, and to decrease with the size of the bureaucratic organization. Even under optimal circumstances, the impact of any given decision maker's personality is indirect and subject to numerous intervening factors (Kegley & Wittkopf, 1991; M. Hermann, 1978). In practice, Margaret Hermann (1978) notes that this narrows the scope of this factor significantly: "The personal characteristics of only a few high level policy makers affect foreign policy and, even then, only under certain conditions" (p. 68).

Because proliferation-response issues have generally been formulated and implemented below the ministerial level in both Washington and Canberra, leadership theory suggests that personality is unlikely to be a major causal factor. The fact that the patterns in question have spanned multiple leaders reinforces this presumption. In fact, the few glaring instances of idiosyncratic leadership in the case studies all bear a negative causal relationship. The most notable example of this is President George H. W. Bush's personal commitment to the CWC, the source of which was apparently his mother, whose father had been grievously injured by poison gas in World War I. Other examples include on the U.S. side the deep personal commitment of a single member of the Clinton NSC staff named Elisa Harris to support negotiations for a BWC verification protocol despite the unanimous objections of the interagency, and on the Australian side Disarmament Assistant Secretary Ron Walker's personal dedication to the nascent Australia Group process. In each of these instances, the governments were impelled closer to their nonproclivity approach than otherwise would have been likely.

Summary Analysis: What Is the Explanation?

It is impossible at this juncture to isolate a definitive ranking of explanations for the divergence of U.S. and Australian proliferation-response preferences. This is partly due to the explanatory weakness of many elements of extant theory, and partly an inherent limitation of the small-n problem in any two-actor comparison. That said, the preceding analysis does suggest at least a notional hierarchy of explanations.

The single most persuasive variable is the difference in the balance of threats faced by each of the subject actors vis-à-vis CB/M proliferation. Although other factors are also significant influences, threat discrepancy nonetheless stands out as the most compelling, straightforward, and independent variable. It seems reasonable to surmise with a high degree of confidence that geopolitics is a key factor in determining national proliferation-response preferences. Beyond this primary variable, other factors also appear to play meaningful causal roles to varying extents.

There is unquestionably a significant link between differences in the subjective worldviews of the relevant policy elites—along roughly realist–neorealist versus liberal–Grotian–neoliberal lines—and the inclination to support capability-denial and consequence-management versus nonpossession norm-building. At the same time, it is open to interpretation whether this represents a root cause or a secondary manifestation of other factors such as geopolitics.

Competing subnational interests represent a complex set of influences on national proliferation response. However, no such factor can be seen to have contributed consistently to the preference of either actor over time and across proliferation areas. In some instances competing interests have reinforced overall national preferences, but in others they have been countervailing pressures against those preferences. Although these factors therefore must be taken into account as significant causal variables when examining any particular instance of proliferation-response behavior, they do not individually or collectively explain the consistent overall divergence in national preferences.

Differences in national identity may be a relevant factor in shaping antiproliferation preferences. However, existing theory in this area provides too few tools with which to gauge this variable. The similarity in national identities between the two subject actors would seem to minimize this consideration in the present case, although it may not be entirely irrelevant.

Differences in national attributes, governmental and bureaucratic structures, and domestic politics all appear to be marginal or negligible as primary influences on divergent national preferences. Idiosyncratic leadership, to the extent that it has influenced national approaches, has been a countervailing factor.

NOTES

1. Most suggestions of American exceptionalism are not based on size or power factors but rather on agent-specific factors such as system of government, national identity, and so on.

2. It should be noted that data from one of the few existing comparative studies on national proliferation response (Center for Counterproliferation Research, n.d.) suggests that several NATO states may lean toward the Australian approach and away from the U.S. approach as defined and observed in the present study. However, the differences in focus, scope, and methodology make it difficult to compare findings.

3. This highlights a problematic nuance of middle-power theory. As Thakur (1991) points out, whereas Australia is a medium power globally, it is a major power regionally. The implication is that even regarding global issues such as proliferation, Australia may employ non-middle-power tactics in its regional dealings.

4. This illustrative list is not intended as a definitive grouping of comparable middle powers. In fact, the question of how to define and quantify the attributes that should be used to group countries (e.g., geographic size, population, economic capabilities, military strength) remains an active subject of debate in the middle-power literature (Holbraad, 1984; Thakur, 1991). Ergo, the actors listed are merely characteristic examples of a rudimentary definition of middle powers as actors that have less influence than major powers and more influence than weak or small powers.

5. Walt (1987) formulates the notion of balance of threats specifically in regard to alliance formulation, rather than foreign policy behavior generally. However, the fundamental premise is widely applicable, particularly for the present case, in which the Western antiproliferation coalition could be seen as an alliance of sorts.

6. Other than the law enforcement threat of WMD terrorism. That said, many analysts argue that a terrorist attack (state sponsored or otherwise) is the most likely scenario for a WMD attack.

7. Cheeseman (1997) observes that the same dynamic explains the relative lack of Australian enthusiasm for constraints on conventional arms transfers.

8. Both Australian and U.S. officials note in interviews that some other Western states (France, Germany, Japan) have been more reluctant than either the United States or Australia to embrace supply-side measures, precisely because they accord higher priority to their economic interests. This suggests that this factor could be significant in explaining differences in other cases.

9. The English School Grotian perspective sees the international system characterized by neither the realists' anarchy nor the liberals' rule of law, but instead as a "society" of states that interact according to a web of conventions, including international law, balance of power, and force. Kerr (1999) finds that the English School, although often described as a variation on realism, lies closer to neoliberalism than neorealism.

10. Verney (1992) notes that "parliament" in this sense is almost always used to denote the "assembly" component in a parliamentary system as distinct from the "government" component, both of which are technically part of the parliament.

11. To the extent that ideology is important, as already discussed, control of the U.S. Senate could be seen as a key variable in U.S. attitudes toward treaty norms. However, since treaty ratification requires a two-thirds supermajority, and the minority retains significant influence under Senate rules, a significant degree of bipartisan support is almost always required, no matter which party holds the majority.

Chapter 6

Conclusion: Common Ends, Divergent Means

The primary finding of this two-actor study has broad ramifications for the viability of overall U.S. cooperation with its Western antiproliferation partners. This, in turn, raises serious questions regarding the wider prospects for effective international responses to the burgeoning proliferation threat.

The upshot of the study—that there has been a significant, consistent pattern of divergence between the United States and a key "like-minded" Western antiproliferation partner—implicitly challenges the prevalent assumption that Western states have responded collectively to proliferation with an essentially cohesive strategy. Given that Washington is an essential leader in virtually all antiproliferation ventures, and that the United States and Australia represent "similar cases," it is reasonable to infer that this type of divergence is probably not exceptional. It seems likely, in fact, that the United States and Australia do not represent an especially extreme instance of national divergence, if for no other reason than Australia's special commitment to supply-side efforts derived from its unique association with the Australia Group. Thus, the major finding of the present study strongly suggests a wider divergence among Western supplier states, and in particular between Washington and its various partners.

This generalizable conclusion, albeit tentative, is consistent with the few brief studies that examine the antiproliferation proclivities of other Western states (Jabko & Weber, 1998; Center for Counterproliferation Research, n.d.). Clearly, additional research on the national antiproliferation strategies of other states is sorely needed. Absent such comparable data on other countries, any wider inferences about Western divergence from the present findings remain suggestive rather than conclusive. Nonetheless, the present study's findings seem more than sufficient to justify treating broader Western divergence—or, at a minimum, divergence between the United States and some number of its allies—as a plausible working assumption. Given that this has been a long-standing pattern, it is also plausible to project that it will continue into the foreseeable future. If anything, the new Bush administration's apparent intention to redouble Washington's emphasis on capability-denial, and even more so consequence-management (e.g., its determination to develop robust national missile defenses), augurs for a sharpening of differences in the coming years.

The notion of a fractured Western antiproliferation coalition raises challenging policy issues. Quite simply, if key Western states do not agree on the best means to respond to proliferation, it is unlikely that proliferation can be thwarted as effectively as otherwise might be possible. It is indisputable that the effectiveness of all antiproliferation strategies depends to some extent on cooperation among many states. Even the world's lone superpower, while enjoying its "unipolar moment," cannot hope to prevent and manage proliferation on its own. The extent of cooperation required, of course, varies among the three main approaches to proliferation response. Treaty norms require extremely broad participation by a variety of types of states, with near-universal subscription being the ultimate goal for success. Supply-side nonproliferation requires the cooperation of all significant suppliers, and ideally all alternative suppliers, potential suppliers, and trans-shipment states. Consequence-mitigation requires at least some cooperation among states that are likely to face proliferation threats together (e.g., any alliance or coalition in which at least some members are potentially in harm's way). Because each of these groupings include at least all of the major Western states, this grouping collectively can be judged to represent the core antiproliferation coalition, whose cooperation is required for any of these approaches to be fully effective.

As we have seen, many observers argue that no one approach is optimal, and that what is needed instead is a web of antiproliferation strategies that incorporates all of the available tools. Unfortunately, this laudable sentiment fails to acknowledge the inherent tensions between the parallel approaches being employed. Consequently, whereas states may agree that all of these approaches have a legiti-

mate role to play—as do all Western states, and many others too—
they cannot avoid decisions that involve tradeoffs. Moreover, these
tradeoffs can involve either competing proliferation response approaches or unrelated competing national interests, or both at once.
The result is that states must choose (whether explicitly, implicitly, or
unwittingly) a hierarchy of antiproliferation preferences.

Significant divergence within the core Western antiproliferation coalition regarding the proper balance of this hierarchy cannot help but
have an enervating impact on its constituent parts. This is evident even
in the present study's narrow, two-actor comparison. For example,
there can be no doubt whatsoever that nonpossession norm-building
has been rendered far weaker than it would have been due to
Washington's ambivalence. If the United States had opted to be more
helpful, both the CWC and especially the BWC could have been more
stringent more quickly, and a real global missile norm might have been
seriously explored. Washington's rejection of the CTBT provides another obvious example of this dynamic in the nuclear area. By the same
token, it is equally certain that capability-denial tools have been far
less effective than otherwise would have been the case if Australia
(along with other Western governments) had unreservedly supported
U.S. efforts to further institutionalize multilateral export-control regimes, and had actively supported U.S. efforts to widen and aggressively enforce stringent export-control norms. Moreover, given its
leading role in the Australia Group, Australia has probably been more
supportive of supply-side measures than some other Western states.
Finally, American efforts to manage the consequences of proliferation
through military countermeasures will be hampered if other Western
states mirror Australia's halfhearted support for CB/M deterrence and
counterproliferation. European resistance to missile defense provides
an obvious example.

It is important to avoid either overstating or understating the problem. Even assuming a worst-case interpretation of the present study's
tentative generalizable conclusions—that Australia does not represent
an unusual or perhaps even a particularly severe case of Western divergence from U.S. priorities—Washington and its allies will almost
certainly continue to stave off overt rifts. Unfortunately, as long as
there is core divergence on fundamental priorities, this appearance of
"like-mindedness" will likely be attained by papering over various
and sundry disagreements with least-common-denominator compromises. While this type of muddling-through approach may permit
Western states to downplay public ruptures, it is certainly not the way
to achieve robust outcomes.

The bottom line is that by failing to agree on a common balance
between competing approaches, Western states are severely under-

cutting their ability to pursue a collective strategy with maximum vigor and effectiveness. The question that this gloomy conclusion begs, of course, is whether there are any policy steps that might help to forge greater Western cohesion. Unfortunately, it seems unrealistic to hope that states with strong, long-standing preferences could be persuaded to subordinate their respective national priorities for the sake of Western unity. Assuming that the hypothesis that Western divergences stem to a significant degree from systemic factors such as geopolitics is correct, then the problem may well prove to be relatively intractable. If the present study demonstrates anything it is that the fundamental logic for each of the major antiproliferation approaches is perfectly sound, as are the reasons why Western states might differ in their preferences.

The most promising avenue for identifying policy prescriptions to promote Western unity probably lies in recognition of both the problem and its causes. Taking this perspective, there may be policy options that states on each side of equation could use to maximize cooperation. For example, states like Australia that stress the normative approach could consider a strategy that takes into account the greater balance of threats that the United States and others may face. This could involve a conscious effort to build ad hoc coalitions by using intelligence sharing and diplomacy to heighten awareness of local threats on a country-by-country basis. To cite only the most obvious example, North Korea's missile tests over Japan would seem to provide an opportunity to secure heightened Japanese support for missile technology controls or cooperation on theater missile defense. More generally, Washington's leadership of the post–September 11 anti-terrorist coalition offers the prospect that the United States can garner wide international support to target extremely stringent supply-side measures against those few proliferators that are shown to actively support Al-Qaida and other global terror networks. While admittedly such tactics are unlikely to solve the fundamental problem, they may assist in broadening the scope for vigorous supply-side and consequence management cooperation against some of the worst cases.

It remains to be seen to what extent the United States and its Western allies will prove willing or able to narrow their differences in order to better achieve common antiproliferation goals. The reality of an international security environment that has been fundamentally transformed by the new war on terrorism provides both the opportunity and impetus to find new common ground on this longstanding common cause. Recognizing that a significant problem exists and striving to understand one another's perspectives would represent an important first step in meeting this urgent challenge.

Bibliography

BOOKS AND ARTICLES

Some journal articles obtained via electronic databases or inter-library loan do not include page numbers. The author apologizes for these unavoidable omissions.

Allison, Graham T. (1971). *Essence of decision: Explaining the Cuban missile crisis.* Boston: Little, Brown.

Bailey, Kathleen C. (1993a). Missile defense and nonproliferation. *Comparitive Strategy, 12,* 15–22.

———. (1993b). Non-proliferation export controls: Problems and alternatives. In Kathleen Bailey & Robert Rudney (Eds.), *Proliferation and export controls* (pp. 49–55). Lanham, MD: University Press of America.

———. (1993c). Problems with the Chemical Weapons Convention. In Benoit Morel & Kyle Olson (Eds.), *Shadows and substance: The Chemical Weapons Convention* (pp. 17–36). Ridgway Series in International Studies. Boulder, CO: Westview Press.

Ball, Desmond. (1985). *The ties that bind: Intelligence cooperation between the UKUSA countries—the United Kingdom; the United States of America; Canada; Australia and New Zealand.* Sydney: Allen and Unwin.

Ball, Desmond, & Kerr, Pauline. (1996). *Presumptive engagement: Australia's Asia–Pacific security policy in the 1990s.* St. Leonards, NSW: Allen and Unwin.

Berkowitz, Bruce D. (1995). Portending the future of proliferation. *Orbis, 39* (2), 279–285.

Bertsch, Gary K., & Cuppitt, Richard T. (1993). Non proliferation in the 1990s: Enhancing international cooperation on export controls. *Washington Quarterly, 16* (4), 53–70.

Bertsch, Gary K., Cuppitt, Richard T., & Yamamoto, Takehiko. (1997). Trade, export controls, and non-proliferation in the Asia–Pacific region. *Pacific Review, 10* (3), 407–425.

Bertsch, Gary K., & Zaborsky, Victor. (1997). Bringing Ukraine into the MTCR: Can U.S. policy succeed? *Arms Control Today, 27* (2). Available at: http://www.armscontrol.org.

Blechman, Barry M. (1990). *The politics of national security: Congress and U.S. defense policy.* Oxford: Oxford University Press.

Bowen, Wyn Q. (1997). U.S. policy on ballistic missile proliferation: The MTCR's first decade (1987–1997). *Nonproliferation Review, 5* (1), 21–39.

Bowen, Wyn Q., & Dunn, David H. (1996). U.S. proliferation strategy. In *American security policy in the 1990s: Beyond containment* (pp. 115–146). Aldershot, UK: Dartmouth.

Boutin, J. D. Kenneth. (1994). Obstacles to the effective verification of controls on technology transfers. In David Mutimer (Ed.), *Control but verify: Verification and the new non-proliferation agenda* (pp. 57–68). Toronto: York University.

Bull, Hedley. (1965). *The control of the arms race: Disarmament and arms control in the nuclear age* (2d ed.). Westport, CT: Praeger.

Burck, Gordon M., & Flowerree, Charles C. (1991). *International handbook on chemical weapons proliferation.* Westport, CT: Greenwood Press.

Burrows, William E., & Windrem, Robert. (1994). *Critical mass: The dangerous race for superweapons in a fragmenting world.* New York: Simon and Schuster.

Butler, Richard. (1990). Australia and disarmament. In Desmond Ball (Ed.), *Australia and the world: Prologue and prospects* (pp. 393–415). Canberra: Strategic and Defence Studies Centre, Australian National University.

———. (1998, June 19). *Can the Security Council enforce international law?* Keynote address to the sixth annual conference of the Australian and New Zealand Society of International Law, Canberra.

Carus, W. Seth. (1990). *Ballistic missiles in the Third World: Threat and response.* Washington Papers no. 146. Westport, CT: Praeger.

———. (1992a). *Cruise missile proliferation in the 1990s.* Westport, CT: Praeger.

———. (1992b). The proliferation of chemical weapons without a convention. In Brad Roberts (Ed.), *Chemical disarmament and U.S. security* (pp. 47–56). Boulder, CO: Westview Press.

Center for Counterproliferation Research. (n.d.). *Allied perceptions of WMD proliferation.* Washington, DC: National Defense University Press.

Chafetz, Glenn, Spirtas, Michail, & Frankel, Benjamin. (1998–1999). The political psychology of the nuclear nonproliferation regime. *Journal of Politics, 57* (3), 743–775.

Cheeseman, Graeme. (1997). Conventional arms control, conventional wisdom. In Richard Leaver & Dave Cox (Eds.), *Middling, meddling, muddling: Issues in Australian foreign policy* (pp. 160–181). St. Leonards, NSW: Allen and Unwin.

Cheney, Richard B., et al. (1996, September 6). *Letter to Senator Lott regarding the Chemical Weapons Convention.* Washington, DC: Center for Security Policy. Available at: http://www.security-policy.org/papers/other/chemltr.01.html.

Chevrier, Marie Isabelle. (1995). Impediment to proliferation? Analysing the Biological Weapons Convention. *Contemporary Security Policy, 16* (2), 72–102.

———. (1996). Strengthening the biological weapons convention: Progress and peril in the ad hoc group to strengthen the BWC. *Disarmament Diplomacy, 7*, 11–14.

Chow, Brian G. (1993). *Emerging national space launch programs: Economics and safeguards.* Santa Monica, CA: RAND.

Clark, Theodore Hotchkiss. (1993). *The proliferation of surface-to-surface missiles and weapons of mass destruction and the emerging role of tactical missile defense: Israel, Syria and Iran.* Diss. Fletcher School of Law and Diplomacy, Tufts University. Ann Arbor, MI: University Microfilms International.

Clarke, Duncan L., & Johnston, Robert J. (1999). U.S. dual-use exports to China, Chinese behavior, and the Israel factor: Effective controls? *Asian Survey, 39* (2), 193–213.

Clinton, David W. (1994). Defining the national interest. In David W. Clinton (Ed.), *The two faces of national interest* (pp. 50–70). Baton Rouge: Louisiana State University Press.

Cooper, Andrew Fenton. (1997). Niche diplomacy: A conceptual overview. In Andrew Fenton Cooper (Ed.), *Niche diplomacy: Middle powers after the Cold War* (pp. 1–24). London: Macmillan.

Cooper, Andrew Fenton, Higgott, Richard A., & Nossal, Kim Richard. (1991). Bound to follow? Leadership and followership in the Gulf War. *Political Science Quarterly, 106* (3), 391–410.

———. (1993). *Relocating middle powers: Australia and Canada in a changing world order.* Vancouver: VBC Press.

Cooper, David A. (1999). Common ends, divergent means: U.S. and Australian responses to proliferation (chemical, biological, missile). Unpublished Ph.D. diss., Australian National University, Canberra.

Dalby, Simon. (1996). Continent adrift? Dissident security discourse and the Australian geopolitical imagination. *Australian Journal of International Affairs, 50* (1), 59–76.

Dando, Malcolm. (1992). *Arms control after the Cold War: An optimistic perspective.* Occasional Paper Series no. 13. Nedlands, Western Australia: Indian Ocean Centre for Peace Studies, University of Western Australia.

———. (1995). Strengthening the biological weapons convention: Slow and difficult, but possible. *Pacific Research, 8* (2), 39–42.

———. (1997). Strengthening the biological weapons convention: Moving towards the endgame. *Disarmament Diplomacy, 21*, 10–14.

Davis, Zachary S. (1999). The convergence of arms control and nonproliferation: Vive la différence. *Nonproliferation Review, 6* (3), 98–107.

DeSutter, Paula A. (1997). *Denial and jeopardy: Deterring Iranian use of NBC weapons.* Washington, DC: National Defense University Press.

Dougherty, James E., & Pfaltzgraff, Robert L., Jr. (1990). *Contending theories of international relations: A comprehensive survey* (3d ed.). New York: Harper and Row.

Dunn, Lewis A. (1998). Proliferation watch: Some reflections on the past quarter century. *Nonproliferation Review, 5* (3), 59–77.

Dunn, L., Bernstein, P., Cusack, M., Doyle, J., Gentry, L., Giles, G., Gregory, B., Hallenbeck, R., Kern, S., Lutinski, H., Murray, P., Nahas, N., Starr, K., Tomashoff, J., & Yager, J. (1992). *Global proliferation: Dynamics, acquisition strategies, and responses* (Vols. 1, 3–5). Alexandria, VA: Center for Verification Research.

Dunn, Peter. (1989). *Australian diplomatic and technical inputs into the control of chemical weapons.* Working Paper Series no. 65. Canberra: Peace Research Centre, Australian National University.

Eisenstein, Maurice. (1993). *Countering the proliferation of chemical weapons.* Santa Monica, CA: RAND.

Elleman, Michael, & Harvey, John. (1993). The proliferation of ballistic missiles: What is the threat? In Kathleen Bailey & Robert Rudney (Eds.), *Proliferation and export controls* (pp. 17–38). Lanham, MD: University Press of America.

Endicott, Stephen, & Hagerman, Edward. (1999). *The United States and biological warfare: Secrets from the early Cold War and Korea.* Bloomington: Indiana University Press.

Escudé, Carlos. (1998). An introduction to peripheral realism and its implications for the interstate system: Argentina and the Cóndor II missile project. In Stephanie G. Neuman (Ed.), *International relations theory and the Third World* (pp. 55–76). London: Macmillan.

Evans, Gareth. (1997). The labour tradition: A view from the 1990s. In David Lee & Christopher Waters (Eds.), *Evatt to Evans: The labour tradition in Australian foreign policy* (pp. 11–22). St. Leonards, NSW: Allen and Unwin.

Evans, Gareth, & Grant, Bruce. (1991). *Australia's foreign relations in the world of the 1990s.* Carlton, Victoria: Melbourne University Press.

Fergusson, James. (1991). The changing arms control agenda: New meanings, new players. *Arms Control, 12* (2), 191–210.

———. (1994). Spilldown and stability: An alternative perspective on the UN Register of Conventional Arms. In David Mutimer (Ed.), *Control but verify: Verification and the new non-proliferation agenda* (pp.181–193). Toronto: York University.

———. (1995). Non-proliferation, arms control, and confidence building: A case for institutional and technical spilldown. In David Mutimer (Ed.), *Moving beyond supplier controls in a mature technology environment* (pp. 69–88). Toronto: York University.

———. (1996). *From counter-proliferation to non-proliferation: An alternative perspective on ballistic missile defence.* Unpublished manuscript.

Findlay, Trevor. (1989). Getting the chemistry right. *Pacific Research, 2* (4), 6–7.

———. (1991a). Desperately seeking a CWC: Neutering challenge OSI. *Pacific Research, 4* (4).

———. (1991b). *The making of a moral ornament: Australian disarmament and arms control policy 1921–1991.* Working Paper Series no. 107. Canberra: Peace Research Centre, Australian National University.

———. (1992a). CWC: Australia to the rescue. *Pacific Research, 5* (2), 20–21.

———. (1992b). *Disarming cooperation: The role of Australia and New Zealand in disarmament and arms control.* Working Paper Series no. 114. Canberra: Peace Research Centre, Australian National University.

———. (1993). *Peace through chemistry: The new chemical weapons convention.* Canberra: Peace Research Centre, Australian National University.

Flank, Steven M. (1994). Nonproliferation policy: A quintet for two violas? *Nonproliferation Review, 1* (3), 71–81.

Flowerree, Charles C. (1991). Countering chemical weapons proliferation: An introduction. In Trevor Findlay (Ed.), *Chemical weapons and missile proliferation: With implications for the Asia/Pacific region* (pp. 65–74). Boulder, CO: Lynne Rienner.

Forsberg, Randal, Driscoll, William, Webb, Gregory, & Dean, Jonathan. (1995). *Nonproliferation primer: Preventing the spread of nuclear, chemical, and biological weapons.* Cambridge: MIT Press.

Fox, Annette Baker. (1977). *The politics of attraction: Four middle powers and the United States.* New York: Columbia University Press.

Frankel, Joseph. (1970). *National interest.* London: Pall Mall Press.

Freedman, Lawrence. (1993). The proliferation problem and the new world order. In Efraim Karsh, Martin S. Navial, & Philip Sabin (Eds.), *Nonconventional-weapons proliferation in the Middle East: Tackling the spread of nuclear, chemical, and biological capabilities* (pp. 163–178). Oxford: Clarendon Press.

Freeman, Shirley E., & Mathews, Robert J. (1988). Verification of non-production of chemical weapons and their precursors by the civilian chemical industry. In S. J. Lundin (Ed.), *Non-production by industry of chemical-warfare agents: Technical verification under a chemical weapons convention* (pp. 45–52). SIPRI Chemical and Biological Warfare Studies no. 9. Oxford: Oxford University Press.

Gebhard, Paul R. S. (1995). Not by diplomacy or defense alone: The role of regional security strategies in U.S. proliferation policy. *Washington Quarterly, 18* (1), 167–179.

George, Jim. (1997). Australia's global perspectives in the 1990s: A case of old realist wine in new (neo-liberal) bottles? In Richard Loaves & Dave Cox (Eds.), *Middling, meddling, muddling: Issues in Australian foreign policy* (pp. 44–68). St. Leonards, NSW: Allen and Unwin.

Goldfischer, David. (1998). Long-term nuclear policy planning after the Cold War. *Security Studies, 7* (4), 165–194.

Gompert, David C. (1998). *Rethinking the role of nuclear weapons.* Strategic Forum no. 141. Washington, DC: National Defense University Press.

Goodby, James E. (1993). Arms control in changing times. In Benoit Morel & Kyle Olson (Eds.), *Shadows and substance: The Chemical Weapons Convention* (pp. 263–278). Ridgway Series in International Studies. Boulder, CO: Westview Press.

Gormley, Dennis M. (1998). Hedging against the cruise-missile threat. *Survival, 40* (1), 92–111.

Gray, Colin S. (1993). Arms control does not control arms. *Orbis, 37* (3), 333–352.

Haas, Richard N. (1995). Paradigm lost. *Foreign Affairs, 74* (1), 43–58.

————. (1997). Fatal distraction: Bill Clinton's foreign policy. *Foreign Policy*, 108, 112–122.

Hackett, James T. (1996). *CBWs: The arms control approach.* Lancaster, UK: CDISS, Lancaster University. Available at: rpt.www.cdiss.org. column2.htm.

Hagan, Joe D. (1987). Regimes, political oppositions, and the comparative analysis of foreign policy. In Charles F. Aermann, Charles W. Kegley, Jr., & James N. Rosenau (Eds.), *New directions in the study of foreign policy* (pp. 339–365). Boston: Allen and Unwin.

Halperin, Morton H. (1974). *Bureaucratic politics and foreign policy.* Washington, DC: Brookings Institution.

Handel, Michael. (1981). *Weak states in the international system.* London: Frank Cass.

Harris, Elisa D. (1987). The Biological and Toxin Weapons Convention. In Albert Carnesale & Richard N. Haas (Eds.), *Superpower arms control: Setting the record straight* (pp. 223–274). Cambridge, MA: Ballinger.

Herby, Peter. (1991). Beyond partial measures: Nonproliferation and the chemical disarmament negotiations. In Trevor Findlay (Ed.), *Chemical weapons and missile proliferation: With implications for the Asia/Pacific region* (pp. 74–80). Boulder, CO: Lynne Rienner.

Hermann, Charles F. (1978a). Decision structure and process influences on foreign policy. In Maurice A. East, Stephen A. Salmore, & Charles F. Hermann (Eds.), *Why nations act: Theoretical perspectives for comparative foreign policy studies* (pp. 69–102). Beverly Hills, CA: Sage.

————. (1978b). Foreign policy behaviour: That which is to be explained. In Maurice A. East, Stephen A. Salmore, & Charles F. Hermann (Eds.), *Why nations act: Theoretical perspectives for comparative foreign policy* (pp. 25–48). Beverly Hills, CA: Sage.

Hermann, Margaret G. (1978). Effects of personal characteristics of political leaders on foreign policy. In Maurice A. East, Stephen A. Salmore, & Charles F. Hermann (Eds.), *Why nations act: Theoretical perspectives for comparative foreign policy studies* (pp. 44–68). Beverly Hills, CA: Sage.

Hiestand, Trevor. (1995). Swords into plowshares: Considerations for 21st century export controls in the United States. *Emory International Law Review*, 9 (2) [On-line]. Available at: www.law.emory.edu/EILR/eilrhome.htm.

Hilsman, Roger. (1990). *The politics of policy making in defense and foreign affairs: Conceptual models and bureaucratic politics* (2d ed.). Englewood Cliffs, NJ: Prentice Hall.

Hirsh, Michael. (1998). The great technology giveaway? Trading with potential foes. *Foreign Affairs*, 77 (5), 2–9.

Hocking, Brian. (1997). Finding your niche: Australia and the trials of middle-powerdom. In Andrew F. Cooper (Ed.), *Niche diplomacy: Middle powers after the Cold War* (pp. 129–146). London: Macmillan.

Holbraad, Carsten. (1984). *Middle powers in international politics.* New York: St. Martin's Press.

Hudson, Valerie M. (1993). *Gaddis' lacuna: Foreign policy analysis and the end of the Cold War.* Working Paper Series no. 5. Canberra: Department of International Relations, Australian National University.

————. (1995). Foreign policy analysis yesterday, today and tomorrow. *Mershon International Studies Review, 39* (suppl. 2), 209–238.

Isaacs, John. (1990). Legislative needs. In Susan Wright (Ed.), *Preventing a biological arms race* (pp. 291–299). Cambridge: MIT Press.

Jabko, Nicolas, & Weber, Steven. (1998). A certain idea of nuclear weapons: France's nuclear nonproliferation policy in theoretical perspective. *Security Studies, 8* (1), 108–150.

Jensen, Lloyd. (1987). *Explaining foreign policy.* Englewood Cliffs, N.J.: Prentice Hall.

Jepperson, Ronald L., Wendt, Alexander, & Katzenstein, Peter J. (1996). Norms, identity, and culture in national security. In Peter J. Katzenstein (Ed.), *The culture of national security: Norms and identity in world politics* (pp. 33–75). New York: Columbia University Press.

Jones, Rodey W., & McDonough, Mark G. (1998). Missile proliferation, 1995–1997. In *Tracking nuclear proliferation* (pp. 253–269). Washington, DC: Carnegie Endowment for International Peace.

Joseph, Robert, & Lehman, Ronald. (1998). *U.S. nuclear policy in the 21st century.* Strategic Forum no. 145. Washington, DC: National Defense University.

Kamal, Nazir. (1999). Pakistani perception and prospects of reducing the nuclear danger in South Asia. Cooperative Monitoring Center Occasional Paper no. 6. Albuquerque, NM: Sandia National Laboratories.

Karp, Aaron. (1989). *The United States and the Soviet Union and the control of ballistic missile proliferation in the Middle East.* Boulder, CO: Westview Press.

————. (1993). Ballistic missile control. In Trevor Findlay (Ed.), *Arms control in the post–Cold War world: With implications for Asia/Pacific* (pp. 245–270). Canberra: Peace Research Centre, Australian National University.

————. (1996). *Ballistic missile proliferation: The politics and technics.* Oxford: Oxford University Press.

————. (1998). Lessons of Iranian missile programs for U.S. nonproliferation policy. *Nonproliferation Review, 5* (3), 17–26.

Kay, David A. (1995). Denial and deception practices of WMD proliferators: Iraq and beyond. *Washington Quarterly, 18* (1), 85–106.

Keating, Tom. (1993). *Canada and world order: The multilateralist tradition in Canadian foreign policy.* Toronto: University of Toronto Press.

Keeley, James F. (1994). Weapons of mass destruction as mature technologies. In David Mutimer (Ed.), *Control but verify: Verification and the new nonproliferation agenda* (pp. 171–180). Toronto: York University.

————. (1995). Non-proliferation and verification response strategies in a maturing technological environment. In David Mutimer (Ed.), *Moving beyond supplier controls in a mature technology environment* (pp. 11–30). Toronto: York University.

Keeny, Spurgeon M. (1994). What price counterproliferation? *Arms Control Today, 24* (5), 2.

Kegley, Charles W., Jr., & Wittkopf, Eugene R. (1991). *American foreign policy: Patterns and process* (4th ed.). New York: St. Martin's Press.

Kelle, Alexander. (1997a). Implementation of the CWC after the second session of the conference of states parties. *Disarmament Diplomacy, 21,* 15–19.

————. (1997b). Setting up the Organization for the Prohibition of Chemical Weapons. *Disarmament Diplomacy, 15*, 9–10.

Keller, William W., & Nolan, Janne E. (1997–1998). The arms trade: Business as usual? *Foreign Policy, 109*, 113–125.

Kerr, Pauline. (1999). *Labor's security policy, 1983–1996: Towards a liberal-realist explanation?* Unpublished Ph.D. diss., Australian National University, Canberra.

Khromov, Gennady. (1997). The threat of cruise missile proliferation requires urgent coordinated actions. *The Monitor: Nonproliferation, Demilitarization and Arms Control, 3/4 (4/1)*, 3–6.

————. (1998). Problems of missile proliferation. (Translation, FBIS-SOV-98-119). *Yadernyy Kontrol, 37*, (1), 38–45.

King, Jonathan, & Strauss, Harlee. (1990). The hazards of defensive biological warfare programs. In Susan Wright (Ed.), *Preventing a biological arms race* (pp. 120–132). Cambridge: MIT Press.

Knoth, Artur. (1995). Counterproliferation at the crossroads. *International Defense Review, 28* (10).

Kortunov, Sergei. (1994). Nonproliferation and counterproliferation: The role of BMD. *Comparative Strategy, 13* (1).

Kowert, Paul A. (1998–1999). National identity: Inside and out. *Security Studies, 8* (2–3), 1–34.

Larsen, Randall J. (1995). *Bio war: A threat to America's current deployable force.* Arlington, VA: Aerospace Education Foundation.

Leaver, Richard. (1997a). Middle power "niche diplomacy" and nuclear non-proliferation: The failure in success. In Richard Leaver & Dave Cox (Eds.), *Middling, meddling, muddling: Issues in Australian foreign policy* (pp. 182–201). St. Leonards, NSW: Allen and Unwin.

————. (1997b). Nuclear non-proliferation, international norms, and labour traditions. In David Lee & Christopher Waters (Eds.), *Evatt to Evans: The labour tradition in Australian foreign policy* (pp. 165–180). St. Leonards, NSW: Allen and Unwin.

Ledogar, Stephen J. (1991). Interview: Ambassador Stephen J. Ledogar: Closing in on a chemical weapons ban. *Arms Control Today, 21* (4), 3–7.

Letts, Martine. (1992). The year of the CWC? *Pacific Research, 5* (3), 6–9.

Lijphart, Arend. (1971). Comparative politics and the comparative method. *American Political Science Review, 65*, 682–693.

Lumpe, Lora. (1994). Zero ballistic missiles and the Third World. *Arms Control, 14* (1).

Lundbo, Sten. (1997). Non-proliferation: Expansion of export control mechanisms. *Aussen Politik, 48* (2), 137–147.

Lynn-Jones, Sean M. (1987). Lulling and stimulating effects of arms control. In Albert Carnesale & Richard N. Haass (Eds.), *Superpower arms control: Setting the record straight* (pp. 223–274). Cambridge, MA: Ballinger.

Lyons, Gene M. (1995). International organizations and national interests. *International Social Science Journal, 47* (2), 261–276.

MacEachin, Douglas J. (1998). Routine and challenge: Two pillars of verification. *CBW Conventions Bulletin, 39*, 1–3.

MacLean, John. (1988). Belief systems and ideology in international relations: A critical approach. In Richard Little & Steve Smith (Eds.), *Belief systems and international relations* (pp. 57–82). Oxford: Basil Blackwell.

Mathews, Robert J., & McCormack, Timothy L. H. (1995). Australian security, weapons of mass destruction and international law. In Anthony Bergin & Shirley V. Scott (Eds.), *International law and Australian security.* Canberra: Australian Defence Studies Centre.

McColl, Angus. (1997). Is counterproliferation compatible with nonproliferation? Rethinking the defense counterproliferation initiative. *Airpower Journal, 11* (1), 99–109.

McCormack, Timothy L. H. (1993). Some Australian efforts to promote chemical weapons non-proliferation and disarmament. *Australian Year Book of International Law, 14,* 157–178.

McDougall, Robert. (2001). New approaches to combatting missile proliferation. *Missile proliferation and defences: Problems and prospects* (pp. 28–35). Occasional Paper no. 7. Monterey: Center for Nonproliferation Studies and Mountbatten Center for International Studies.

McElroy, Robert Walter. (1989). America's renunciation of chemical and biological warfare. In *Morality and American foreign policy: The role of moral norms in international affairs* (pp. 145–202). Diss. Stanford University. Ann Arbor, MI: University Microfilms International.

Mediansky, F. A. (1992). The development of Australian foreign policy. In P. J. Boyce & J. R. Angel (Eds.), *Diplomacy in the marketplace: Australia in world affairs 1981–90* (pp. 15–29). Melbourne: Longman Chesire.

Miller, J.D.B. (1988). Parties and foreign policy the Australian way. *Current Affairs Bulletin, 65* (1), 4–13.

Moodie, Michael. (1995). Beyond proliferation: The challenge of technology diffusion. In Brad Roberts (Ed.), *Weapons proliferation in the 1990s.* Cambridge: MIT Press.

Müller, Harold. (1994). Specific approaches: Nuclear, chemical and biological proliferation. In Serge Sur (Ed.), *Disarmament and arms limitation obligations: Problems of compliance and enforcement* (pp. 251–272). Aldershot, UK: Dartmouth.

———. (1997). Neither hype nor complacency: WMD proliferation after the Cold War. *Nonproliferation Review, 4* (2), 62–71.

———. (1998). The death of arms control? *Disarmament Diplomacy, 29,* 2–5.

Mussington, David. (1995). Verifying end-use restrictions on dual-use technology transfers: A technology transparency hierarchy. In David Mutimer (Ed.), *Moving beyond supplier controls in a mature technology environment* (pp. 31–56). Toronto: York University.

Mutimer, David. (1994). Non-proliferation and international security. In David Mutimer (Ed.), *Control but verify: Verification and the new non-proliferation agenda* (pp. 3–13). Toronto: York University.

———. (1998). Reconstituting security? The practices of proliferation control. *European Journal of International Relations, 4* (1), 99–129.

Nathan, James A., & Oliver, James K. (1983). *Foreign policy making and the American political system.* Boston: Little, Brown.

Nolan, Janne E. (1991). *Trappings of power: Ballistic missiles in the Third World.* Washington, DC: Brookings Institution.

———. (1992). Technology and non-proliferation in a changing world order. *Transnational Law and Contemporary Problems, 2* (2).

Nossal, Kim Richard. (1993). Middle power diplomacy in the changing Asia–Pacific order: Australia and Canada compared. In Richard Leaver & James L. Richardson (Eds.), *The post–Cold War order: Diagnoses and prognoses* (pp. 210–223). St. Leonards, NSW: Allen and Unwin.

———. (1994). *Rain dancing: Sanctions in Canadian and Australian foreign policy.* Toronto: University of Toronto Press.

Ogilvie-White, Tanya. (1996). Is there a theory of nuclear nonproliferation? An analysis of the contemporary debate. *Nonproliferation Review, 9* (1).

Olson, William, & Onuf, Nicholas. (1985). The growth of a discipline: Reviewed. In Steve Smith (Ed.), *International relations: British and American perspectives.* New York: Blackwell.

Ozga, Deborah A. (1994). A chronology of the Missile Technology Control Regime. *Nonproliferation Review, 1* (2). Available at: www.cns.miis.edu/pbus/npr/.

Papadakis, Maria, & Starr, Harvey. (1987). Opportunity, willingness, and small states: The relationship between environment and foreign policy. In Charles F. Hermann, Charles W. Kegley, Jr., & James N. Rosenau (Eds.), *New directions in the study of foreign policy* (pp. 409–432). Boston: Allen and Unwin.

Payne, Keith. (1995). Post–Cold War deterrence and missile defense. *Orbis, 39* (2), 201–224.

Pearson, Graham S. (1993a). Biological weapons: Their nature and arms control. In Efraim Karsh, Martin S. Navias, & Philip Sabin (Eds.), *Nonconventional weapons proliferation in the Middle East: Tackling the spread of nuclear, chemical and biological capabilities* (pp. 99–134). Oxford: Clarendon Press.

———. (1993b). Prospects for chemical and biological arms control: The web of deterrence. *Washington Quarterly, 16* (2), 145–162.

———. (1997). *The necessity for non-challenge visits.* Strengthening the Biological Weapons Convention Briefing Paper no. 2. Bradford, UK: Department of Peace Studies, University of Bradford. Available at: http://www.brad.ac.uk/acad/sbtwc/briefing/bp2.htm.

Pengelley, Rupert. (1994). Betting each way on proliferation. *International Defense Review, 27* (2).

Perkovich, George. (1998). Nuclear proliferation. *Foreign Policy, 112,* 12–23.

Pilat, Joseph F., & Kirchner, Walter K. (1995). The technological promise of counterproliferation. *Washington Quarterly, 18* (1), 153–166.

Pikayev, Alexander A. (2001). The global control system. *Missile proliferation and defences: Problems and prospects* (pp. 21–27). Occasional Paper no. 7. Monterey: Center for Nonproliferation Studies and Mountbatten Center for International Studies.

Pikayev, Alexander A., Spector, Leonard S., Kirichenko, Lina V., & Gibson, Ryan. (1998). *Russia, the U.S. and the Missile Technology Control Regime.* Adelphi Paper no. 317. London: Oxford University Press.

Plischke, Elmer. (1988). National interests. In Elmer Plischke (Ed.), *Foreign relations: Analysis of its anatomy* (pp. 9–49). Westport, CT: Greenwood Press.

Porter, Evan H. (1996–1997). Niche diplomacy as Canadian foreign policy. *International Journal, 52* (1), 25–38.

Price, Richard. (1995). A genealogy of the chemical weapons taboo. *International Organization, 49* (1), 73–103.

Putnam, Robert D. (1988). Diplomacy and domestic politics: The logic of two-level games. *International Organization, 42* (3), 427–460.

Rauf, Tariq. (1998). Proliferation of nuclear, chemical and biological weapons after the Cold War. In Ramesh Thakur (Ed.), *Keeping proliferation at bay* (pp. 39–59). Jakarta, Indonesia: CSIS.

Ravenhill, John. (1998). *Cycles of middle power activism: Constraint and choice in Australian and Canadian foreign policies.* Unpublished manuscript.

Redick, John. (1995). *Nuclear illusions: Argentina and Brazil.* Washington, DC: Stimson Center.

Richardson, Bill. (1993). The threat of chemical and biological proliferation. In Kathleen Bailey & Robert Rudney (Eds.), *Proliferation and export controls* (pp. 15–18). Lanham, MD: University Press of America.

Richardson, J. L. (1986). *Arms control in the later 1980s: The implications of the strategic defense initiative.* Working Paper Series no. 3. Canberra: Peace Research Centre, Australian National University.

Ripley, Brian. (1993). Psychology, foreign policy, and international relations theory. *Political Psychology, 14* (3), 403–416.

Roberts, Brad. (1993). The Chemical Weapons Convention and world order. In Benoit Morel and Kyle Olson (Eds.), *Shadows and substance: The Chemical Weapons Convention* (pp. 1–16). Ridgway Series in International Studies. Boulder, CO: Westview Press.

———. (1995). 1995 and the end of the post–Cold War era. *Washington Quarterly, 18* (1), 5–28.

———. (1998). Evaluating global non-proliferation instruments. In Ramesh Thakur (Ed.), *Keeping proliferation at bay* (pp. 60–74). Jakarta, Indonesia: CSIS.

Robinson, Julian Perry. (1987). *Chemical warfare arms control: A framework for considering policy alternatives.* SIPRI Chemical and Biological Warfare Studies no. 2. Oxford: Oxford University Press.

———. (1991). Chemical weapons proliferation: The problem in perspective. In Trevor Findlay (Ed.), *Chemical weapons and missile proliferation: With implications for the Asia/Pacific region* (pp. 19–36). Boulder, CO: Lynne Rienner.

———. (1992). The supply-side control of the spread of chemical weapons. In Jean-Francois Rioux (Ed.), *Limiting the proliferation of weapons: The role of supply-side strategies* (pp. 57–74). Ottawa: Carleton University Press.

Rosenau, James N. (1976). The study of foreign policy. In James N. Rosenau, Kenneth W. Thompson, & Gavin Boyd (Eds.), *World politics: An introduction* (pp. 15–35). New York: Free Press.

———. (1980). *The scientific study of foreign policy* (rev. enlg. ed.). London: Francis Pinter.

Rosenberg, Barbara Hatch. (2001). Allergic reaction: Washington's response to the BWC protocol. *Arms Control Today, 31* (6), 3–8.

Rothstein, Robert L. (1968). *Alliances and small powers*. New York: Columbia University Press.

Salmore, Barbara G., & Salmore, Stephen A. (1978). Political regimes and foreign policy. In Barbara G. Salmore & Stephen A. Salmore (Eds.), *Why nations act: Theoretical perspectives for comparative foreign policy studies* (pp. 103–122). Beverly Hills, CA: Sage.

Sampson, Martin W., III. (1987). Cultural influences on foreign policy. In Charles F. Hermann, Charles W. Kegley, Jr., & James N. Rosenau (Eds.), *New directions in the study of foreign policy* (pp. 384–408). Boston: Allen and Unwin.

Schelling, Thomas C., & Halperin, Morton H. (1961). *Strategy and arms control*. New York: Twentieth Century Fund.

Schneider, Barry R. (1994). Nuclear proliferation and counterproliferation: Policy issues and debates. *Mershon International Studies Review, 38* (suppl. 2), 209–234.

Schwartz, Stephen I. (1998). Miscalculated ambiguity: U.S. policy on the use and threat of use of nuclear weapons. *Disarmament Diplomacy, 23*, 10–15.

Simpson, John. (1998). Strengthening non-proliferation barriers. In Ramesh Thakur (Ed.), *Keeping proliferation at bay* (pp. 121–128). Jakarta, Indonesia: CSIS.

Sims, Nicholas A. (1990a). National Implementation of international obligations: Experience under the multilateral treaty regime of the 1972 convention on biological and toxin weapons. In Tomas Stock & Ronald Sutherland (Eds.), *National implementation of the future chemical weapons convention* (pp. 55–63). SIPRI Chemical and Biological Warfare Studies no. 11. Oxford: Oxford University Press.

———. (1990b). The second review conference on the biological weapons convention. In Susan Wright (Ed.), *Preventing a biological arms race* (pp. 267–288). Cambridge: MIT Press.

Siracusa, Joseph M., & Cheong, Yeong-Han. (1997). *America's Australia, Australia's America: A guide to issues and reference*. Claremont, CA: Regina Books.

Smith, Mark. (2001). Verifiable control of ballistic missile proliferation. *Trust and Verify* (95), 1–3.

Smith, Steve. (1988). Belief systems and the study of international relations. In Richard Little and Steve Smith (Eds.), *Belief systems and international relations* (pp. 11–36). Oxford: Basil Blackwell.

———. (1995). The self-images of a discipline: A genealogy of international relations theory. In K. Booth and Steve Smith (Eds.), *International relations theory today*. Cambridge: Polity Press.

Smithson, Amy E. (1995). Dateline Washington: Clinton fumbles the CWC. *Foreign Policy, 99*, 169–182.

———. (1997a). Bungling a no-brainer: How Washington barely ratified the Chemical Weapons Convention. In *The battle to obtain U.S. ratification of the Chemical Weapons Convention* (pp. 7–33). Occasional Paper no. 35. Washington, DC: Henry L. Stimson Center.

———. (1997b). From engine to caboose: The United States and the chemical weapons convention. In James Brown (Ed.), *Arms control issues for the twenty-first century* (pp. 241–266). Albuquerque, NM: Sandia National Laboratories.

————. (1998a). Man versus microbe: The negotiations to strengthen the Biological Weapons Convention. In *Biological weapons proliferation: Reason for concern, courses of action*. Chemical and Biological Nonproliferation Project Report no. 24. Washington, DC: Henry L. Stimson Center.

————. (1998b). *Rudderless: The Chemical Weapons Convention at 1 ½ (executive summary)*. Washington, DC: Henry L. Stimson Center. Available at: http://stimson.org/pubs/cwc/execsum.htm.

Sokolski, Henry D. (1995a). Curbing proliferation's legitimization. *Nonproliferation Review*, 2 (2), 60–63.

————. (1995b). Nonapocalyptic proliferation: A new strategic threat? In Brad Roberts (Ed.), *Weapons proliferation in the 1990s*. Cambridge: MIT Press.

————. (1996). Next century nonproliferation: Victory is still possible. *Nonproliferation Review*, 4 (1), 90–97.

Solingen, Etel. (1995). The new multilateralism and nonproliferation: Bringing in domestic politics. *Global Governance*, 1 (2), 205–227.

Sopko, John F. (1996–1997). The changing proliferation threat. *Foreign Policy*, 105, 3–20.

Spector, Leonard S. (1996). Export controls: Is hardware the key today? In William Clark, Jr. & Ryukichi Imai (Eds.), *Next steps in arms control and non-proliferation: Report of the U.S.–Japan study group on arms control and non-proliferation after the Cold War* (pp. 173–181). Washington, DC: Carnegie Endowment for International Peace.

Speier, Richard H. (1995). *The Missile Technology Control Regime: Case study of a multilateral negotiation*. Unpublished manuscript.

————. (1999). *Can the MTCR be repaired?* Unpublished manuscript.

Spillman, Lyn. (1998, March 19). *Explaining national identities: The United States and Australia compared*. Unpublished seminar paper, sociology program lecture series, Australian National University.

Stanley Foundation. (1996). *Weapons of mass destruction: Are the nonproliferation regimes falling behind?* Report of the 37th Strategy for Peace, U.S. foreign policy conference. Muscatine, IA: Stanley Foundation. Available at: http://www.stanleyfdn.org/confrpts/USFP/SPC96/ WMD93.pdf.

Starr, Barbara. (1997). Asymmetrical warfare threat makes CWC a tough one to sell. *Jane's Defence Weekly*, 27 (8), 16.

Steiner, Miriam. (1983). The search for order in a disorderly world: Worldviews and prescriptive decision paradigms. *International Organization*, 37 (3), 373–413.

Stock, Thomas, & De Geer, Anna. (1995). *Chemical trade control and Article XI of the CWC* (rev. ed.). Chemical Weapons Convention Implementation Paper no. 4. Stockholm: SIPRI. Available at: http://www.sipri.se/cbw/research/ssf-cwc-paper4.html.

Subrahmanyam, K. (1993). Export controls and the North–South controversy. *Washington Quarterly*, 16 (2), 135–144.

Talbott, Strobe. (1999). Dealing with the bomb in South Asia. *Foreign Affairs*, 78 (2), 110–122.

ter Haar, Barend. (1991). *The future of biological weapons*. CSIS Washington Paper no. 151. Westport, CT: Praeger.

Thakur, Ramesh. (1991). The elusive essence of size: Australia, New Zealand, and small states in international relations. In R. Higgot & J. L. Richardson (Eds.), *International relations: Global and Australian perspectives on an evolving discipline* (pp. 241–287). Studies in World Affairs no. 30. Canberra: Australian National University Press.

Thomas, Ann Van Wynen, & Thomas, A. J., Jr. (1970). *Legal limits on the use of chemical and biological weapons*. Dallas: Southern Methodist University Press.

Thraenert, Oliver. (1997). Biological weapons and the problems of nonproliferation. *Aussen Politic, 48* (2), 148–157.

Tigner, Brooks. (2001, July 9–15). EU hopes Code of Conduct will cool missile proliferation. *Defense News*.

Tucker, Jonathan B. (1998a, July 29). Chemical weapons treaty: U.S. signed, so it should comply. Monterey, CA: MIIS. Available at: http://cns.miss.edu. pubs/reports/tuck_csm.htm.

———. (1998b). Putting teeth in the biological weapons ban. *MIT Technology Review* [On-line]. Available at: http://www.techreview.com.

———. (1998c). Strengthening the BWC: Moving toward a compliance protocol. *Arms Control Today, 28* (1).

Turpen, Elizabeth A., & Kadner, Steven P. (1997). Counterproliferation versus nonproliferation: A case for prevention versus post factum intervention. *Fletcher Forum of World Affairs, 21* (1), 153–171.

Ungerer, Carl. (1997). Australia and the world: A seminar report. *Australian Journal of International Affairs, 51* (2), 255–262.

United Nations Association of the United States of America. (1995). Confronting the proliferation danger: The role of the UN Security. *Nonproliferation Analysis, 1* (1). Available at: http://infomanage.com/nonproliferation/najournal/unsecouncilrole.html.

Utgoff, Victor A. (1997). *Nuclear weapons and the deterrence of biological and chemical warfare*. Occasional Paper no. 36. Washington, DC: Henry L. Stimson Center.

Vachon, Gordon K. (1994). Chemical weapons: Verifying controls. In David Mutimer (Ed.), *Control but verify: Verification and the new non-proliferation agenda* (pp. 35–38). Toronto: York University Press.

———. (1997). The biological weapons negotiations and transparency: Framing the debate. In James Brown (Ed.), *Arms control issues for the twenty-first century* (pp. 55–64). Albuquerque, NM: Sandia National Laboratories.

Van Ham, Peter. (1993). *Managing non-proliferation regimes in the 1990s: Power, politics, and policies*. London: Pinter.

Verney, Douglas V. (1992). Parliamentary government and presidential government. In Arend Lijphart (Ed.), *Parliamentary versus presidential government* (pp. 31–47). Oxford: Oxford University Press.

Vital, David (1967). *The inequality of states: A study of small powers in international relations*. Oxford: Clarendon Press.

Wallerstein, Mitchel B. (1998). *Responding to proliferation threats*. Strategic Forum no. 138. Washington, DC: National Defense University Institute for National Strategic Studies.

Walsh, Jim. (1997). Surprise down under: The secret history of Australia's nuclear ambitions. *Nonproliferation Review, 5* (1), 1–20.

Walt, Stephen M. (1987). *The origins of alliances.* Ithaca, NY: Cornell University Press.

Wendt, Alexander. (1994). Anarchy is what states make of it: The social construction of power politics. *International Organization, 41* (3), 391–425.

Wheelis, Mark L. (1992). Strengthening biological weapons control through global epidemiological surveillance. *Politics and the Life Sciences, 2* (2), 179–189.

Wilson, James Q. (1989). *Bureaucracy: What government agencies do and why they do it.* New York: Basic Books.

Wood, Bernard. (1988). *The middle powers and the general interest.* Middle Powers in the International System Series no. 1. Ottawa: North–South Institute.

Woollett, Gillian R. (1998). Industry's role, concerns, and interests in the negotiation of a BWC compliance protocol. In *Biological weapons proliferation: Reasons for concern, courses of action.* Chemical and Biological Nonproliferation Project Report no. 24. Washington, DC: Henry L. Stimson Center.

Wright, Susan. (1993). Biological arms control. In Trevor Findlay (Ed.), *Arms control in the post–Cold War world: With implications for Asia/Pacific* (pp. 139–179). Canberra: Peace Research Centre, Australian National University.

Yasmeen, Samina. (1999). South Asia after the nuclear tests: Prospects for arms control? *Pacifica Review, 11* (3), 239–256.

Yin, Robert K. (1984). *Case study research: Design and methods.* Applied Social Research Methods Series no. 5. Beverly Hills, CA: Sage.

Zanders, Jean Pascal. (1997). Chemical weapons between disarmament and nonproliferation. *The Monitor: Nonproliferation, Demilitarization and Arms Control, 3* (3), 18–23.

INTERVIEWS (INT.)

Some interview subjects listed here have asked not to be cited directly. In these cases, names and dates are not included in citations; affiliation and rank are provided when this does not risk revealing identities.

Alessi, Victor. (1998, 27 August). (U.S.) Special Assistant to the Director ACDA (1994–1995); Director Arms Control and Nonproliferation, DOE (1987–1994); various nuclear disarmament postions, ACDA (pre–1987). Personal interview, Alexandria, Virginia.

Berry, Kenneth B. (1998, 29 January). (AUS) Assistant Secretary, Peace, Arms Control and Disarmament Branch, DFAT (1987–present). Personal interview, Canberra.

Bird, Gillian. (1998, 27 October). (AUS) Assistant Secretary, Peace, Arms Control and Disarmament Branch, DFAT (1995–1996). Personal interview, Canberra.

Buckley, Sheila. (1998, 4 September). (U.S.) Director Multilateral Negotiations, OSD (1978–1994). Personal interview, McClean, Virginia.

Bushong, Col. Jim. (1999, 9 September). (U.S.) Assistant for Multilateral Negotiations, OSD (1989–1992). Telephone interview.

Butler, Amb. Richard W. (1998, 11 September). (AUS) Ambassador for Disarmament (1983–1988). Personal interview, United Nations, New York.

Cacci, Ralph A. (1998, 14 November). (U.S.) Senior Assistant for Counterproliferation Assessment and Response, OSD (1994–1997); Assistant for Negotiations, OSD (1990–1994). Telephone interview.

Carayanides, Anastasia. (1998, 17 November). (AUS) Director Biological Disarmament Section, DFAT (1997–present); Director Chemical and Biological Disarmament Section, DFAT (1996–1997). Personal interview, Canberra.

Carter, Hon. Ashton B. (1999, 30 June). (U.S.) Assistant Secretary of Defense for International Security Policy (1993–1996). Telephone interview.

Costmeyer, Robbie. (1998, 14 October). (AUS) Director Strategic Trade Policy and Operations, DOD (1994–present). Personal interview, Canberra.

Courtney, Jill. (1998, 24 November). (AUS) Director Conventional and Nuclear Disarmament Section, DFAT (1991–1994). Telephone interview and electronic correspondence.

Cousins, Ian. (1998, 13 November). (AUS) First Assistant Secretary, International Security Division, DFAT (1993–1997). Personal interview, Canberra.

Donadio, CDR (Ret) Giuseppe. (1998, 20 August). (U.S.) Desk Officer for CW Negotiations, JCS (1991–1994). Personal interview, Springfield, Virginia.

Dorling, Philip. (1998, 6 November). (AUS) Adviser to the Shadow Minister for Foreign Affairs, House of Representatives (1996–present); Desk Officer Conventional and Nuclear Disarmament Section, DFAT (1994–1996). Personal interview, Canberra.

Evans, Hon. Gareth. (1998, 26 November). (AUS) Deputy Labour Party Leader, House of Representatives (1996–1998); Minister for Foreign Affairs and Trade (1988–1996). Personal interview, Canberra.

Feith, Douglas J. (1998, 14 November). (U.S.) Deputy Assistant Secretary of Defense for Negotiations Policy (1984–1986); Special Counsel to the Assistant Secretary of Defense for International Security Policy (1982–1984); Director Middle East Affairs, NSC (1981–1982). Telephone interview.

Findlay, Trevor. (1998, 24 September). (AUS) Disarmament Branch, DFAT (1984); Delegation to the Conference on Disarmament (1979–1983). Personal interview, London (UK).

Fitzgibbon, Gerald M. (1998, 9 September.) (U.S.) Deputy Director Nonproliferation Policy (previously Negotiations and Implementation), OSD (1993–present); Director Proliferation Controls and Countermeasures, OSD (1990–1993). Personal interview, Arlington, Virginia.

Furlonger, Peter. (1998, 3 November). (AUS) Disarmament Analyst, Office of National Assessments (1997–present); Director Chemical and Biological Disarmament Section, DFAT (1992–1997); Assistant Director Chemical and Biological Disarmament Section, DFAT (1991–1992). Personal interview, Canberra.

Gallucci, Amb. Robert L. (1998, 1 September). (U.S.) Assistant Secretary of State for Politico-Military Affairs (1992–1993); Special negotiator for North Korea (1993–1994). Personal interview, Washington, DC.

Gee, John. (1998, 21 October). (AUS) Head of CWC Negotiations Support Unit, DFAT (1992–1993); Director Chemical and Biological Disarmament Section, DFAT (1991); Desk Officer Disarmament Branch (previously Disarmament Pool), DFAT (1982–1986). Personal interview, The Hague, Netherlands, and electronic correspondence.

George, Anna. (1998, 27 September). (AUS) Alternative Representative to the OPCW (1995–present); Desk Officer Chemical and Biological Weapons Section, DFAT (1993–1995). Personal interview, Sussex United Kingdom.

Goodby, Amb. James. (1998, 6 August). (U.S.) Head of Delegation to the BW Trilateral Process Working Group (1995–1996). Personal interview, Washington, DC.

Griffin, John. (1998, 13 October). (AUS) Director Conventional and Nuclear Disarmament Section, DFAT (1995–present). Personal interview, Canberra.

Hammer, Brendan. (1998, 13 November). (AUS) Political Counsellor Embassy Washington (1995–1998); Chemical and Biological Disarmament Section, DFAT (1993–1995); Strategic Weapons Analyst (1989–1993). Personal interview, Canberra.

Harris, Stuart J. (1999, 2 June). (AUS) Secretary, DFAT (formerly DFA) (1984–1988). Personal interview, Canberra.

Higgins, Col. Don. (1998, 9 November). (AUS) Director Peacekeeping and Arms Control Section, DOD (1998–present). Telephone interview.

Hinds, Jim E. (1998, 28 October). (U.S.) Deputy Assistant Secretary of Defense for Negotiations Policy (1987–1989). Telephone interview.

Inglee, William. (1998, 3 September). (U.S.) Acting Assistant Secretary of Defense for International Security Policy (1993); Principal Deputy Assistant Secretary of Defense for International Security Policy (1992–1993); Deputy Assistant Secretary of Defense for Conventional Forces and Arms Control Policy (1990–1992). Personal interview, Washington, DC.

Jones, Clive R., "Kim." (1998, 28 October). (AUS) Deputy Secretary DFAT (1993–present); First Assistant Secretary, Disarmament, Security and Nuclear Division, DFAT (1988–1991); Acting Deputy Secretary Department of Prime Minister and Cabinet (1987–1988). Personal interview, Canberra.

Karika, Lt. Col. Janet. (1998, 1 September). (U.S.) Desk Officer for Space and Missile Nonproliferation Policy, ACDA (1995–1998). Personal interview, Arlington, Virginia.

Ledogar, Amb. Steven. (1998, 2 September). (U.S.) Representative to the Conference on Disarmament (1990–1997). Telephone interview.

Letts, Amb. Martine. (1998, 6 November). (AUS) Adviser to the Minister for Foreign Affairs and Trade (1992–1994); Special Coordinator for CWC Draft Text, DFAT (1991–1992); Delegation to the Conference on Disarmament (1990–1991). Telephone interview.

Mahley, Amb. Donald. (1998, 26 and 28 August). (U.S.) Special Negotiator for Chemical and Biological Weapons (1998–present); Deputy Assistant Director ACDA for Multilateral Affairs (1994–1998); Associate Assistant Director ACDA for Multilateral Affairs (1990–1994); Director Defense Policy and Arms Control, NSC (1984–1990); Deputy Director Defense Plans Division, U.S. Mission NATO (1980–1984). Personal interviews, Washington, DC.

Mathews, Bob. (1998, 11 November). (AUS) Disarmament Cell, Defence Science Technology Organisation (1984–present). Personal interview, Canberra, and electronic correspondence.

McNamara, Amb. Thomas E. (1998, 10 September). (U.S.) Assistant Secretary of State for Politico-Military Affairs (1993–1998); Deputy Assistant Secretary of State for Politico-Military Affairs (1983–1986). Personal interview, Washington, DC.

Miller, Col. William (1998, 18 September). (U.S.) Representative to the OPCW (1998–present); Alternate Representative to the OPCW (1996–1998); Deputy Director Chemical and Biological Negotiations Policy, ACDA (1995–1996); Assistant for Negotiations, OSD (1991–1995); Program Officer for Binary Weapons, Department of the Army (1984–1987). Personal interview, The Hague, Netherlands.

Moodie, Hon. Michael. (1998, 18 August). (U.S.) Assistant Director ACDA for Multilateral Affairs (1990–1993). Personal interview, Alexandria, Virginia.

Moores, Anne. (1998, 17 November). (AUS) Director Chemical Disarmament Section, DFAT (1997–present). Personal interview, Canberra.

Nelson, Ron (1998, 9 September). (U.S.) Representative of the Secretary of Defense to the Conference on Disarmament (1985–1989, 1990–1993). Personal interview, The Hague, Netherlands.

O'Sullivan, Amb. Paul T. (1998, 5 August). (AUS) Deputy Chief of Mission Embassy Washington (1996–present); Ambassador for Disarmament (1991–1994); Director Chemical and Biological Disarmament Section, DFAT (1986–1990). Personal interview, Washington, DC.

Perle, Hon. Richard N. (1998, 4 November). (U.S.) Assistant Secretary of Defense for International Security Policy (1981–1987). Telephone interview.

Poneman, Daniel. (1998, 13 September). (U.S.) Special Assistant to the President and Senior Director Nonproliferation and Export Controls, NSC (1993–1996); Director Defense Policy and Arms Control, NSC (1990–1993). Telephone interview.

Reese, Amb. David H. (1998, 22 November). (AUS) Deputy Director, Office of National Assessments (1990–1997); Ambassador for Disarmament (1989–1990); Political Counsellor Embassy Washington (1985–1988). Personal interview, Canberra.

Rostow, Victor A. D. (1998, 18 August). (U.S.) Acting Deputy Assistant Secretary of Defense for Conventional Forces and Arms Control Policy (1993); Principal Director Conventional Forces and Arms Control Policy (previously Negotiations Policy), OSD (1986–1993); Director Long Range Planning (Negotiations Policy), OSD (1985–1986). Personal interview, Alexandria, Virginia.

Rybka, LTC (Ret.) Constance. (1997, 12 November). (U.S.) Assistant for Negotiations, OSD (1992–1997). Personal interview, Port Tobacco, Virginia.

Saboe, Steven. (1998, 10 September). (U.S.) Director Nonproliferation and Disarmament Fund, State Department (1994–present); Special Assistant to the Ambassador-at-Large for Strategic Arms Transfers, State Department (1987–1993); Special Assistant for Nonproliferation and Technology Transfer to the Undersecretary of State for Security Assistance, Science and Technology (1985–1987). Personal interview, Washington, DC.

Smoldone, Joseph (1998, 25 August). (U.S.) Chief Weapons and Technology Control Division, ACDA (1988–present); Director Arms Licensing, State Department (1980–1988). Personal interview, Washington, DC.

Snidle, Giovanni. (1998, 6 November). (U.S.) Desk Officer for CBW Nonproliferation Policy, ACDA (1988–1994). Telephone interview.

Sokolski, Henry. (1998, 8 September). (U.S.) Deputy for Nonproliferation, DOD (1989–1993). Telephone interview.

Speier, Richard H. (1998, 4 August). (U.S.) Assistant for Counterproliferation Assessment and Response, OSD (1994); Assistant for Nonproliferation, OSD (1982–1993). Personal interview, Reston, Virginia, and electronic correspondence.

Starr, Amb. Richard G. (1998, 16 September). (AUS) Ambassador for Disarmament (1994–1996); Assistant Secretary, Peace, Arms Control and Disarmament Branch, DFAT (1990–1993). Personal interview, Madrid, Spain.

VanDiepen, Vann. (1998, 25 August). (U.S.) Director Chemical, Biological and Missile Nonproliferation, State Department (1991–present); Strategic Forces Analyst, State Department (1982–1989). Personal interview, Washington, DC.

Walker, Amb. Ronald A. (1998, 13 February and 23 June). (AUS) First Assistant Secretary, Disarmament, Defence and Nuclear Division, DFAT (1986–1988); Special Disarmament Adviser to the Foreign Minister (1984–1986); Assistant Secretary, Disarmament and Arms Control Branch, DFAT (1983–1984); Representative to the Conference on Disarmament (1979–1983). Personal interviews, Canberra.

Wallerstein, Mitchel B. (1998, 21 August). (U.S.) Deputy Assistant Secretary of Defense for Counterproliferation Policy (1993–1997). Personal interview, Washington, DC.

Wendt, Amb. Alan. (1998, 31 August). (U.S.) Ambassador-at-Large and Special Assistant to the Secretary of State for Strategic Arms Transfers, State Department (approx. 1987–1993). Telephone interview.

White, Hugh J. (1999, 2 June). (AUS) Deputy Secretary, DOD (1995–present); First Assistant Secretary, International Policy Division, DOD (1994–1995); Assistant Secretary, North America and Intelligence Branch, DOD (1993–1994); Assistant Secretary, Strategic Analysis Branch, Office of National Assessments (1992–1993); Senior Advisor for International Relations, Office of the Prime Minister (1990–1991); Advisor to the Minister for Defense (1985–1990). Personal interview, Canberra.

Zimmerman, John. (1998, 4 September). (U.S.) Director Strategic Technology Affairs, State Department (1987–1989). Telephone interview.

OFFICIAL MATERIALS (OFF.)

Previously classified and/or unpublished official documents that have been released for the first time pursuant to this research through Freedom of Information or other means are identified by an asterisk (*). Titles represent the author's position at the time of promulgation.

ACDA. (1992). *Nonproliferation*. Washington, DC: Author.

———. (1997a). Adherence to and compliance with arms control agreements. In *1997 ACDA annual report.* Washington, DC: Author. Available at: http://www.acda.gov/reports/ annual/comp97.htm.

———. (1997b). *Fact sheet: Australia Group.* Washington, DC: Author. Available at: http://www.acda.gov/factshee/wmd/cw/aus496.htm.

———. (1998). *Fact sheet: U.S.–Russian Wyoming Memorandum of Understanding on Chemical Weapons.* Washington, DC: Author. Available at: http://www.acda.gov/factshee/wmd/cw/cwmou.htm.

Assembly of Western European Union. (2000, November). *Transatlantic cooperation on anti-missile defence.* Report submitted on behalf of the Technological and Aerospace Committee. Available at: http://www.weu.int/assembly/eng/reports/1717c.

Attorney General's Department (AUS). (1998). *Chemical Weapons (Prohibition) Act 1994.* Act no. 26 of 1994 as amended, includes amendments up to Act no. 9 of 1998. Canberra: Author.

*Australia. (1991). *Biological Weapons Convention: Australian position paper.* Unpublished.

*———. (1995). *Missile Technology Control Regime Montreaux seminar: Working paper by Australia: A multilateral ballistic missile and space vehicle launch notification agreement.* Unpublished.

*Australia Group (AG). (1990). *Awareness-raising on BW proliferation: Australian experience* (AG/Dec90/BW/AUS). Unpublished.

Australian Labour Party. (1998). *A better plan for foreign affairs.* Canberra: Author. Available at: http://www.alp.org.au/campaign/policy/betterplans/foraffairs.html1#a194c.

*Bird, Gillian. (AUS) Assistant Secretary, DFAT, Peace, Disarmament and Arms Control Branch. (1994a, 6 May). *Ministerial submission 940604 on subject: Australia Group: May 1994 meeting.* Unpublished.

*———. (1994b, 28 July). *Ministerial submission 941046 on subject: Strengthening the Biological Weapons Convention.* Unpublished.

*———. (1994c, 18 November). *Ministerial submission on subject: Australia Group: November 1994 meeting.* Unpublished.

Bush, George H. W. (U.S.) President. (1990). *National security strategy of the United States: 1990–1991.* Washington, DC: Brassey's.

———. (1992). *Address to the United Nations General Assembly in New York City.* (21 September 1992). College Station, Texas: Bush Presidential Library. Available at: http://www.csdl.tamu.edu/bush/cgi.

*Canada. (1994). *Canadian discussion paper: Elements for a multilateral approach to a missile non-proliferation instrument (MTCR plenary).* Unpublished.

Canberra Commission. (1996). *Report of the Canberra Commission on the Elimination of Nuclear Weapons.* Canberra: DFAT. Available at: http://www.dfat.gov.au/cc/cchome.html.

Clarke, Richard A. (U.S.) Assistant Secretary of State for Politico-Military Affairs. (1989a). Outstanding questions: What needs to be done by government and by industry? Discussants' paper, Workshop I: Concluding the Chemical Weapons Convention: Government–industry cooperation. In *Final record: Government–Industry Conference Against Chemical Weapons: Canberra, September 1989* (pp. 59–65). Canberra: DFAT.

———. (1989b). Plenary statement: Delegation of the United States. In *Final record: Government–Industry Conference Against Chemical Weapons: Canberra, September 1989* (pp. 408–409). Canberra: DFAT.

Clinton, William J. (U.S.) President. (1995). *National security strategy of the United States 1994–1995: Engagement and enlargement.* Washington, DC: Brassey's.

———. (1998, November 12). *Letter to the Speaker of the House and the President of the Senate on weapons of mass destruction.* Monterey, CA: MIIS. Available at: http://cns.miis.edu.news.other.wmdlet.htm.

Commission to Assess the Ballistic Missile Threat to the United States. (1998, July 15). *Executive summary: Report of the Commission* (preproduction copy). Washington, DC: U.S. Cong. House. Available at: http://www.house.gov/nsc/testimony/105thcongress/BMThreat.htm.

Congressional Research Service (CRS). (1991). *Weapons nonproliferation policy and legislation.* Washington, DC: Author.

———. (1997). *Nuclear, biological, chemical, and missile proliferation sanctions: Selected current law.* Washington, DC: Author.

*Cousins, Ian. (AUS) First Assistant Secretary, DFAT, International Security Division. (1991a, 15 May). *Ministerial submission 910833 on subject: Chemical Weapons Convention: New U.S. position on challenge inspections.* Unpublished.

*———. (1991b, 15 July). *Ministerial submission 911242 on subject: Chemical Weapon [sic] Convention: New U.S. position on challenge inspections.* Unpublished.

*———. (1994, 15 December). *Ministerial submission 941088 on subject: Missile non-proliferation: Possible treaty instruments.* Unpublished.

*Dauth, John (AUS) First Assistant Secretary, DFAT, International Security Division. (1992a, 25 February). *Ministerial submission 920202 on subject: Biological Weapons Convention: Indonesian ratification.* Unpublished.

*———. (1992b, 27 March). *Ministerial submission 920487 on subject: Biological Weapons Convention: Experts verification meeting.* Unpublished.

*———. (1992c, 24 November). *Ministerial submission 909130 on subject: Chemical weapons: Australia Group: December 1992 meeting.* Unpublished.

Defence, Department of (AUS). (1987). *The Defence of Australia (1987 Defence White Paper).* Canberra: Author.

———. (1994). *Defending Australia (1994 Defence White Paper).* Canberra: Author.

———. (1997). *Australia's strategic policy.* Canberra: Directorate of Publishing and Visual Communications.

———. (1998a). *Annual report: Exports of defence and strategic goods from Australia: 1994/95, 1995/96 and 1996/97.* Canberra: Defence Publishing and Visual Communications.

———. (1998b). *Australian export controls: A general information guide for Australian industry.* Canberra: Defence Publishing and Visual Communications.

———. (1998c). *Australian export controls: An information guide for industry, universities and the general public: The Weapons of Mass Destruction (Prevention of Proliferation) Act 1995 (WMD Act).* Canberra: Defence Publishing and Visual Communications.

*Defense Science Board (U.S.). (1995). *Report of the Defense Science Board Summer Study Task Force on cruise missile defense.* Washington, DC: Office of the Undersecretary of Defense for Acquisition and Technology.

*DFAT. (n.d.a). *Australian regulations on biological weapons materials*. Unpublished.

*————. (n.d.b). *Background issues paper: Missile policy issues*. Unpublished.

*————. (n.d.c). *The Biological Weapons Convention: A possible verification regime*. Unpublished.

*————. (n.d.d). *Missile Technology Control Regime Non-paper*. Unpublished.

*————. (n.d.e). *Missile Technology Control Regime (replacement—following your discussions in Beijing)*. Unpublished.

————. (1987). *An A to Z of Australian disarmament and arms control initiatives and activities*. Canberra: AGPS.

*————. (1989, 6 November). *Cable O.CE799445 to Australian Embassy Washington on subject: Missile Technology Control Regime*. Unpublished.

*————. (1990a). *Australia Group: Briefing for pre-consultations, Dec. 1990*. Unpublished.

*————. (1990b, 1 June). *Cable O.CE885820 to Australian Embassy Tokyo on subject: Biological Weapons Convention review conference: Preliminary paper*. Unpublished.

*————. (1990c, July). *Missile Technology Control Regime (MTCR): Suggested talking points for Senator Evans*. Unpublished.

*————. (1990d, 11 July). *Draft no. 2 of 11 July for possible release early week beginning 15 July (cleared with Dept of Defence and DND) please hold until we advice that we have completed necessary formalities on subject: Australia to become member of the Missile Technology Control Regime*. Unpublished.

————. (1990e, 20 July). *Cable O.UNC to posts on subject: Missile Technology Control Regime: Joint ministerial release*. Unpublished.

*————. (1990f, 21 September). *Ministerial submission 910834 on subject: Missile Control Technology Regime [sic]*. Unpublished.

*————. (1990g, 11 December). *Cable O.CE967206 to Australian Embassy Washington on subject: Iraq/Kuwait: U.S. initiative on CBW, nuclear and missile proliferation*. Unpublished.

*————. (1991a). *Bilateral with Indonesia—regional arms control/chemical and biological weapons*. Unpublished.

*————. (1991b). *Bilateral with Japan—regional arms control issues*. Unpublished.

*————. (1991c). *Bilateral with Malaysia—regional arms control/chemical and biological weapons*. Unpublished.

*————. (1991d). *Biological Weapons Convention: Review conference*. Unpublished.

*————. (1991e). *Brief for the Australian delegation to preparatory committee for the third review conference of the Biological Weapons Convention, Geneva, 8–12 April 1991*. Unpublished.

*————. (1991f). *Missile Technology Control Regime*. Unpublished.

*————. (1991g). *Polmil talks (biological weapons)*. Unpublished.

*————. (1991h, 15 February). *Cable O.CE991409 to posts on subject: Biological weapons seminar and follow-up action*. Unpublished.

*————. (1991i, 4 April). *Tokyo meetings of the Missile Technology Control Regime (MTCR) 18–20 March*. Unpublished.

*————. (1991j, 3 May). *Cable O.CE21571 to Australian Embassy The Hague on subject: Chemical and biological weapons: Australia Group*. Unpublished.

*————. (1991k, 24 May). *Cable O.PA87164 from Australian Embassy Paris on subject: CW/BW: Australia Group: Meeting 21–23 May*. Unpublished.

————. (1991l, 18 July). Cable O.CE52148 to Australian Embassy Geneva on sub-ject: Biological weapons: Western papers: Australian views. Unpublished.

————. (1991m, 10 September). Cable O.CE72002 to Australian Embassy Geneva on subject: Biological weapons third revcon: Delegation instructions. Unpublished.

————. (1991n, 27 September). Cable O.GE94724 from Australian Embassy Geneva on subject: Biological Weapons Convention review conference: Out-comes. Unpublished.

————. (1992a). Verification of the Biological Weapons Convention. Unpublished.

————. (1992b, 18 May). Cable O.CH656747 to posts on subject: Australia Group: The Group's future. Unpublished.

————. (1992c, 5 June). Cable O.PA92841 from Australian Embassy Paris on sub-ject: Australia Group: June 1992 meeting: Delegation report. Unpublished.

————. (1992d, 2 December). Cable O.BJ52711 from Australian Embassy Beijing on subject: Disarmament talks with China. Unpublished.

————. (1993a, 22 April). Cable O.CE272929 to Australian Embassy The Hague on subject: Global non-proliferation arrangements: G7 consideration. Unpublished.

————. (1993b, 24 May). Cable O.CE283022 to posts on subject: MTCR China demarche. Unpublished.

————. (1993c, 7 June). Cable O.CE287408 to Australian Embassy Paris on sub-ject: MTCR: Vienna licensing and enforcement meeting. Unpublished.

————. (1993d, 15 July). Cable O.CE299248 to posts on subject: MTCR: India. Unpublished.

————. (1993e, 3 September). Cable O.CE314609 to Australian High Commis-sion New Delhi on subject: Biological Weapons Convention: VEREX IV: India's position. Unpublished.

————. (1993f, 27 September). Cable O.CE99941 from Australian Embassy Geneva (UNGA 48) on subject: BWC: Revised briefing for Senator Evans's [sic] bilat-eral meetings. Unpublished.

————. (1993g, 10 October). Cable O.CE331864 to DFAT posts on subject: Biological Weapons Convention: Special conference: Representations. Unpublished.

————. (1993h, 15 October). Cable O.CE328493 to Australian UN Office New York on subject: UNGA: First Committee statement. Unpublished.

————. (1993i, 21 October). Cable O.CE330470 to posts on subject: Biological weapons: Wilton Park arms control seminar. Unpublished.

————. (1993j, 6 December). Cable O.PA101019 from Australian Embassy Paris on subject: Australia Group: December 1993 meeting: Delegation report. Unpublished.

————. (1993k, 10 December). Cable O.PA101019 from Australian Embassy Paris on subject: Australia Group: December 1993 meeting: Delegation report. Unpublished.

————. (1994a, 22 March). Cable O.CE376505 to posts on subject: Australia Group: May 1994 meeting—key issues. Unpublished.

————. (1994b, 20 May). Cable O.PA102843 from Australian Embassy Paris on sub-ject: Australia Group: May 1994 meeting—delegation report. Unpublished.

————. (1994c, 22 July). Cable O.CE417254 to posts on subject: Biological Weap-ons Convention: Brazilian seminar. Unpublished.

————. (1994d, 19 September). Cable O.CE43601 to posts on subject: Biological Weapons Convention: Special conference—representations. Unpublished.

*————. (1994e, 30 October). *Cable O.CE440354 to posts on subject: Australia Group: November 1994 meeting—key issues.* Unpublished.

————. (1994f, November). Australia cooperates with region on CWC. *Peace and Disarmament News*, 17–18.

*————. (1995a, 7 April). *Cable O.CE497318 to Australian Embassy Washington on subject: Missile Technology Control Regime: Seminar on missile non-proliferation treaty instruments: U.S. request for comment.* Unpublished.

*————. (1995b, 20 October). *Cable O.PA108365 from Australian Embassy Paris on subject: Australia Group: October 1995 meeting—delegation report.* Unpublished.

————. (1996a, March). ICJ hearings on legality of nuclear weapons. *Peace and Disarmament News*, 15–16.

*————. (1996b, 18 October). *Cable O.PA1528 from Australian Embassy Paris on subject: Australia Group meeting: October 1996 meeting—delegation report.* Unpublished.

————. (1997a). *In the national interest: Australia's foreign and trade policy white paper.* Canberra: Author.

*————. (1997b, 3 June). *Cable O.CE719399 to Australian Embassy Caracas on subject: BWC: Iranian proposal to amend the convention: Discussion with Columbia.* Unpublished.

*————. (1997c, 18 August). *Cable O.CE739075 to posts on subject: Australia Group: 1997 meeting: Key issues.* Unpublished.

*————. (1998, 7 October). *Annexures 9, 12: Documents totally exempt under part iv provisions of the FOI Act.* Unpublished.

Dibb, Paul. (1986). *Review of Australia's defense capabilities: Report to the Minister for Defence.* Canberra: AGPS.

Downer, Alexander. (1997, March). Address by the Hon. Alexander Downer MP, Minister for Foreign Affairs, to the Conference on Disarmament, Geneva, 30 January 1997. *Peace and Disarmament News*, 8–11.

————. (1998). *Government initiative to strengthen the Biological Weapons Convention.* Statement by Australian Foreign Minister Alexander Downer, 2 March 1998. Canberra: DFAT. Available at: http://www.dfat.gov.au.

*Evans, Gareth (AUS) Minister for Foreign Affairs and Trade. (1991a, 27 March). *Letter to HE Mr. Ali Alatas Minister for Foreign Affairs Jakarta.* Unpublished.

*————. (1991b, 28 May). *Cable O.CH62456 to DFAT posts on subject: Arms control and disarmament: A chance of progress.* Unpublished.

*————. (1993a). *Controlling missile proliferation.* Address by Senator Gareth Evans, Minister for Foreign Affairs and Trade to open the Canberra plenary session of the Missile Technology Control Regime partners, Canberra, 9 March 1993. Unpublished.

————. (1993b, February). Crucial to prepare for CWC membership after years of work are crowned with success: Senator Evans. *Peace and Disarmament News*, 11.

*————. (1994a, 7 February). *Letter to Minister for Defence Senator the Hon. Robert Ray.* Unpublished.

————. (1994a, 7 May). Australia ratifies the Chemical Weapons Convention (Press Release [Minister for Foreign Affairs]). Canberra: DFAT.

*Executive Office of the President. (1989a, 4 May). *Legislative referral memorandum on subject: State and GSA reports on H.R. 963, a bill establishing sanctions for the enforcement of the Missile Technology Control Regime.* Bush Presidential Library.

*————. (1989b, 28 June). *Legislative referral memorandum on subject: State draft respone on CBW legislation.* Bush Presidential Library.

*Fox, Henry (AUS) Head Chemical and Biological Disarmament Section, DFAT. (1990). *Australia–United States disarmament officials talks: 26–27 November 1990, Canberra: Record.* Unpublished.

————. (1991). *The biological weapons review conference: The political challenges.* Unpublished.

GAO (U.S.) (1992). *Arms control: U.S. and international efforts to ban biological weapons.* Report to the Honorable Albert Gore, Jr., U.S. Senate. Gaithersburg, MD: Author.

Hayden, Bill (AUS) Minister for Foreign Affairs. (1984). *Uranium, the joint facilities, disarmament and peace: speech by the Minister for Foreign Affairs at the official lunch hosted by the Soviet Foreign Minister, Mr. Gromyko, Moscow 29 May 1984.* Canberra: AGPS.

Holum, John D. (U.S.) Director ACDA. (1996, November 26). *Remarks to the Fourth Review Conference of the Biological Weapons Convention (as prepared for delivery).* Washington, DC: ACDA. Available at: http://www.acda.gov/speeches/holum/bwcrev.htm.

*Jones, Kim. (1991, 15 March). *Ministerial submission 910456 on subject: Missile Technology Control Regime: Australian approach at Tokyo meeting.* Unpublished.

McLachlan, Ian. (1997, 8 August). *Australia and the United States co-operate in missile detection.* Press release. Canberra: Department of Defence.

"Missile Technology Control Regime (MTCR) guidelines." Washington, DC: ACDA. Available at: http://www.acda.gov.

OSD. (1996). *Proliferation: Threat and response.* Washington, DC: U.S. Government Printing Office.

————. (1997a). *Proliferation: Threat and response.* Washington, DC: U.S. Government Printing Office.

————. (1997b). *Relevant texts of U.S. nonproliferation sanctions laws and related documents: Staff summary compiled with the assistance of RAND Corporation for the Office of Nonproliferation Policy (OSD).* Unpublished.

O'Sullivan, Paul. (1991, 12 September). *Statement by Ambassador Paul O'Sullivan, head of the Australian delegation to the third review conference of the parties to the Biological Weapons Convention.* DFAT FOI/Cooper, Ref. 98014, Annexure 1, Doc. No. 14, released 7 October 1998. Unpublished.

Parliament of the Commonwealth of Australia. (1986). *Disarmament and arms control in the nuclear age.* Report from the Joint Committee on Foreign Affairs and Defence. Canberra: AGPS.

————. House. (1994, 9 February). *Parliamentary debates (Hansard).* Canberra: CGP.

————. Senate. (1994a, 2 February). *Parliamentary debates (Hansard).* Canberra: CGP.

————. (1994b, 3 February). *Senate Journals* (56), 1201.

————. (1994c, 9 February). *Senate Journals* (59), 1242.

————. (1995, 8 June). *Senate Journals* (166), 3388.

Poneman, Daniel (U.S.) Special Assistant to the President and Senior Director for Nonproliferation and Export Control, NSC. (1994, February 18). *Memorandum to Robert Gallucci, Assistant Secretary of for Political-Military Affairs (Department of State) and Ashton Carter, Assistant Secretary for Nuclear Security and Counterproliferation (Department of Defense) on subject: Agreed definitions*. Unpublished.

Reagan, Ronald (U.S.) President. (1982, November 30). *National security decision directive 70: Nuclear capable missile technology transfer policy*. Unpublished.

———. (1988). *National security strategy of the United States*. Washington, DC: Pergamon-Brassey's.

Rennack, Dianne E. (1996). *China: U.S. economic sanctions*. CRS Report for Congress no. 96-272F. Washington, DC: Congressional Research Service.

*Rowen, Henry S. (U.S.) Assistant Secretary of Defense for International Security Affairs. (1991, July 31). *Memorandum for Secretary of Defense on subject: OSD's nonproliferation effort*. Unpublished.

*Sinclair, Jill E. (Canada) Chair, MTCR Montraeux Seminar. (1995). *Montraeux seminar: Chairman's paper*. Unpublished.

*Starr, Richard. (1991a, 21 January). *Ministerial submission 910085 on subject: Biological weapons: Dutch seminar: National position paper (and attachment)*. Unpublished.

*———. (1991b, 22 August). *Ministerial submission 911495 on subject: Biological Weapons Convention: Third Review Conference: Australian approach*. Unpublished.

*———. (1993, 26 October). *Ministerial submission 901778 on subject: Missile Technology Control Regime plenary, Interlaken, Switzerland, 29 November–2 December 1993*. Unpublished.

State, Department of (U.S.). (1983, March). *Missile technology controls*. Unpublished.

———. (1994). U.S. and South Africa sign missile non-proliferation agreement. *U.S. Department of State Dispatch, 5* (42), 694.

———. (1997). Memorandum prepared in the Department of State. In *Foreign relations of the United States, 1964–1968: Vol. 9. International devlopment and economic defense policy; commodities*. Doc. no. 196. Washington, DC: U.S. Government Printing Office.

———. (1999). *NDF: Nonproliferation and disarmament fund*. Washington, DC: Author. Available at: http://www.ndf.org.

*Steele, Rory (AUS) Acting First Assistant Secretary, DFAT, International Security Division. (1993, 25 May). *Ministerial submission 930658 on subject: Australia Group: June 1993 meeting*. Unpublished.

*———. (1996, 9 October). *Ministerial Submission 961412 on subject: Australia Group: October 1996 meeting*. Unpublished.

*Taubman, Tony (AUS) Delegation to OPCW PrepCom. (1994, 27 March). *DFAT telememo from Australian Embassy The Hague on subject: OPCW Prepcom: Export control issue*. Unpublished.

United States & Union of Soviet Socialist Republics. (1990). Joint statement on non-proliferation. In U.S. Cong. House. *Proliferation and arms control* (pp. 135–141). 101st Cong., 2nd sess. Washington, DC: U.S. Government Printing Office.

U.S. Cong. House. (1993). *Countering the chemical and biological weapons threat in the post-Soviet world: Report of the special inquiry into the chemical and biological threat of the Committee on Armed Services*. 102nd Congress, 2nd sess.

U.S. Cong. Office of Technology Assessment. (1993). *Proliferation of weapons of mass destruction: Assessing the risks.* Washington, DC: U.S. Government Printing Office.

U.S. Cong. Senate. (1997, April 24). *Senate executive resolution 75: Advice and consent to ratification of the CWC. Cong. Rec.*, S3537-S3658.

———. (1998). *Proliferation Primer: Majority report of the Subcommittee on International Security, Proliferation, and Federal Services of the Committee on Governmental Affairs.* Available at: http://www.senate.gov/~gov_ af fairs/prolifpr.htm.

*Walker, Ronald A. (AUS) First Assistant Secretary, DFA, Disarmament, Security and Nuclear Division. (1987, 27 May). *Ministerial submission on subject: Controls on exports of missile technology.* Unpublished.

White House, Office of the Press Secretary. (1991, 21 May). *Fact sheet on the Middle East arms control initiative.* Washington, DC: Author.

———. (1993, 27 September). *Fact sheet: Nonproliferation and export control policy.* Washington, DC: Author.

*Wolfowitz, Paul (U.S.) Undersecretary of Defense for Policy. (1991, 16 April). *Memorandum for distribution on subject: Resumption of the Proliferation Countermeasures Working Group (PCWG).* Unpublished.

LEGISLATIVE TESTIMONY (TST.)

Legislative testimony includes Congressional testimony by current and former U.S. executive branch officials only (i.e., not nongovernment experts), and Parliamentary statements by current Australian ministers or their representatives and testimony by government experts. Titles represent position at time of testimony unless otherwise noted.

ACDA & Department of State. (1990). Written responses to additional questions submitted for the record. In U.S. Cong. House. *Proliferation and arms control* (Appendix 1). Washington, DC: U.S. Government Printing Office.

Adelman, Hon. Kenneth L. (U.S.) Director ACDA. (1984). Testimony before the Senate Committee on Foreign Relations and the Subcommittee on Energy, Nuclear Proliferation and Government Processes of the Senate Committee on Governmental Affairs. In U.S. Cong. Senate. *Chemical warfare: Arms control and nonproliferation.* 98th Cong., 2nd sess. Washington, DC: U.S. Government Printing Office.

Bartholomew, Amb. Reginald (U.S.) Undersecretary of State for Security Assistance, Science and Technology. (1989a). Testimony before the Senate Committee on Governmental Affairs. In U.S. Cong. Senate. (1990). *Nuclear and missile proliferation.* 101st Cong., 1st sess. Washington, DC: U.S. Government Printing Office.

———. (1989b). Testimony before the Subcommittee on International Finance and Monetary Policy of the Senate Committee on Banking, Housing and Urban Affairs. In U.S. Cong. Senate. (1990). *Chemical and biological weapons proliferation: How to control the production and use and proliferation of chemical and biological weapons.* 101st Cong., 1st sess. Washington, DC: U.S. Government Printing Office.

Brabin-Smith, Richard (AUS) Chief Defence Scientist/head of DSTO. (1997). Testimony before the Joint Standing Committee on Foreign Affairs, Defence and Trade (6 August). In Joint Committees. *Level of funding for Defence*. Canberra: Parliament. Available at: http://www.aph.gov.au.

Brereton, Hon. Laurie (AUS) "Shadow" Foreign Minister. (1998). Statement during Parliamentary debate (1 June). In Parliament of the Commonwealth of Australia. House. *Parliamentary debates (Hansard)*. Canberra: Parliament.

Bryen, Stephen D. (U.S.) former Deputy Undersecretary of Defense for Trade Security Policy and Director Defense Technology Security Administration. (1989). Testimony before the Senate Committee on Foreign Relations. In U.S. Cong. Senate. *Chemical and biological weapons threat: The urgent need for remedies*. 101st Cong., 1st sess. Washington, DC: U.S. Government Printing Office.

Burns, Maj. Gen. William F. (U.S.) Director ACDA. (1989a). Testimony before the Senate Committee on Foreign Relations. In U.S. Cong. Senate. *Chemical and biological weapons threat: The urgent need for remedies*. 101st Cong., 1st sess. Washington, DC: U.S. Government Printing Office.

————. (1989b). Testimony before the Senate Committee on Governmental Affairs and its Permanent Subcommittee on Investigations. In U.S. Cong. Senate. *Global spread of chemical and biological weapons*. 101st Cong., 1st sess. Washington, DC: U.S. Government Printing Office.

Clarke, Hon. Richard A. (U.S.) Assistant Secretary of State for Politico-Military Affairs. (1989). Testimony before the Senate Committee on Foreign Relations. In U.S. Cong. Senate. (1990). *National security implications of missile proliferation*. 101st Cong., 1st sess. Washington, DC: U.S. Government Printing Office.

————. (1990). Testimony before the House Committee on Foreign Affairs and its Subcommittee on Arms Control, International Security and Science. In U.S. Cong. House. *Proliferation and arms control*. 101st Cong. 2nd sess. Washington, DC: U.S. Government Printing Office.

————. (1991). Testimony before the Subcommittee on Technology and National Security of the Joint Economic Committee. In U.S. Cong. Joint. *Arms trade and nonproliferation* (I). 101st Cong., 2nd sess. Washington, DC: U.S. Government Printing Office.

————. (1996). Testimony before the Senate Committee on Foreign Relations. In U.S. Cong. Senate. *Convention on chemical weapons*. Washington, DC: Federal Document Clearing House. Available at: LEXIS–NEXIS (Library: LEGIS, File: CNGTST).

Christopher, Hon. Warren (U.S.) Secretary of State. (1996). Testimony before the Senate Committee on Foreign Relations. In U.S. Cong. Senate. *Convention on Chemical Weapons*. Washington, DC: Federal Document Clearing House. Available at: LEXIS–NEXIS (Library: LEGIS, File: CNGTST).

Davis, Hon. Lynn E. (U.S.) Undersecretary of State for International Security Affairs. (1993). Testimony before the House Committee on Foreign Affairs. In U.S. Cong. House. *U.S. nonproliferation policy*. 103rd Cong, 1st sess. Washington, DC: U.S. Government Printing Office.

————. (1996). Testimony before the House Committee on International Relations. In U.S. Cong. House. *Nonproliferation policy*. Washington, DC: Federal Document Clearing House. Available at: LEXIS–NEXIS (Library: LEGIS, File: CNGTST).

Deutch, Hon. John M. (U.S.) Deputy Secretary of Defense. (1994). Testimony before the Senate Committee on Armed Services. In U.S. Cong. Senate. *Military implications of the Chemical Weapons Convention (CWC)*. 103rd Cong, 2nd sess. Washington, DC: U.S. Government Printing Office.

Duffy, Gloria C. (U.S.) Deputy Assistant Secretary of Defense and Deputy Head, Negotiations on Safe and Secure Dismantlement. (1994). Testimony before the Subcommittee on Europe and the Middle East of the House Committee on Foreign Affairs. In U.S. Cong. House. *U.S. assistance to the Newly Independent States*. Washington, DC: Federal Document Clearing House. Available at: LEXIS–NEXIS (Library: LEGIS, File: CNGTST).

Eckert, Hon. Sue E. (U.S.) Assistant Secretary of Commerce for Export Administration. (1994). Testimony before the Subcommittee on Technology, Environment and Aviation of the House Committee on Science, Space and Technology. In U.S. Cong. House. *Export control and high technology*. Washington, DC: Federal Document Clearing House. Available at: LEXIS–NEXIS (Library: LEGIS, File: CNGTST).

Einhorn, Robert J. (U.S.) Deputy Assistant Secretary of State for Nonproliferation. (1997). Testimony before the Subcommittee on International Security, Proliferation, and Federal Services of the Senate Committee on Governmental Affairs. In U.S. Cong. Senate. *Proliferation of weapons from Russia*. Washington, DC: Federal Document Clearing House. Available at: LEXIS–NEXIS (Library: LEGIS, File: CNGTST).

Emery, David F. (U.S.) Deputy Director ACDA. (1984). Testimony before the House Committee on Armed Services. In U.S. Cong. House. *Full committee briefing on the recently proposed chemical arms treaty*. 98th Cong., 2nd sess. Washington, DC: U.S. Government Printing Office.

Erlick, Barry J. (U.S.) Biological Weapons Analyst, Department of the Army. (1989). Testimony before the Senate Committee on Governmental Affairs and its Permanent Subcommittee on Investigations. In U.S. Cong. Senate. *Global spread of chemical and biological weapons*. 101st Cong., 1st sess. Washington, DC: U.S. Government Printing Office.

Evans, Sen. Gareth (AUS) Minister Representing the Minister for Foreign Affairs. (1987). Statement in response to question during Parliamentary debate (28 May). In Parliament of the Commonwealth of Australia. Senate. *Parliamentary debates (Hansard)*. Canberra: Parliament.

Freedenberg, Hon. Paul (U.S.) former Undersecretary of Commerce for International Trade. (1989). Testimony before the Senate Committee on Governmental Affairs and its Permanent Subcommittee on Investigations. In U.S. Cong. Senate. *Global spread of chemical and biological weapons*. 101st Cong., 1st sess. Washington, DC: U.S. Government Printing Office. (Note: testimony provided the day after leaving office).

Gaffney, Frank J., Jr. (U.S.) former Acting Assistant Secretary of Defense for International Security Policy. (1989). Testimony before the Senate Committee on Governmental Affairs and its Permanent Subcommittee on Investigations. In U.S. Cong. Senate. *Global spread of chemical and biological weapons*. 101st Cong., 1st sess. Washington, DC: U.S. Government Printing Office.

Goldberg, David (U.S.) Chemical Weapons Analyst, Department of the Army. (1989). Testimony before the Senate Committee on Governmental Affairs and its Permanent Subcommittee on Investigations. In U.S. Cong. Senate. *Global spread of chemical and biological weapons*. 101st Cong., 1st sess. Washington, DC: U.S. Government Printing Office.

Gordon, Bradley (U.S.) Assistant Director for Nuclear and Weapons Control, ACDA. (1990). Testimony before the House Committee on Foreign Affairs and its Subcommittee on Arms Control, International Security and Science. In U.S. Cong. House. *Proliferation and arms control*. 101st Cong., 2nd sess. Washington, DC: U.S. Government Printing Office.

Harrison, Roger (U.S.) Deputy Assistant Secretary of State for Politico-Military Affairs. (1989). Testimony before the Senate Committee on Governmental Affairs and its Permanent Subcommittee on Investigations. In U.S. Cong. Senate. *Global spread of chemical and biological weapons*. 101st Cong. 1st sess. Washington, DC: U.S. Government Printing Office.

Hawke, Hon. Robert J. L. (AUS) Prime Minister. (1989). Statement in response to question during Parliamentary debate. In Parliament of the Commonwealth of Australia. House. *Parliamentary debates (Hansard)* (H. of R. 166). Canberra: CGP.

Hayden, Hon. William (AUS) Minister of Foreign Affairs. (1986). Statement in response to question during Parliamentary debate. In Parliament of the Commonwealth of Australia. House. *Parliamentary debates (Hansard)* (H. of R. 151). 34th Parliament, 4th period. Canberra: CGP.

———. (1989). Statement in response to question during Parliamentary debate (2 November). In Parliament of the Commonwealth of Australia. House. *Parliamentary debates (Hansard)*. Canberra: Parliament.

Hinds, Jim E. (U.S.) Deputy Assistant Secretary of Defense for Negotiations Policy. (1989a). Testimony before the Senate Committee on Governmental Affairs and its Permanent Subcommittee on Investigations. In U.S. Cong. Senate. *Global spread of chemical and biological weapons*. 101st Cong., 1st sess. Washington, DC: U.S. Government Printing Office.

———. (1989b). Testimony before the Subcommittee on Defense Industry and Technology of the Senate Committee on Armed Services. In U.S. Cong. Senate. *Ballistic and cruise missile proliferation in the Third World*. 101st Cong., 1st sess. Washington, DC: U.S. Government Printing Office.

Holmes, Amb. Allen H. (U.S.) Assistant Secretary of State for Politico-Military Affairs. (1989a). Testimony before the House Committee on Foreign Affairs and its Subcommittees on Arms Control, International Security and Science, and on International Economic Policy and Trade. In U.S. Cong. House. *Chemical weapons proliferation*. 101st Cong., 1st sess. Washington, DC: U.S. Government Printing Office.

———. (1989b). Testimony before the Senate Governmental Affairs Committee and its Permanent Subcommittee on Investigations. In U.S. Cong. Senate. *Global spread of chemical and biological weapons*. 101st Cong., 1st sess. Washington, DC: U.S. Government Printing Office.

———. (1989c). Testimony before the Subcommittee on Defense Industry and Technology of the Senate Committee on Armed Services. In U.S. Cong. Senate. *Ballistic and cruise missile proliferation in the Third World*. 101st Cong., 1st sess. Washington, DC: U.S. Government Printing Office.

Holum, Hon. John D. (U.S.) Acting Undersecretary of State for Arms Control and International Security Affairs. (1998). Testimony before the House Committee on International Relations. In U.S. Cong. House. *Export of missile-related technology to China.* Washington, DC: Federal Document Clearing House. Available at: LEXIS–NEXIS (Library: LEGIS, File: CNGTST).

Landry, Maj. Gen. John R. (U.S.) National Intelligence Officer for General Purposes Forces, CIA. (1994). Testimony before the Senate Committee on Armed Services. In U.S. Cong. Senate. *Military implications of the Chemical Weapons Convention (CWC).* 103rd Cong., 2nd sess. Washington, DC: U.S. Government Printing Office.

Lehman, Hon. Ronald F., II (U.S.) Director ACDA. (1989). Testimony before the Senate Committee on Governmental Affairs. In U.S. Cong. Senate. *Nuclear and missile proliferation.* 101st Cong., 1st sess. Washington, DC: U.S. Government Printing Office.

———. (1992). Testimony before the Subcommittee on Arms Control, International Security and Science of the House Committee on Foreign Affairs. In U.S. Cong. House. *The future of U.S. arms control policy.* 102nd Cong., 2nd sess. Washington, DC: U.S. Government Printing Office.

LeMunyon, James M. (U.S.) Deputy Assistant Secretary of Commerce for Export Administration. (1989a). Testimony before the Senate Committee on Governmental Affairs and its Permanent Subcommittee on Investigations. In U.S. Cong. Senate. *Global spread of chemical and biological weapons.* 101st Cong., 1st sess. Washington, DC: U.S. Government Printing Office.

———. (1989b). Testimony before the Subcommittees on Arms Control, International Security and Science, and International Economic Policy and Trade of the House Committee on Foreign Affairs. In U.S. Cong. House. *Missile proliferation: The need for controls (Missile Technology Control Regime).* 101st Cong., 1st sess. Washington, DC: U.S. Government Printing Office.

———. (1990). Testimony before the Subcommittee on Technology and National Security of the Joint Economic Committee. In U.S. Cong. Joint. *Arms trade and nonproliferation (I).* 101st Cong., 2nd sess. Washington, DC: U.S. Government Printing Office.

———. (1991). Testimony before the Subcommittee on Technology and National Security of the Joint Economic Committee. In U.S. Cong. Joint. *Arms trade and nonproliferation (I).* 102nd Cong., 1st sess. Washington, DC: U.S. Government Printing Office.

McNamara, Amb. Thomas E. (U.S.) Assistant Secretary of State for Politico-Military Affairs. (1995). Testimony before the Subcommittee on International Finance and Monetary Policy of the Senate Committee on Banking, Housing, and Urban Affairs. In U.S. Cong. Senate. *Dual-use export control program.* Washington, DC: Federal Document Clearing House. Available at: LEXIS–NEXIS (Library: LEGIS, File: CNGTST).

Miller, Franklin C. (U.S.) Acting Assistant Secretary of Defense for International Security Policy. (1997). Testimony before the Subcommittee on Strategic Forces of the Senate Committee on Armed Services. In U.S. Cong. Senate. *Weapons proliferation and FY98 budget—Defense.* Washington, DC: Federal Document Clearing House. Available at: LEXIS–NEXIS (Library: LEGIS, File: CNGTST).

Oehler, Gordon C. (U.S.) Director Nonproliferation Center, CIA. (1995). Testimony before the Permanent Subcommittee on Investigations of the Senate Committee on Governmental Affairs. In U.S. Cong. Senate. *Proliferation of weapons of mass destruction*. Washington, DC: Federal Document Clearing House. Available at: LEXIS–NEXIS (Library: LEGIS, File: CNGTST).

———. (1996). *Testimony before the Senate Committee on Armed Services*. Washington, DC: Federation of American Scientists. Available at: http://www.fas.org/irp/cia/product/go_toc_032796.html.

Olmer, Hon. Lionel H. (U.S.) Undersecretary of Commerce for International Trade. (1984). Testimony before the Senate Committee on Foreign Relations and the Subcommittee on Energy, Nuclear Proliferation and Government Processes of the Senate Committee on Governmental Affairs. In U.S. Cong. Senate. *Chemical warfare: Arms control and nonproliferation*. 98th Cong., 2nd sess. Washington, DC: U.S. Government Printing Office.

Perry, William. (1996). Testimony before the Senate Committee on Foreign Relations. In U.S. Cong. Senate. *Convention on chemical weapons*. Washington, DC: Federal Document Clearing House. Available at: LEXIS–NEXIS (Library: LEGIS, File: CNGTST).

Punch, Hon. Gary F. (AUS) Minister for Defence Science and Personnel. (1995). Statement in response to question during Parliamentary debate. In Parliament of the Commonwealth of Australia. House. *Parliamentary debates (Hansard)* (H. of R. 201). 37th Parliament, 7th period. Canberra: CGP.

Ray, Sen. Robert (AUS) Minister for Defense. (1990). Statement in response to question during Parliamentary debate (19 July). In Parliament of the Commonwealth of Australia. Senate. *Parliamentary debates (Hansard)*. Canberra: Parliament.

———. (1991). Statement in response to question during Parliamentary debate (8 October). In Parliament of the Commonwealth of Australia. Senate. *Parliamentary debates (Hansard)*. Canberra: Parliament.

———. (1995). Statement in response to question during Parliamentary debate (22, 23 August). In Parliament of the Commonwealth of Australia. Senate. *Parliamentary debates (Hansard)*. Canberra: Parliament.

Shalikashvili, Gen. John M. (U.S.) Chairman of the Joint Chiefs of Staff. (1994). Testimony before the Senate Committee on Armed Services. In U.S. Cong. Senate. *Military implications of the Chemical Weapons Convention (CWC)*. 103rd Cong., 2nd sess. Washington, DC: U.S. Government Printing Office.

Slocombe, Hon. Walter B. (U.S.) Undersecretary of Defense for Policy. (1994). Testimony before the Senate Committee on Foreign Relations. In U.S. Cong. Senate. *Chemical Weapons Convention*. Washington, DC: Federal Document Clearing House. Available at: LEXIS–NEXIS (Library: LEGIS, File: CNGTST).

———. (1997). Testimony before the Subcommittee on International Security, Proliferation and Federal Services of the Senate Committee on Governmental Affairs. In U.S. Cong. Senate. *Nuclear deterrence policy*. Washington, DC: Federal Document Clearing House. Available at: LEXIS–NEXIS (Library: LEGIS, File: CNGTST).

Sokolski, Henry (U.S.) Deputy for Nonproliferation Policy, OSD. (1989a). Testimony before the Senate Committee on Foreign Relations. In U.S. Cong. Senate. *National security implications of missile proliferation*. 101st Cong., 1st sess. Washington, DC: U.S. Government Printing Office.

———. (1989b). Testimony before the Subcommittees on Arms Control, International Security and Science, and on International Economic Policy and Trade of the House Committee on Foreign Affairs. In U.S. Cong. House. *Missile proliferation: The need for controls (Missile Technology Control Regime).* 101st Cong., 1st sess. Washington, DC: U.S. Government Printing Office.

———. (1990a). Testimony before the House Committee on Foreign Affairs and its Subcommittee on Arms Control, International Security and Science. In U.S. Cong. House. *Proliferation and arms control.* 101st Cong., 2nd sess. Washington, DC: U.S. Government Printing Office.

———. (1990b). Testimony before the Subcommittee on Technology and National Security of the Joint Economic Committee. In U.S. Cong. Joint. *Arms trade and nonproliferation* (I). 101st Cong., 2nd sess. Washington, DC: U.S. Government Printing Office.

———. (1991). Testimony before the Subcommittee on Technology and National Security of the Joint Economic Committee. In U.S. Cong. Joint. *Arms trade and nonproliferation* (I). 102nd Cong., 1st sess. Washington, DC: U.S. Government Printing Office.

———. (1996). *Testimony before the Subcommittee on Acquisitions and Technology of the Senate Committee on Armed Services (prehearing draft).* Unpublished.

Tarbell, Dave (U.S.) Director Defense Technology Security Administration. (1995). Testimony before the Subcommittee on International Finance and Monetary Policy of the Senate Committee on Banking, Housing, and Urban Affairs. In U.S. Cong. Senate. *Dual-use export control program.* Washington, DC: Federal Document Clearing House. Available at: LEXIS–NEXIS (Library: LEGIS, File: CNGTST).

Verville, Elizabeth (U.S.) Deputy Assistant Secretary of State for Politico-Military Affairs. (1990). Testimony before the Subcommittee on Technology and National Security of the Joint Economic Committee. In U.S. Cong. Joint. *Arms trade and nonproliferation* (I). 101st Cong., 2nd sess. Washington, DC: U.S. Government Printing Office.

Wallerstein, Mitchel B. (U.S.) Deputy Assistant Secretary of Defense for Counterproliferation Policy and Senior Department of Defense Representative for Trade Security Policy. (1997). Testimony before the Subcommittee on International Security, Proliferation and Federal Services of the Senate Committee on Governmental Affairs. In U.S. Cong. Senate. *Weapons proliferation: U.S. export controls.* Washington, DC: Federal Document Clearing House. Available at: LEXIS–NEXIS (Library: LEGIS, File: CNGTST).

———. (1998). Testimony before the Senate Committee on Armed Services. In U.S. Cong. Senate. *U.S. export control and nonproliferation policy.* Washington, DC: Federal Document Clearing House. Available at: LEXIS–NEXIS (Library: LEGIS, File: CNGTST).

Webster, Hon. William (U.S.) Director of Central Intelligence. (1989a). Testimony before the Senate Committee on Foreign Relations. In U.S. Cong. Senate. *Chemical and biological weapons threat: The urgent need for remedies.* 101st Cong., 1st sess. Washington, DC: U.S. Government Printing Office.

———. (1989b). Testimony before the Senate Committee on Governmental Affairs and its Permanent Subcommittee on Investigations. In U.S. Cong. Senate. *Global spread of chemical and biological weapons.* 101st Cong., 1st sess. Washington, DC: U.S. Government Printing Office.

Woolsey, Amb. James R. (U.S.) Director of Central Intelligence. (1993a). Testimony before the House Committee on Foreign Affairs. In U.S. Cong. House. *U.S. security policy toward rogue regimes.* 103rd Cong., 1st sess. Washington, DC: U.S. Government Printing Office.

———. (1993b). Testimony before the Senate Committee on Governmental Affairs. In U.S. Cong. Senate. *Proliferation threats of the 1990s.* 103rd Cong., 1st sess. Washington, DC: U.S. Government Printing Office.

———. (1994). Testimony before the Senate Committee on Foreign Relations. In U.S. Cong. Senate. *Chemical Weapons Convention.* Washington, DC: Federal Document Clearing House. Available at: LEXIS–NEXIS (Library: LEGIS, File: CNGTST).

Wulf, Norman A. (U.S.) Deputy Assistant Director for Nuclear and Weapons Control, ACDA. (1989a). Testimony before the Senate Committee on Foreign Relations. In U.S. Cong. Senate. (1990). *National security implications of missile proliferation.* 101st Cong., 1st sess. Washington, DC: U.S. Government Printing Office.

———. (1989b). Testimony before the Subcommittees on Arms Control, International Security and Science, and on International Economic Policy and Trade of the House Committee on Foreign Affairs. In U.S. Cong. House. *Missile proliferation: The need for controls (Missile Technology Control Regime).* 101st Cong., 1st sess. Washington, DC: U.S. Government Printing Office.

———. (U.S.) Acting Assistant Director for Nonproliferation and Regional Arms Control, ACDA. (1993). Testimony before the House Committee on Foreign Affairs. In U.S. Cong. House. *U.S. nonproliferation policy.* 103rd Cong., 1st sess. Washington, DC: U.S. Government Printing Office.

NEWSPAPERS AND NEWS SERVICES

Arms Control Today (News and negotiations section)

Associated Press wire service (from 12/97)

Australian Financial Review

Canberra Times (from 12/97)

Chemical Weapons Convention/CBW Conventions Bulletin (News chronology section)

Disarmament Diplomacy (News review section) (1/96–1/98)

International Herald Tribune (from 12/97)

New York Times (from 12/97)

Pacific Research (6/89–8/93) (*CBW Bulletin* section)

Reuters wire service (from 12/97)

Sydney Morning Herald (from 1/92)

Washington Post

Washington Times

Index

Japan, 73, 85, 92, 129, 146, 158–159, 180, 210, 219 n.8
Joint Facilities, 138, 156, 185, 187 n.1
Joseph, Robert, 100

Keating government, 141, 185, 188 n.11, 209
Keating, Paul, 139
Kurds, CW use against, 70, 78

Labor Party of Australia, 138, 141, 183–185
Lampedusa, Libyan attack on, 1
Ledogar, Stephen J., 76, 149
Lehman, Ronald, 160
Libralism–neolibralism, theory of, 206–210, 218, 220 n.9
Liberal-National Coalition, Australian political party, 139, 210
Libya, 24, 36, 56, 65, 70, 73, 82, 100, 122, 132 n.7, 198. *See also* Lampedusa, Libyan attack on; Rabta
Lott, Trent, 95, 96

M-9 missile, sale of, 120
M-11 missile, sale of, 120
Malaysia, 176, 204–205
Malta summit, U.S.–USSR, 91
Managed access, 92, 158–160, 174
MEADS (Medium Extended Air Defense System), 128
Mendoza Agreement, 25, 97
Middle power behavior, theory of, 186, 193–197
Missile: ban proposals, 55–56, 124–126, 181–184; defense. *See* Counterproliferation; free zones 25, 127, 184; talks, U.S.–DPRK, 119, 135 n.33
Missile proliferation: Australian responses to 177–185; threats of 60; U.S. responses to, 110–130, 178
Missile Technology Control Act, 122. *See also* Sanctions
Mountbatten Centre, Southampton University, 135 n.36
MTAG (Missile Technology Analysis Group), 120

MTCR (Missile Technology Control Regime), 15, 20–21, 55–56, 110–116, 117–128 passim, 134 nn.25–30, 135 nn.31, 32, 34, 177–184, 207. *See also* Code of Conduct Against Missile Proliferation, MTCR

NAM (non-aligned movement) states, 74–76, 92, 101, 149–150, 153, 156, 162, 167, 169, 187 n.8, 204
National attributes, theory of, 192–197, 219
National Guard, 98
National identity–political-strategic culture, theory of, 197, 215, 218–219
National interest (competing subnational interests), theory of 62, 200–205, 214, 218
National Security Act of 1947, 212
National Security Action Memorandum-294, 110
National Security Strategy, 1990, 63
National trial inspections, 156, 174
NATO (North Atlantic Treaty Organization), 1, 67, 114, 155
Navy, missile defense systems, 128
Neoliberalism, theory of. *See* Liberalism–neoliberalism
Neorealism, theory of. *See* Realism–neorealism
Netherlands, The, 146, 161
New York Times, 60
New Zealand, 7 n.4, 171, 188 n,13
NIE-95-19 (National Intelligence Estimate-95-19), 129
Nixon, Richard M., 110
NMD (National Missile Defense). *See* Counterproliferation
Nonpossession Norms. *See* Norm-bulding.
Nonproliferation treaties. *See* BWC; CWC; CTBT; Norm-building; NPT
Norm-building, nonproliferation strategy: Australian policies of, 92–93, 125, 140–141, 154–164, 169–176, 181–184; complementarity with capability-denial, 52–53, 55–56, 57;

ABOUT THE AUTHOR

David A. Cooper is Deputy Director at the Office of Strategic Arms Control Policy, U.S. Department of Defense (Office of the Secretary of Defense).